CISTERCIAN STUDIES S[...]

ASPECTS OF MONASTICISM

Published originally by Editions de la Source as
Aspects du monachisme hier et aujourd'hui (Paris, 1968).

© Cistercian Publications, Inc., 1978

Ecclesiastical permission for publication of this
volume has been given by Bernard J. Flanagan, Bishop
of Worcester, 20 June 1974.

Available in Europe and the Commonwealth
from A. R. Mowbray & Co Ltd., St Thomas House
Becket Street, Oxford OX1 1SJ.

ISBN 0 87907 807 3

CISTERCIAN PUBLICATIONS INC
Kalamazoo, Michigan
49008

Printed in the United States of America

CISTERCIAN STUDIES SERIES: NUMBER SEVEN

Aspects of Monasticism

by
Jean Leclercq

Translated by Mary Dodd

CISTERCIAN PUBLICATIONS, INC.
Kalamazoo, Michigan
1978

CONTENTS

PREFACE TO THE ENGLISH EDITION

I T IS ALWAYS UNSEEMINGLY for a monk to talk about himself. He should never do it. But sometimes honesty toward himself and toward others demand it, especially as he gets along in years. For then, like anyone who has been writing for a long time, he finds himself exposed to two dangers. The first consists in not modifying his views in any way, which would amount to saying that he had always been and continues to be right. This could happen because he is anxious to safeguard a threatened reputation, or because he is no longer capable, psychologically, of changing his mind. It has been pointed out how difficult it is for an author to shed the views acquired before he turned forty. But the opposite danger would be for him to indulge himself, to luxuriate in self-criticism, to confess publicly that he has been wrong, thus applying to himself the words spoken to Clovis, the first of the barbarian kings to become a Christian: "Burn what you have worshipped, and worship what you have burned." Such confessions are made today under psychological, social or political pressures—either in civil or religious spheres—or, if one is completely free, as a result of a conversion. One must be prepared for such a conversion. He has no right to remain unchanged at a time when in society at large and in the Church many things are changing. On the other hand, one must not change simply to yield to current fashion, or to "play at being young" when one is sixty years old. Fortunately, between a state of immobility and one of radical change, there is room for a third attitude. An old monk I knew, who was told that he was not saying the same things he had said twenty years earlier, replied, "I do not change, I develop." Evolution is regressive when one returns to positions he had formerly abandoned, as is the case with people who once seemed "advanced" but who are today considered reactionary. But evolution is progressive when one goes along with the movement which may be called "the Church on the march," which at times may seem like "the Church on the run."

When the essays assembled in this volume appear, six or seven years will have elapsed since they were published for the first time. When they appeared in the French edition of 1968, they were freshly gathered, so to speak. Some few went back to 1965, a few to 1966, but most of them were from 1967. This volume was a continuation of three earlier collections of the same kind which had appeared during the three preceding years. And each year since, until 1971, a new collection has been published. New problems are continually cropping up—not indeed demanding instant solutions, but stimulating new research and encouraging new hypotheses. At the time (August 1971) when I was asked to write this preface, the last papers given at the summer's congress were at the printer. One of these, which was delivered, then written down, last July, and which will be published in the November issue of *Nouvelle revue théologique,* deals with one of the questions of greatest interest in current religious thought, namely the relations existing between the realities of salvation and the cultural "given" in which they were accomplished and continue to be experienced. The application of this problematic of monasticism is opening new horizons for historical research and for critical analysis of the traditions by which we live: a period of transition such as ours is favorable only to the "provisory." The time is gone when a theologian could entitle his work *Theologia definitiva.* Few, if any, can pretend to create a major work, a *magnum opus,* which will be epoch-making. Let us willingly accept the role of making provisory progress, if it can be of service.

What statements are all these preambles leading up to? They simply introduce a short "retractatio", in the sense in which the ancients — including Augustine — used the word. It does not mean that one "retreats", but that one is "treating (a subject) anew." It will be short, I say, because the points I might enlarge upon can already be found, in part, in volumes previously published. The present volume contains two parts. The first expresses a conviction; the second tries to show how it has been worked out at different times in different parts of the world. The text of the first part was written during, or shortly after, the Second Vatican Council, chiefly following its texts. At that time the question was not so much solving concrete problems, practical applications — renewal had only just begun — as recalling some basic truths concerning the religious life, and discerning what was, for monasticism, its so-called identity.

And now, a few years later, as a consequence of what is called the acceleration of history, the Council (in the opinion of some) has already entered the sphere of legend. Its texts are questioned. Are they not the source of a great deception? Instead of renewing, have they not introduced into the Church a new series of problems and debates, and produced insecurity for many — in short worsened the crisis? Does the abundance and variety of publications, sometimes contradicting each other, to which the Council has given rise not prove that the Council has not succeeded in creating unanimity? Today people dream of Vatican III or Jerusalem II. In this connection, people refer to the "dynamism of the Council." According to them the best way to be faithful to it is to go further than the Council went. Now, this is true, if one means to go in the same direction, but not if one intends to change the main direction the Council has given to the life of the Church and of monasticism. In fact, the main problems discussed today were propounded at the time of the Council, and the doctrinal solutions given now would not seem to be fundamentally different from those given less than ten years ago. A certain number of hopes expressed at the Council have not been realized. If only we could gradually put into practice all the program it elaborated, we would be making a great leap forward along the road to renewal. True, Vatican II has given rise to a large corpus of thought in many different fields. To synthesize the first results of this intense research, I would have to be competent in several different disciplines. I would have to be a biblicist, an historian, a theologian, a psychologist, a sociologist — very difficult, when I have spent thirty-five years of my life studying only one discipline, history. Nothing of this sort, then, should be expected in the following pages.

Another difficulty, which must necessarily be overcome today, if one would be up-to-date, consists in responding to the aspirations of "contemporary man," "modern man," or "today's youth." In this connection, however, two questions arise immediately: Who is being referred to? and, if it is possible to know that, then what value should be attached to his aspirations? There is not one kind of "modern man." Some men seek "action now" — be it doctrinal, social, political, revolutionary, or some other. And some of them seek a life of prayer; these are less numerous than they once were (though this is not altogether certain), but they exist and have a right to exist.

The "youth of today" are often adults projecting on to youth their own frustrations or aspirations. On the other hand, it is revealing, and amazing to us, to hear real young people's opinions of a man of forty-five. Some of our genuine youth react against the infatuations of men of action with technology, production, and efficiency. And those among them who come to monasteries do not wish the world to be the norm of monasticism; if they did, they would have stayed in the world. They come because they believe that the monastic life offers them a way of life which they could not find elsewhere. They do not expect us to change it fundamentally. They even feel themselves strangers to some of the institutional or psychological forms with which we have associated it, but they sometimes pay less attention than we to "observances," and to the anachronistic character of some of them. Today's young generation has not known the battles we had to fight in order to free ourselves from the past. They wish that we adults would gradually come to forget our conflicts and stop talking about them. There were "things" that had to be changed; they have been changed. Now we must reaffirm the values which do not change. Seen in this way, the ideas we attribute to "the man of today" are perhaps really only temptations; the modern man is also in certain respects a carnal man, and his aspirations are not necessarily the absolute criteria of renewal in the Holy Spirit. Just as it would be a grave mistake to ignore the authentic desires of our Christian youth, so it would be equally dangerous to reverse the formula of St. Benedict, making him give this advice: "do only what conforms with the example of the young."

In communities where there are no young people, men of forty are tempted to believe that they are young and can speak in the name of youth. Now the reality of today's youth moves extremely fast. In the past, one "generation" lasted a quarter of a century. Later, it lasted ten years, then five. At the present time, there are countries in the West where young people have new problems every two years. Hence they feel all the more a need of stability in their concept of life. They willingly consent to prayer, to work, to the observance of the Rule, they even launch into them in a more personal and diversified way, which can only enrich the community. Clearsighted as they are, and very early formed in habits of critical judgment, they quickly see that the older monks have defects; but at least these latter know what they want, and remain faithful to their vocation, to their first love for Jesus Christ, and they bring to their young brothers a spiritual security and trust in the Holy Spirit for which many weaknesses will be forgiven them. The important thing is to have a program, or more precisely an ideal, even better, a conviction, a faith, in the value to the Church of monasticism. Such a criterion allows one to reduce to its exact value the evidence often drawn from an abundance of recruits, as if the fact that a community has many novices means that the form is good, and that it is willed by God. This is only the sign of a fixed identity, which is not necessarily the best. Still, we have to have one in order to test it, to compare it to the Gospel, with tradition, and with the *sensus Ecclesiae*.

A new question has been, if not yet asked, at least made more urgent, by the Council and the chain of events it initiated: the question of the relationship between monasticism and the world. We take it for granted that monasticism continues to be the most challenged on this point. Oversimplified presentations, even caricatures, of the real problem circulate unceasingly, sometimes coming from monastic pens. New abstract words ending in "ism" or "ty" are created to characterize the problem: manicheism, pharisaism, supernaturalism, impersonalism, artificiality, credibility gap. If one wanted to play this game, one could speak, in this connection, of caricaturism, psychologism, sociologism. An author judges all the time until he reached forty years of age as an uninterrupted succession of deviations, aberrations, guilt feelings and, of course, alienations. And he proclaims from on high that everything was erroneous, illusory and unhealthy. And if he consents to offer proof, he will sum up in half a page all of contemplative history — which stemming from that inspired pagan, Plato, through St Thomas and into the present day, is not even Christian. And he will reduce *ascesis* to a minimum of those unavoidable inconveniences which belong to the human condition. Devotion to man will be the only prayer, and all the past, in contrast to what the present is going to be, will be described in black and white: a long night followed, at last, by a bright light.

These negative sentiments, often clearly expressed, inspired by valuable data borrowed from Marx and Freud, and presented with a subtle dialectic, have the advantage of provoking among many, in reaction, a rediscovery of the traditional values. There is a "sense of Christ", a sort of Christian instinct, which has allowed saints and scholars from antiquity to our day to discern what must be safeguarded in the inheritance received from God, and what can and ought to be transformed by the new man whom the Holy Spirit created anew in Jesus Christ and in those who live in Him. It is some of these voices whose echo I have tried to transmit in the pages of the present book. It would not have been possible to treat each problem completely. Some aspects — for instance, those concerning communion and the service of the community, the *koinonia* and the *diakonia* — are not described. They have been, or will be, described elsewhere.

One problem which remains a source of irritation, and becomes more and more irritating, is that of vocabulary. Very recently, a specialist in the language of the New Testament published a study on the *Dangers of Eschatology*, in which he showed how this word, which is relatively recent, is now used in the most varied, and sometimes the vaguest, of senses. And yet, on this point as on all the others, the texts of Vatican II, in which eschatology occupies an important place, remain a valid source of reference, because the redactors of the Constitutions and Decrees took pains to define the terms they were using. The same can be said of the notion of "contemplative life" as a way of life. This is why a study had to be undertaken with regard to these texts; their exegesis is confirmed by the testimony of those who, during the Council and immediately after it, stated their understanding of the realities of which they were speaking. Vatican II should not become a myth, or a series of different myths, which each person invents either in order to attack them, or to make them support his own private opinions. Equivalents can indeed be found for "contemplative life"; one must find some if he wants to explain lucidly what it is all about. But there is in every technical vocabulary a precision which one is duty-bound to respect. Some writers question the link established by the Council and in accord with tradition, between "contemplation" as a personal activity, and the "contemplative life" — as if the former could not be the intent of an institution, and of a way of life meant to foster the activity of contemplative prayer. And yet, the past as well as the present bear testimony that it is a reality, a fact. Before rejecting it, one should make an effort to grasp its real meaning. Then, if one safeguards what is essential and inherent in it, one is all the more free with regard to the forms in which it has been associated. The contemplative life is essentially a "life of adoration": it is a life, that is to say, a state not a transitory action, just as the moral life is something more than a "good act". It tends toward "adoration", in the sense this word occupies in Scripture and Christian tradition — not, as was perhaps the case in certain platonic traditions, merely intellectual speculation, but an attitude of love, of waiting, of desire, prayer and *ascesis*. One may say that the word "contemplation" points toward the subjective viewpoint of the man who contemplates, and the word "adoration" toward the objective aspect of the God whom he adores. But since these are two aspects of the same reality, it is better not to distinguish them too much, nor multiply subtle nuances about each of them. There is a *sensus monasticus* as well as a *sensus Ecclesiae*, neither of which is misleading.

Since the problems treated in this book were set forth in the light of the Council, others have appeared which will stimulate new reflections and new advances. One of the most recent is the very delicate subject of feminine monasticism, its religious and cultural motivations, its theological justifications, and its psychological and juridical aspects. In this area, it will probably again be necessary to advance several hypotheses before the exact perspective can be found.

Lastly, the second part of this work tries to illustrate with some examples the convictions formulated in the first part. It seems that the saints and their *milieux*, although far from us in time, have a distinct reality. One reads sometimes that monasticism is built on a "rejection of culture", but the monks alluded to here have enjoyed to the fullest the culture that their epoch and civilization could provide. One hears it said that monasticism is a "refuge from action", but St

Columban, St Maieul, St Bernard and so many others have been all the more active because they were monks. They were exceptional, no doubt, but nonetheless symbolic of a reality too rich to allow itself to be formulated in negative terms. Renouncing is not refusing, it is outrunning.

Some concrete examples must conterbalance oversimplified judgments, generalizations, and caricatures. We must show how the ideal was realized in certain individuals who could not have existed but for the *milieux* in which they grew up.

Since the Epilogue of this book was written, I have come across the admirable pages in which Karl Barth exercised his critical judgment on Christian monasticism. They express with more nuances than I had done myself the riches and the risks of this reality in the Church which is monasticism. And because, according to the avowal of this theologian as of so many other witnesses of this tradition, it is part of the Church, we must also maintain a solid conviction and the freedom of judgment which the Holy Spirit manages to keep alive in what Paul called "the obedience of faith."

Jean Leclercq

Trappe N.D. d'Oka
September, 1971

ABBREVIATIONS

AA SS	*Acta Sanctorum*, Antwerp, 1643 —; Paris-Rome, 1863-1870.
Acta Aps	*Acta apostolicae sedis*. Rome, 1909 —
CCSL	*Corpus Christianorum, Series Latina*, Turnholt: Brepols, 1953 —
CSEL	*Corpus scriptorum ecclesiasticorum latinorum. Editum consilio et impensis Acamiae Litterarum Caesareae Vindobonensis.* Vienna 1866.
Collectanea OCR	*Collectanea Ordinis Cisterciensium Reformatorum.* Westmalle.
LThK	*Lexikon für Theologie und Kirche.* Freiburg im Breisgau: Herder, 1957 —
MGH SS	*Monumenta Germaniae Historica, Scriptores.* Leipzig, Hannover, Hann, 1826-1934.
PL	J. P. Migne, *Patrologia latina.* Paris, 1844—
RTAM	*Recherches de théologie ancienne et médiévale.* Louvain: Abbaye du Mont Cesar, 1929
SCH	*Sources Chrétiennes.* Paris: Editions du Cerf, 1942 —

PART ONE:

PROBLEMS IN MONASTICISM

FOREWORD

THE IDEAL AND MANKIND

THIS BOOK IS MADE UP of a series of essays originally lectures delivered to various audiences drawn from
the religious or university life. They will not therefore
make up a homogeneous whole. And yet in all of them one
and the same question will be asked and, in rough outline,
an answer given.

The subjects will be doctrine and history. In expounding
the former, say those who teach it, one receives at times the
somewhat discouraging impression that it is sublime and on
that account unreal. Who can attain to that contemplative
prayer in which the *magisterium* and the saints of the Church
train monks, and even demand of them. Are the many objections raised today to such a life completely without justification? Do advances in psychology, or simply an awareness of
the world's wretchedness, not give man an increasing sense of
his limitations? He grows in knowledge, in the mastery of
cosmic powers; he becomes more astute but at the same time
he knows himself capable of the worst; he learns every day of
horrors occuring in some corner of the globe. Surely it is
action that will deliver him, give him the chance of becoming
and proving himself better, of transforming his environment and his universe, and of bringing them nearer to God?
The aims of the contemplative life seem idealistic, out of
reach, an escape. There is no doubt that certain traditional
maxims, for various reasons, justify this impression. Taken
out of the context which softened any note of finality they

15

may have had, words are given abstract connotations which they certainly did not have originally. They are interpreted in the light of the speculations of an age not their own. When these statements are put back into the whole context which illuminates them, they can be seen not as inducements to fly from reality, but as safeguards of all aspects of reality. The teaching of the Church today as yesterday is accessible to the Christian who has received the contemplative vocation.

The first series of essays will attempt to present different, complementary, aspects of the conception which the Church, in the person of her leaders and her members, has of the monastic life in our day. These will show that, if no concessions are made as far as the ideal is concerned, its expression is adaptable to men of our time. Still that might not be enough; we must turn to the test of history and accomplishments. And so the second part of the volume will recall monks as they have been and still are, with their aspirations, which come from the Holy Spirit, and their weaknesses, which come from their own nature. The rages of St Columban, the confessions of St Bernard, the astuteness of St John of Gorze, the falterings of institutions, the gropings of the present day, will be reminders of everything that is human in monasticism, as in everything which is real in the Church.

After all, is it not this combination of the sublime and the mundane which gives value to the Christian adventure? Is weakness not the fulfilment of strength? To admit the fallible condition of every man, to offer it and to open it to the radiance of the Spirit is to participate in the mystery of him who, being God, identified himself with the wretchedness of his creature in order to rescue him from it. Rich, he made himself poor to enrich us with his divinity. He emptied himself, taking the form of a slave, even to death, and that the death of the Cross. And accepting his sacrifice, the Father raised him up. His Spirit henceforth sanctifies our limitations and, above all, our falterings. In earthen vessels, constantly threatened, we carry a treasure, provided only that we believe in grace.

THE CONTEMPLATIVE LIFE AND MONASTICISM
IN THE LIGHT OF VATICAN II.*

SURPRISING AS IT MAY SEEM, the document in which the Council speaks with the greatest insistence of the life of contemplation is the Decree on the Missionary Activity of the Church. Among those who were engaged in preparing the Decree on the Religious Life itself were found some who were not only ready to contest the legitimacy of a 'life of contemplation', but who even—in the course of a discussion of this formula—threw doubt on the existence of any concrete reality at all beneath the label. And yet, at precisely the same time, those upon whom rests the responsibility for the Church's activity in lands where needs are greatest, were unhesitatingly maintaining the sheer necessity of such a way of life. Just another example, no doubt, of the way in which theory can lag behind actual fact! For quite unmistakably, what confronts us here is no mere bright idea but an unqualified assertion: 'Either by their prayer (*sive oratione*) or active work, Religious of both sexes render indispensable service in making the kingdom of God take root in souls, giving it a firmer footing there and spreading it still further' (No. 15). And soon afterwards the wish is expressed that 'Even from the time when the Church is first being established in a region, the Religious life must be sedulously promoted' (No. 18). One of the tasks assigned to it to 'ex-

*Previously published in *Gregorianum*, 47 (1966) 495-516, in Italian in *Vita contemplativa e monachesimo* (Sorrente, 1947) 13-28; in English in *Cistercian Studies*, 1 (1966) 53-57. [Because several of the chapters have previously appeared in British and American journals, some variation in punctuation and spelling occurs in the volume—ed.]

17

amine carefully how those ascetical and *contemplative* traditions—whose seeds God has at times deposited in ancient
cultures even before the preaching of the Gospel—can be
assimilated into the Christian religious life' (no. 18). This
particular chapter ends:

> Worthy of special mention are the various attempts at mak-
> ing *the contemplative life* take root. In making such an
> attempt, some, while retaining the essential elements of
> monasticism, strive to implant the rich traditions of their
> Order, whereas others return to the simpler forms of an-
> cient monasticism. All, however, should strive after a genu-
> ine adaptation to local conditions. For *since the contempla-
> tive life belongs to the fullness of the Church's presence, it
> ought to be established everywhere in the infant Churches.*

In this forthright passage, the life of contemplation and the
monastic life are, as we see, equated and identified. Furthermore, attempts of those foundations which are rediscovering
their original simplicity are recognized, accepted and spurred
on. Equally welcome are those which adhere to the essential
elements alone of an Order which, though heir to a valuable
tradition, no longer possesses this simplicity. The one condition is that all alike must strive for an 'adaptation' which will
clearly be rendered easier by simplicity and by 'return' to the
sources. In conclusion, the contemplative life is given a place
within the Mystery of the Church among the elements necessary for the fullness of its presence: *ad plenitudinem praesentiae Ecclesiae pertinet.*

In a Decree which deals with missionary activity this mention might have been deemed sufficient — but far from it.
Towards the end, another complete paragraph is devoted to
'Religious Institutes of *the contemplative* and the active life'.
Both, it is stated, 'have thus far made, and still make, the
greatest contribution to the evangelization of the world . And
so they are spoken of yet again, and here, as in all the Council's Decrees, a significant priority is accorded to those under
consideration in this article. The passage runs as follows:

Institutes of the contemplative life are of paramount importance in the conversion of souls through their prayers, works of penance and trials, since it is God Who, when asked to do so, sends laborers into his harvest (cf. Mt. ix, 38), opens the minds of non-Christians to listen to the Gospel (cf. Acts, xvi, 14), and makes the word of salvation fruitful in their hearts (cf. 1 Cor. iii, 7). These Institutes are even asked to make foundations in mission countries, as many of them have already done, so that by living there in a manner adapted to the genuinely religious traditions of the people, they may bear splendid witness among non-Christians to the majesty and love of God, as well as to union in Christ (No. 40).

This declaration is condensed in the extreme and packed with teaching. Austerity is inherent in the life of contemplation and to the penitential practices which are part of the every-day observance are added those sufferings which — described by the Biblical word 'trials' (*tribulationes*) — are never far to seek. The efficacy of such a life is established by reference to the words of Our Lord himself and to those of his Apostles. And since, according to the Dogmatic Constitution on the Church, the primary office of all religious, the one common to all of them, is to bear witness, a careful description is given of the way in which this is to be done by contemplatives who live in the midst of non-Christians. It is noteworthy that the mention of God's majesty and love was added only during the final revision of the text. Yet it is an addition which catches the attention of all who, as result of having lived among many of the non-Christian peoples of the Near and Far East, and Africa, know well how widespread among them is an awareness of the awe-inspiring grandeur of the godhead, and know, too, how this very awareness itself can sometimes lead to the notion that mere man is scarcely able to enjoy any kind of intimacy with It at all.

Contemplatives, however, through a total consecration to God alone which engages them in a way of life that seems, to all appearances at least, capricious, escapist and downright futile, proclaim that God is so great that it is no more than his due that that there should be some who are set apart for the sole purpose of praising him, and that these very men and women, far from feeling themselves to be in any way remote from him are, on the contrary, engaged in returning to him, on behalf of the rest of men, his own love for this same humanity, a love with which they themselves are filled. They are witnesses to Love, to Charity. This can only, of course, become truly effective in Christ, through the Spirit sent by him, for it is the living reality of the *'cor unum'* set at the beginning of the Acts of the Apostles as an example to the entire Christian community.

In conclusion, let us draw attention to a renewed insistence upon the necessity of adapting the practices and precepts of the life of contemplation to the religious traditions of non-Christian peoples. A bare transplantation of spiritual traditions or observances derived from ancient forms of Christianity, whether Western or Eastern, is no longer tolerable.

DOCTRINE

The Story behind a Text.

So the way of life known as contemplative does, indeed, exist in the Church. But how? What form does it take?

The first proof of its identity must be some link with the Person of Christ, making clear that it is one way of participating in his Mystery, of imitating his example, of following his teaching. In the Constitution on the Church a comprehensive doctrinal instruction is provided which covers the religious life in all its various forms. No more than a bare mention can be made of each of these in particular, but the mention is there, and it is significant.

'Religious must make it their careful aim that through them the Church may daily be increasingly enabled to show Christ — to both believers and unbelievers alike — *in contemplation on the mountainside,* proclaiming God's kingdom to the crowds, healing the sick and maimed, and converting sinners into wholesome fruit, blessing children, doing good to all, and in all things obeying the Will of the Father Who sent Him' (No. 46)[1].

Here, the Council, instead of using explicit Scriptual quotations, whose application to the religious life mught be disputed, draws upon actual concrete events in the life of the Saviour. In this way, it is clearly established that Jesus himself, in his own Person, engaged in many different forms of activity of which the one common element was that in whatever did he was always accomplishing his mission of salvation by doing what would please his Father; in other words, he was obedient. And first and foremost amongst all these activities came prayer: *sive in monte contemplantem.* 'Jesus went up onto the mountain by himself to pray'.[2]

How can the nature of this life given up to prayer be accurately described?

While the third version of the Decree on the Religious Life was being worked out, a controversy arose over the expression 'contemplative life', which was taxed with being pagan in origin, of purely philosophical import, and incompatible with the demands made by the Gospel. In some eyes, everything to do with 'contemplation' and 'monasticism' aroused suspicions of platonism, dualism, pessimism and, as a final thrust, sheer egoism. Those Christians, however, who were perfectly well aware that they had, themselves, received just such a vocation from God, remained quite unmoved by all this, and it became apparent that no arguments drawn from history or from pure speculation could possibly carry weight against confrontation with a concrete reality within the

---

1. Both here and later on, the extracts from the *Dogmatic Constitution* on the Church are taken from the translation made by Rev. Fr. Th. Camelot, in the "Unam Sanctam" cole., vol 51 (1965).

2. Mt. xiv, 23; cf. Jn vi, 15; Lk. v, 16, etc. . .; these passages have been collected and studied by D.L. De Lorenzi, "La preghiera anima del Evangelo," in C. Vagaggini—G. Penco, *La Preghiera* (Rome, 1964) p. 129-136. The relationship between monastic prayer and Jesus' solitary prayer on the mountainside was established by Cassian, *Conlationes*, X, *De oratione*, 6, CSEL 3 (1886) p. 292, and by many others after him.

Church. All that was at issue was the need to reach agreement as to the wording, while reminding those to whom such a call had not been personally addressed to have due respect for one of the Church's charismata not entrusted to them.

In the event, the practical result of this challenge was to bring into being a lively and beneficial reaction by which, in the end, the Decree was actually enriched—in rather the same way that heresies have resulted in some of those doctrinal definitions which have marked a decisive forward step. Two new paragraphs were added to the text, the origin of which was explained as follows, at the time when the fourth draft was being presented to the Fathers:

> Since it has already been stated in No. 5. that the members of any and every Religious Institute whatsoever 'should combine contemplation, by which they become united with God in mind and heart, with apostolic love' and because many of the Fathers have asked for it, the Commission has thought fit to provide a description of what might be called the types into which all the various religious institutes can be divided, by speaking of institutes 'which are totally devoted to contemplation' (No. 7) and 'those institutes which are devoted to the various works of the apostolate' (No. 8)[3]. In addition, in response to the desires ex-

3. A special number of the review *Collectanea Cisterciensia*, 26 (1965), fasc. 2, was devoted to the problem raised in this controversy. Also, from the very beginning of the discussions, much light was thrown on the problem in an important article by a canonist who is extremely well informed as to the special demands made by the monastic life: the article in question is by Rev. Fr J. Beyer, SJ., "La vie consacrée dans l'Eglise," in *Gregorianum* 44 (1963) p. 32-61: all the elements of the monastic life which an given there, p. 53-54, are again to be found in the definition of the contemplative life given in the conciliar Decree, no. 7, dealt with further on. Fr Beyer always mentioned in conjuction with each other the two traditional—and ever-living—forms of monastic life: the eremitical and the cenobitical. He has developed these notions afresh—and in so doing anticipated the Council—under the title "L'avenir des Instituts séculiers," *ibid.*, 46 (1965) p. 545-594, in particular p. 547 and 592-593. He is a specialist in the law concerning these Secular Institutes, and he has clearly perceived and shown ("La vie consacrée . . ." p. 61) where the distinction lies between 'the monastic eremitical or cenobitical way of life', 'the life of public apostolate' and 'the life of presence in the world'. The Conciliar Decree, as will be seen, does actually point out clearly the special distinctive features proper to each of these differing types of vocation and, in consequence, the institutes in which they may be put into effect.

pressed by several Fathers, the Commission has drafted some fresh paragraphs, namely, No. 9, 'On the faithful observance of the monastic life and conventual way of life'; No. 10, 'On the lay religious life'; and No. 11, 'On secular institutes'. It has not wished to draw up a new statement on the subject of the eremitical way of life.[4]

This means, in effect, that this fourth version is not to be considered as providing a speculative definition of what is meant by the life of contemplation and the monastic way of life, but a 'description' by which these ways of life may be recognized as legitimate and distinct among the forms, the 'types' of religious life. This is also why, 'in order to by-pass certain doctrinal and historical controversies, the Council has of set purpose refrained from making use of the terminology by which distinctions are drawn between the contemplative life, the active life, and the mixed life'.[5] True enough, as we all know, the idea of a mixed life, both in St Thomas and in more recent times, has in practice shown itself to be liable to a whole series of hair-splitting and varied interpretations, not one of which really carries exclusive conviction. So it is a very good thing indeed that the Council, after having firmly asserted the necessity for all religious, the active ones included, of making a place in their personal lives for that form of contemplation which means intimate union with God, should have gone on to make a clear distinction between two 'states' or 'institutions' of life, by which both possess their own special value, without confusing the one with the other.

The practice of the eremetical or solitary life within the Church reaches back in an unbroken line to the very beginnings of the religious state. Ignored by the canonists at the start of the present century, it has once again compelled recognition of itself as one of the concrete realities of the Church, within the religious state. But it is understandable that it should, here, have been accorded no more than passing reference, for there are, on the one hand, as yet few minds

4. *Schema decreti de accommodata renovatione vitae religiosae. Textus recognitus et modi a commissione conciliari de religiosis examinati*, 1965.
5. *Ibid.*, p. 48.

which are sufficiently prepared to grasp its value, while, on
the other, it is very much in order that legislation should in
no way steal a march on life as it is actually being lived. It is
tomorrow's canonists who will find themselves being compelled to focus their attention on the eremitical life as a result of
its renewal. And it is, in addition, inherent in this form of life
to need no more than the very minimum of organization. But
it is at least referred to as authentic and as going right back to
the very sources: 'Since the very beginning, there have been
men and women who . . . have lived . . . in the solitary form
of life . . . .'[6] And already, at the commencement of the
chapter on religious in the Constitution on the Church, we
have been reminded that 'There has come about a growth of
different rules of life, solitary or in community' (No. 43).

The fourth text prepared by the Commission underwent
still further alterations after it had been submitted to the
Fathers' vote in the final session of the Council, but the new
paragraphs dealing with the life of contemplation and the
monastic life were left untouched. Brought into being as the
result of a challenge which never became widespread or more
than superficial, they were in accord with the deep-rooted
and spontaneous conviction of the main body of the bishops.

The Comtemplative State of Life

Here, to begin with, is a translation of paragraph 7. This
will be followed by a commentary on its text.

However urgent the need for an active apostolate, Institutes which are wholly dedicated to contemplation, and
whose members are solely occupied with God in solitude
and silence, in assiduous prayer and willing penance, must
still continue to play a wonderful role in the Mystical Body
of Christ, in which 'all members have not the same office'.
They offer to God an outstanding sacrifice of praise, making God's people resplendent with the rich fruits of holiness; they stir it by their example and give it growth by the
fruitfulness of their hidden apostolate. They are thus a

6. *Ibid.,* p. 30 and 78.

glory to the Church and a fountainhead of graces from heaven. Nevertheless, while preserving intact their withdrawal from the world, and those practices proper to their life of contemplation, their way of life must be revised in accordance with the principles for the adaptation to modern conditions and the renewal laid out above.

In this text, every word counts. It is clearly stated at the outset that the matter in hand has nothing to do with those purely personal vocations by which anyone, whether a member of any institute at all, or of no institute at all, may be 'a contemplative', but with actual institutions themselves. Nor is it a question of 'acts of contemplation', in the meaning which has sometimes been given to this expression in recent times, and by which is meant certain 'states of prayer' which are generally considered as exceptional and quite independent of any kind of institution, and as not being the result of any special way of life.

There are, however, in actual fact, 'institutes' which are directly 'ordered' to certain definite spiritual activities, and it is in this context that the term 'contemplation'—which, if taken in isolation, might lead to ambiguity, but which is used here in the very first sentence—is to be understood, and all that follows is intended to make this meaning clearer and more precise. In this particular context it can only, as we shall see, refer to a state of being, an actual existence completely orientated towards contemplative prayer and ascetical activity, and in which everything is so organized as to foster both. This is the traditional idea, which St Thomas expressed in the word *ordinatio*.[7] And so we have here, right at the start, an assertion that there are within the Church, in actual concrete fact, states of life which are wholly and solely—*integre*—designed so as to allow the fullest development of the kind of existence about to be described.

7. Let it suffice to quote this passage from the 11a 11ae, q. 189, a. 8, ad 2: '*quantum ad alia quae sunt propria monasticae professioni, quae specialiter ad vitam contemplativam ordinatur*'. As I have remarked under the title "La vie contemplative dans S. Thomas et dans la tradition," in RTAM 28 (1961) p. 262, it is the 'profession of the monastic life' which is 'ordered to the contemplative life'. On the meaning of '*contemplatio*', see p. 267.

Three major characteristics are then established: it is organized "in such a way that its adepts may be" before all else, "in solitude and silence" *ita ut eorum sodales in solitudine ac silentio* . . . . All the concrete realities which are part of the Church's life, including those which belong to the religious life, must seek their meaning in relation to the Mystery of Christ. Now Jesus withdrew himself, at times, into the mountains in just this way—into those mountains which had become the symbols of solitude because among them it was still possible to find oneself alone, while in the plains below, clustered around the lakes, or strung out along the valleys, the mass of men was seeking an easier way of life. The only way in which solitude and silence of the life of contemplation can find their justification is as imitations of those periods of solitude and silence in the life of Christ, and as a participation in that profound solitude which he willingly endured as a means of universal salvation. There are some for whom isolation and withdrawal are the necessary conditions for encounter with him and with all those whom he wills to save. In this sense, enclosure stands in the forefront of all the traditional observances of the monastic life. Dom Guéranger used to say: 'It is separation from the world that makes the monk'.

A mere condition, however necessary, does not of itself suffice to fill a life. The Council set out a second characteristic of the contemplative state of life: 'assiduous prayer'. 'Pray without ceasing', wrote St Paul,[8] and Christian spirituality of all ages has made of the pursuit of *oratio continua* one of the main endeavours of those among the faithful who are really in earnest about trying to live in union with their Lord. 'The constant prayer', spoken of by Clement of Alexandria, the continual 'remembrance of God' of so many of the old monastic writers and of the Eastern monks, as well as Western from Cassian down to St Bernard, the 'presence of God' of more recent spiritual writers—all these are brought to mind in those two words. The first of these evokes the idea of a continuity obtained by the succession, the alteration, the

8. 1. Thess. v, 17; cf. Lk. xviii, 1.

repetition of frequent acts: *assiduus potius quam frequens,* as may be read in more than one ancient text on contemplative prayer.[9]

The third characteristic of such a state of life, according to the Council, is austerity. This again is completely traditional. A way of life which was solitary and prayerful, and yet unmarked by mortification, could be no more than an illusion. A way of life, on the other hand, which was austere simply —or even mainly—for austerity's sake, would equally fail in achieving that balance which the Church now, as always, desires to see maintained as one of the components, on the institutional level, of an authentic life of contemplation. And so this necessary tempering of austerity is referred to in two distinct words, the first of which both moderates and completes the second: *in alacri paenitentia.* Alacrity—that joyous zest which is a sign of true vitality. *'Et alacri fide suscipiamus solemne ieiunium...'* said St Leo, speaking of Lent[10], and this way of speaking is still used in the monastic way of life, for it gives a very good idea of the kind of willing penance which is first a preparation for and then an expression of, the opening out and expansion of the soul. It hardly needs adding that, like their solitude and silence, the prayer and mortification of contemplatives are of value only because they are, for them, the means by which they follow in the footsteps of Christ and share in the mystery of his prayer and his suffering. So understood and so lived, they are—in union with his and because of his—of use in the world's salvation.

And now, within the framework of a way of life made up of these three observances, solitude, prayer and austerity — what do the members of contemplative institutes actually *do*?

The answer can be summed up in three words, and they, too, are heavily charged with meaning: *soli Deo vacent.* The

9. In *Etudes sur le vocabulaire monastique du moyen âge,* Studia Anselmiana, 48 (Rome, 1961) p. 133, I have quoted these texts; cf. the word *assiduus* in the index to that work.

10. Sermo 40, 4; PL 54, 270.

first two were used repeatedly by St Gregory the Great in his
life of St Benedict, as well as by many other writers,[11] as a
characteristic description of the monastic and contemplative
vocation, often enough in conjunction with the same verb as
here, (*vacare*),[12] which is borrowed from the language of the
Bible: *Vacate et videte . . .*[13] What is meant is this. Every
form of activity which cannot serve as a help towards constant prayer must be set aside, so that by finding the key to
that freedom from all preoccupation which is so easily lost,
together with that interior tranquillity which is so very much
the opposite of the anxious restlessness which comes so naturally to man, it may become possible to enter into the joyful
possession of the seventh day's rest of the spirit. The life of
contemplation as a state consists simply and solely in this
constant readiness, this complete openness to God, which has
to be unceasingly renewed and ceaselessly regained. But—in
the ordinary course and at the institutional level—it is quite
impossible to attain to this attitude of calm relaxation at the
price of any conditions less stringent than those which have
just been enumerated: solitude, prayer, penance.

Now that we know what makes this way of life what it is,
and what is actually carried on and done within it, we are
faced with the question of how it can find a place relative to
all the other ways of serving Christ. Has it even—in a missionary Church, wide open to the world—any longer any
place at all? Is it not, rather, merely a form of egoism, a
scandalous delusion which needs to be shown up for what it
really is?

The Council did not remain unaware of objections such as
these and dealt with them next. It began with a recognition
of the diversity of the vocations which God gives, and did so
in the words of St Paul: 'in the mystical Body all the mem-

11. Texts quoted in *Etudes sur le vocabulaire*, p. 29-31: "Seul avec Dieu"; cf.
the index, p. 165, under the words *soli Deo.*

12. In *Otia Monastica. Etudes sur le vocabulaire de la contemplation au moyen
âge*, Studia Anselmiana 51. (Rome, 1963), I have quoted these texts: cf. the
index, p. 183, under the words *vacare soli Deo*; also *Etudes sur le vocabulaire*, p.
161, under the word *vaco.*

13. Ps. 45, 11.

bers do not have the same function,'[14]. So *vacatio* is a legitimate vocation. After this appeal to principle, the text went
on to state that the Council was very well aware indeed of
the Church's needs ('however urgent the need for an active
apostolate') and in so saying refuted in advance an objection
which might be raised against the life of contemplation on
the grounds of the immense amount of missionary work to
be done.

This reference to the only too real and difficult situation of
the Church lends additional force to the statement which
follows: 'these institutes must always retain a most excellent
part — *praeclarem partem semper retinent*'. We can recognise
in this a clear allusion to the passage in the Gospel according
to St Luke, in which the Lord tells Martha that Mary has
chosen an excellent part which is never to be taken away
from her. The application of this passage to the contemplative life as a state, long traditional, was contested a few years
back but has since been re-established as a result of fresh
exegetical discoveries. [15] As used here, though, it implies no
comparison between the 'part' of those who belong to contemplative institutes and the part of those who do not. It is
not stated that the first is 'the best', or that it is 'better than
the other'. All that is asserted is, simply, that it remains,
despite all appearances to the contrary and in the face of all
possible objections, of great value: *praeclarem partem semper
retinent*. One might not be far wrong in detecting here an
echo of St Bernard's remark about those who 'living in the
cloister for the sake of God alone, always united with Him,
and concerned only with what pleases Him, have chosen an
excellent part.'[16]

---

14. Rom. xii, 4.
15. F. Puso, "Marta y Maria. Nota exegetica a Lc. x, 38-42 y 1 Cor. vii, 29-35"
in *Estudies ecclesiasticos* 34 (1960) 851-857.
16. 'Ipsi sunt qui optimam partem elegerunt, qui in claustro soli Deo vivunt,
semper Deo adhærentes et eius placitum considerantes', in *Dom. Palmar.* 11, 5;
PL, 183, 258.

So now, after describing the distinguishing features of the life of contemplation and giving it its due place among all the other ways of life in the Church, the conciliar document has just dealt with its function, which it asserts to be most excellent. In what way?

Four fruits or results are enumerated. God is named first of all: *Deo enim eximium sacrificium laudis offerunt....* Monastic prayer, in other words, is presented as a work of praise. The 'people of God' is also mentioned: contemplatives 'make it resplendent with the rich fruits of holiness'; in addition, 'they stir it by their example', and, finally, 'they give it growth by the fruitfulness of an apostolate' which, although it remains 'hidden', is nonetheless real. This idea of an unseen apostolate had already been expressed by Pius XI in speaking of the Carthusians.[17]. In the following phrase, in which these Institutes are compared to fountainheads, the same idea is evoked. A stream can still flow, even when it does not advertise its presence by gushing out in a torrent — but it does not fail, for all that, to water with graces from heaven (*caelestium gratiarum*) the earth through which it flows.

These images and ideas have all been used to illustrate the value to and in the Church of the Institutes in which the life is wholly contemplative. And now, after all this insistence upon the essentials, the Council is free to deal with the ways in which all this has been put into practice, of the existing forms which it has actually assumed. For it is precisely this actual and concrete way in which the life is being lived, *ratio vivendi,* which is to made the object of an *aggiornamento* in conformity with the directives laid down for all religious at the beginning of the Decree. The Latin formula used here — as it always is when *aggiornamento* is in question—gives the key to its meaning: *accommodata renovatio.* Of these two terms, the first evokes the notion of adaptation, the second that of renewal. All reform, in the Church and in each individual Christian, is a renewal of youth (*Reformamini in novi-*

---

17. 'Occulto quodam tacitoque apostolatu', *Constitutionem 'Umbratilem'* in Acta ApS 16 (1924) p. 388.

tate sensus vestri)[18]—a return to the source of all grace. Then the Council, before bringing its declaration to a conclusion, reminds us once more of the two means of grace which belong in a special way to the Institutes with which it has just been dealing. The first of these is 'withdrawal from the world' (*a mundo secessus*) which is the equivalent of the Greek word from which we get our word 'anchoretic'. The second means consists of all the 'exercises of the contemplative life' considered as a whole. So, in the conclusion itself, we have the victorious reassertion of the very phrase which had been disputed earlier. In the designs of Providence, this challenge itself has resulted in bringing about a solemn declaration of the position maintained by the Church of the Council.

The full bearing of the paragraph which has just been analysed is brought out by contrasting it with the one that follows, dealing with the Institutes 'devoted to the various works of the apostolate'. In this case, everything must be organized so as to foster this, for, contrary to what has just been said of the contemplative state, for them, 'apostolic and charitable works are an essential part of the religious life'. And, in the next few lines, *actio apostolica* and *spiritus apostolicus* are again mentioned, twice over. All such expressions had been completely avoided in speaking of contemplatives.

Among the paragraphs which were added to the text in the later stages is, as we have already seen, one—the ninth—which is specially concerned with monks. Traditionally, no doubt, it has always been taken for granted that these belong to the contemplative state of life. But for all that, in the long and lively history of their foundations, actual historical situations have arisen which the Council has been obliged to take into account. In addition, this was an opportune moment for making it quite clear that the monastic life which plays such a large part in the history and organization of the Eastern Churches is equally respected, and even 'venerated', in the West. So the Council took occasion to single it out for praise

18. Rom. xii, 2.

because of all the services which it has rendered 'within the Church and among men all down the ages'. This is true enough but care must be taken, all the same, to avoid the danger of confusion between the monastic life which is, in all its essential characteristics, proper to monks, and things that some monks happen to have done, so to speak, on the side, and not as part of their true purpose.

After this sort of historical introduction, the text goes on to describe what the true function of monks is: 'A monk's main duty is the service, at once both lowly and noble, of the divine Majesty'. The word *servitium* occurs in the Rule of St Benedict, and emphasis is better laid on its humility than on its nobility. . . .[19] But now come three important words: *intra septa monasterii*. The whole of the monks' service, that of each and every one of them, should normally be carried out *'within the enclosure of the monastery'*. There have always been monks who, exceptionally and for a limited time, have had to travel, especially when they left their own enclosure merely to stay for a time in that of another or of several

19. Neither the word *servitium* used here nor the formula *sacrificium laudis* employed earlier need necessarily be understood, even primarily, of the Divine Office, which hermit monks have never celebrated in common. The monastic life is ordered to prayer; as to the idea that it is specified by the Divine Office—*Monachi propter chorum fundati*—that dates only from the nineteenth century and the monastic historian and theologian Dom G. Morin has shown that it cannot be attributed either to the Rule of St Benedict or to tradition: *L'idéal monastique et la vie chrétienne des premiers jours*, 5th. edt. (Maredsous, 1931) p. 96-98. Since then other authors have confirmed these views in such a way that there is no longer any need to insist upon this point to those who are well in touch with monastic tradition. St Benedict allowed for the fact that all the monks of a community would not pray in the same way, but for him, nevertheless, the distinction does not arise from a different way of participating in the Divine Office, but in making the *lectio divina: Regula*, c. 48, 22-23. We should note that on p. 96, still referring to St Benedict, Dom Morin wrote: "as to the professed monks, he does not with them to prefer anything before it" (i.e., the Divine Office), while in the famous phrase *Nihil operi Dei praeponatur, Regula* c. 43, 3, St Benedict is not introducing any distinction between the professed and the rest, and has no intention of expressing a general principle on the value of the Office, but simply a practical rule to be followed: at the moment when the signal for the Divine Office is sounded, no other occupation is to be given preference, and all must go to it immediately.

other houses.[20] But it is in no way normal for a monk, and still less normal for a definite proportion of the members of a community, to live for a long time outside any enclosure at all.[21]

After this reminder, which applies to all alike, the Council goes on to introduce a distinction between two kinds of monastic institutions. There are those whose members 'live in obscurity and devote themselves completely to the worship of God'. *Sive in umbratile vita . . .* this is a way of speaking which is at the same time up-to-date and venerable for it comes from the Bible, and from it there derives a spiritual current of thought which has remained charged with significance throughout the whole course of tradition. It expresses the idea of a form of life which remains hidden and obscure in the sense that it is in no way directed to the fulfilment of any public function to be exercised openly in the Church.[22] But because it also recalls to our minds the glorious cloud in which the divinity of Christ was made manifest, and the overshadowing fruitfulness of the descent of the Holy Spirit upon Mary, it signifies that this obscure life is lived not in darkness but in light.

In a second category, there are monastic foundations which 'have legitimately undertaken some works of the apostolate or of Christian charity'. *Aliqua opera*: here, too, as in the

20. Under the titles "Les relations entre le monachisme oriental et le monachisme occidental dans le haut moyen âge," in *Millénaire du Mount-Athos, 963-1963*, II (Chevetogne, 1965) p. 61-70, and *Aux sources de la Spiritualité occidentale*, p. 35-90 (11. *Monachisme et pérégrination*) Studia Monastica 3, 1, 33ff., I have quoted these texts and facts.

21. Compare this decree of the ecumenical Council of Vienne, in 1311-1312: 'Monachi multi, proh dolor, nomine et habitu monachi tantum, de re et de vita monachili in se nihil habentes, magis cum saeculo mori quam cum Christo in claustro vivere cupientes, in prioratibus ruralibus et alibi bini vel terni mallent, quam in congregatione sui monasterii, conversari', quoted J. Lecler, *Vienne* (Paris, 1964) p. 126. The motives which, in the middle ages, gave rise to this fact of the existence of monks who lived outside their monastery—still, as a rule, in groups— were in part economic: it was a matter of occupying properties and of administering agricultural undertakings. Today, the motives invoked arise rather from the pastoral ministry: parishes or mission stations which are dependent upon monasteries, etc. . .

22. In "La vie cachée," in *Chances de la spiritualité occidentale* (Paris, 1966), I have made a study of this theme of the *vita umbratilis*.

intra septa monasterii, limits are set to the apostolic and charitable activities of monks, who are asked neither to do too much nor to do everything.[23] The whole tone is quite different from that of the preceding paragraph dealing with Institutes dedicated to the apostolic life. To conclude, the Conciliar Decree utters the desire that 'without changing the character of an Order, those ancient traditions which are valuable must be brought up to date and brought into line with the needs of souls today'. Here again the words *renovare* and *accommodatio* recur. Through the *aggiornamento* which they indicate, monasteries are to be living centres 'for the building up of the Christian people'.

Supple yet decisive, this teaching has far-reaching consequences. Some of these concern all Institutes alike, whether of men or of women; others apply with special force to contemplative and monastic Orders in which some of the members are priests. This makes it necessary to consult the various conciliar texts in which such problems are broached.

Pastoral Activity

In the Decree on the Pastoral Office of Bishops, norms were established for the apostolic work of religious in dioceses. It is said, among other things, that:

23. If the designations 'monk' and 'monastic' have come to be no more than qualifications which are applicable to any and every kind of life, then it would be better to let them go altogether and speak instead of the 'cloistered' religious life, as Fr J. Beyer, SJ has begun to do, in *"L'avenir des instituts séculiers,"* Gregorianum 46 (1965) p. 547 and 591-592, in particular 592, note 23: 'Words cannot be misused with impunity! A monk is someone who seeks God in the austerity of a life of silence and solitude and who makes of this the essential mark of his state of life . . .' The 'interim' nature of the pastoral functions which used sometimes to be imposed upon monks in earlier times is clearly shown, p. 591: 'Gregory the Great sent monks to convert England. Would he have sent them if he had had apostolic Orders at his disposal? '

Considering (*praesertim*) the urgent needs of souls and the shortage of diocesan clergy, religious foundations *not dedicated to the purely contemplative life* can be called by the Bishop to help in various pastoral ministrations. He should, however, have regard to the special character of each foundation (No. 35).[24]

The existing formulation of this passage came into being only at the time of the final revision, the two reservations which it contains being introduced as the results of two groups of amendments. The second of these is concerned with all Institutes in general, and no form of activity can be imposed on any of them which runs counter to the functions assigned to them by their founders, their traditions and their constitutions. But over and above this, a quite special exception has been made with regard to those which are dedicated to 'the purely contemplative life', and it is recognized that the acknowledged power of the bishops to call upon religious to help in various pastoral activities does not extend to them. The expression used here: *vita mere contemplativa*, is the equivalent of the one in the Decree on the religious life: *quae integre ad contemplationem ordinantur*. This mention of foundations in which the life is purely, solely and entirely contemplative leads, no doubt, to the conclusion that there are others not so completely exclusive: from this options may follow which will be of such a nature as to clarify certain situations and avoid ambiguities. But henceforward, in the actual words of the chairman who presented the text to the Fathers before the vote, it is an established fact that 'religious institutes in which the life is purely (*mere*) contemplative really cannot be called upon for pastoral ministrations'.[25]

---

24. *Schema decreti de pastorali episcoporum munere in ecclesia. Textus recognitus et mode a commissione conciliari de episcopis et dioecesium regimine examinati,* 1965, p. 94.
    25. *Ibid.,* p. 62.

The Contemplative Life and the Priesthood

Those who belong to Institutes in which the life is contemplative are then excluded from the pastoral ministrations of the Church. In the declarations which concern them in the Decree on the religious life other duties and responsibilities, other ways of serving Christ, which are recognized as possessing an apostolic and not a pastoral efficacy, are assigned to them. Not only women but men as well belong to these foundations, and the question now arises as to the position of these latter with regard to the priesthood. To provide an answer to this question, all that is needed is to consult all the Conciliar texts which are concerned with priests, for they are perfectly clear. There are a good many of them for in all, or nearly all, the Decrees and Constitutions the priestly functions are either mentioned explicitly or at least alluded to, and among all these references there exists a remarkable coherence. For our present purpose, we need only isolate the dominant idea found in every one of them, for it clears up and solves our problem.

The most important document is naturally the Constitution of the Church. From chapter 2 onwards, two ways of 'sharing in the single priesthood of Christ' are clearly distinguished. There is on the one hand 'the common priesthood of the faithful', on the other, 'the ministerial or hierarchical priesthood'. 'The ministerial priest forms and rules the priestly people. Acting in the Name of Christ, he celebrates the Eucharistic Sacrifice and offers it to God in the name of all the people. The faithful, for their part, in virtue of their royal priesthood, join in the offering of the Eucharist. They likewise exercise that priesthood by receiving the sacraments, by prayer and thanksgiving, by the witness of a holy life, and by self-denial and active charity' (No. 10). We should take it to heart that men and women who are religious are even more closely bound to these duties, still more so those, whether men or women, who belong to contemplative foundations.

All the rest of the Constitution continues to lay still further stress upon this dual exercise of the Christian priesthood, that of the faithful (No. 11, 34), and that of the ministers. The priesthood of priests, like the priesthood of the bishops from whom they receive their charge, is always designated and considered as a ministry, that is to say, a form of service which involves three activities: preaching, pastoral work, and the celebration of the Divine service, especially the Eucharist which is a 'proclamation of the Mystery of Christ'. The whole of this long paragraph (No. 28) consists of an exposition of these three 'functions'. In it, the ministerial priesthood is associated with a 'mission' and is consequent upon a 'mission'. The same characteristic is recognized in yet another participation of the ministerial priesthood, the diaconate (No. 29). This idea of function, of active service, as constituting the ministerial priesthood and providing the justification for its reception by one of the faithful, is henceforth either presupposed or invoked (No. 31, 41). In the Decree on the Church's missionary activity, it is stated that: 'Priests are Christ's representatives and collaborate with the order of Bishops in that threefold sacred task which by its very nature bears on the mission of the Church' (No. 39), and the words service, ministry, pastoral charge also recur immediately here (No. 39) as well as elsewhere (No. 16 and 20).

This teaching is applied to religious in the Decree on the pastoral office of bishops: 'Religious who are priests are consecrated to the priestly office so that they may be the devoted collatorators of the episcopal order, and today, in view of the mounting needs of souls, they can be of even greater help to the bishops than ever' (No. 34). In the Decree on the Ministry and Life of Priests still further stress is laid, at considerable length, on the fact that those who receive the priesthood are thereby charged with the exercise of a threefold function: they are ministers of the Word of God, ministers of the Sacraments, and pastors of the People of God. Three paragraphs begin with each of these three phrases: *Verbi Dei ministri . . . , Sacrorum ministri . . . , Populum Dei regentes et pascentes* ... (No. 13). The Council's teaching, then, is both clear cut and firm. It will still, no doubt, remain possible to legitimatize the existence of communities of priests who in no way realize the idea of the priesthood which the Council has chosen to inculcate with such precision, constancy and insistence. Facts like these, representing as they do a legacy from the past—and a comparatively recent past at that[26]— will need to be submitted, from the chronological point of view, to a critical judgement the principle of which will remain the one enunciated by the Commission for the discipline of the clergy and of the Christian people: *ceterum presbyteratus ordinatur ad ministerium.*[27]

Formation and Spirituality

There are other points as well upon which the Council's teaching can help us, as though by contrast, to understand what the Church expects of the contemplative foundations.

The Decree on the Formation of Priests begins its very first sentence with a reminder that the priest is a 'minister', and all the directives which follow are based on this notion: in the seminaries 'true pastors of souls are formed', 'preparation must be given for the ministry of worship and of the means of sanctification, and for the pastoral ministry' (No. 4); 'It is to mankind that they are sent' (No. 8); They must under-

26. Cf. *Chances de la spiritualité occidentale.*

27. The personal problem of those priests who, after having devoted themselves to the ministry, receive the vocation to serve God in the monastic life, whether as hermits or as cenobites, has not been touched on here. From the very fact that they have actually received this vocation, and that it is recognised as authentic, their new way of living their priestly life is legitimate, and its justification from the point of view of their spiritual life is not, for them, a speculative or juridical matter at all. There are priests who actually see, in this second stage of their advance towards God, a way in which that can give a more explicitly universal character to the exercise of their eucharistic ministry. Like the hermit, for example, who habitually celebrates the Holy Sacrifice without any of the faithful being present, and who has placed in front of his altar a small globe of the earth: every day he turns it a little upon its axis, so as to have, turn by turn, under his eyes and in his intention, all the continents, while he is saying Mass before the world.

stand that it is their duty to consecrate themselves entirely
to the service of God and to the pastoral ministry' (No. 9),
and that 'Their spiritual life must draw its strength and vigor,
before all else, from their own pastoral activity' (No. 9).
Further on, their 'pastoral' functions are again enumerated
(No. 19 and again in the conclusion No. 22). Such a programme is obviously inapplicable to members of contemplative foundations and so the conclusion follows that the
priesthood as it is described in this text is not, except by
special exception, to be received by them.

The same distinction makes its appearance very clearly in
the spiritual domain. According to the declaration made by
the Commission for the Discipline of the Clergy and Faithful:
'this text lays the foundation of priestly holiness upon the
very nature of the priestly ministry itself, in other words, in
the sacrament and in the mission which have been received'[28]; 'the true priestly mission to men and true adoration of the Father are so closely bound up with one another
as to be inseparable, in such a way that these two aspects of
the life and ministry of priests cannot be dissociated, the one
from the other'[29]. And while religious who follow the contemplative way of life are to remain 'in solitude and silence',
the ministry of priests demands of them that, without being
conformed to the world, they must nevertheless live within it
side by side with other men (No. 3). All their other obligations spring from this function. While celibacy is simply an
inherent part of the contemplative life as a state, it is represented as befitting priests for many reasons (*multimodam
convenientiam cum sacerdotio habet*), of which the most
outstanding is their 'mission', to which are added 'pastoral
reasons' (No. 16). If priests are 'invited to embrace voluntary
poverty', it is so that they may become 'more obviously
Christlike and more free to discharge their sacred duties' (No.
17). In the same way, 'obedience appears as exacted by the
pastoral ministry, or by pastoral charity', 'it is required by

28. *Schema decreti de ministerio et vita presbyterorum. Textus emendatus et
relationes*, 1965, p. 60.
29. *Ibid.*, p. 54.

the very nature of the pastoral ministry' (No. 15)[30]. For members of contemplative foundations therefore, since they do not possess these functions, the essential characteristics of their true spirituality cannot be determined by the priesthood.

It is easy to see how justifiable are the view of those theologians who have pointed out the originality of a spirituality built up in this way. 'Over and over again in this Council, it has been said that it is necessary to discover a form of spirituality for diocesan priests which is not just a transposition of monastic spirituality'[31]. Instead, it 'breaks away from an overly monastic conception of the secular clergy: the priest is no longer considered a kind of second-hand monk who has somehow wandered out into the world more or less by chance'.[32] Fair enough—but it cuts both ways! The spirituality proper to the contemplative way of life is not a priestly one. The monk is not a priest who has somehow or other wandered off into the cloister.

In the Church and for the World.

The Council's documents have provided us with a clear account of what the contemplative and monastic way of life really is, what are its tasks, its limitations, and its true place within the mystery of God, the mystery of Christ, and the work of the Church. But even declarations which do not directly concern it throw light upon its position and its significance, and so it might be well worth while to conclude with a consideration of those aspects of the Church's presence in the world which it manifests most clearly. For this purpose, two major Constitutions will be of help.

The one dealing with the Church has shown that her office is to save the world by realizing within it the whole mystery of Christ, and in so doing to lead it to its final fulfilment, towards the glory of the kingdom, towards the ultimate

30. *Ibid.,* p. 62.

31. R. Rouquette, "La quatrième session du Concile," in *Etudes* (December 1965) p. 693.

32. R. Laurentin, in *Le Figaro* of 13-14 November 1965.

realities. It is this conviction, the underlying theme of the whole text, which makes of it what we might well call the Magna Carta of Christian hope. Over and over again we are reminded that the Church here below is on the march, in exile, on pilgrimage. A stranger in a strange land, she is on her way to her true homeland, gradually achieving perfect union with her Bridegroom. She is the initial stage, the beginnings of the kingdom to which she is pressing on, and to which she appeals with a confidence which rests upon her faith in the Resurrection of Jesus. She bears witness among men to the Lord Who once time endured suffering but who is now in glory. She herself is still sharing in his Passion but the certainty which she has of one day sharing also in his triumph gives meaning to all she does, to the existence and to the actions of all of her members.

There are some among these who are, so to speak, 'specialists' in this eschatological testimony.

'The People of God have here no abiding city; they are seeking rather the city that is to come. The religious state, while giving to its followers greater independence of earthly cares, gives all believers a clearer demonstration of the good things of heaven which are already present in this age . . . It has a particular way of bringing to light the kingdom of God in its elevated position above all earthly goods and the supremacy of its requirements; it shows all men the supreme and massive dominance of Christ's rule, and the unlimited nature of the Holy Spirit's power at work in the Church in a remarkable way' (No. 44).

But while there are, among religious themselves, those who, occupied in tasks which belong to the apostolic ministry or in active good works, are meant to lead men by means of direct action upon them, there are others who are dispensed even from these offices. All that is asked of them is to lead their brothers towards the Kingdom by reminding them of its existence, by showing the way in which to seek it. These are the members of the contemplative foundations, who imitate Jesus Christ not in his direct action upon men but in his contemplation 'on the mountainside'. Taken in this sense,

not only do they have the office of bearing witness to the
whole body of Christians, whether among the priestly hierarchy or among the laity, but even to religious of the apostolic
way of life. For all and everyone alike they must be a living
reminder of what is known as the 'scale of values', on the
highest rungs of which are ranged the things towards which
the Church is pressing on until - *donec,* and how that word
keeps cropping up in the Constitution - definitive reality is
finally established, in the End of all. This is why they are
dispensed from these immediate tasks, 'however urgent they
may be', in order to be free to devote themselves to others
which, though of apparently less pressing and immediate
necessity, are in reality directed towards the actual presence
of God. Solitude, silence, prayer, willing penance, the freedom to be 'occupied with God alone'—these are their duties,
and hard and demanding ones they are. How ludicrous to
bother to go on asserting that there is nothing Platonic about
them after the Council itself, true to the age-old tradition of
the Church and to the declarations of her magisterium under
recent Popes, has appropriated and consecrated the expression 'life of contemplation', has not only retained its full
Christian significance but has actually confirmed it.

Now we must turn to the Pastoral Constitution on the
Church in the World of Today, for this, surely, has been
drawn up for the express purpose of showing that Catholics
have no right to stand aside from the preoccupations, the
labors and the difficulties of their contemporaries. This being
so, the question must be asked whether it is really still permissible for some to separate themselves from the whole
body of men, turn away into solitude and occupy themselves
only with God.

From the very beginning of the text, we are reminded that
the Church is in exile, 'on her pilgrim way to the Father's
kingdom' (No. 1), until the time at which she will 'be transformed and have achieved her fulfilment' (No. 2). To bear
witness to the death and to the Resurrection of Christ is to
answer one of the 'fundamental questions' mankinds asks
itself: 'What happens after this earthly life? ' (No. 10). The

Christian is a man who has 'the firstfruits of the Spirit', 'the guarantee of our inheritance', who looks forward with complete certainty to the resurrection of his body (No. 22). 'The solidarity of the human race must continue to grow until the day on which it will find its completion—the day on which men saved by grace will give perfect glory to God . . .' (No. 32). And from one end of the document to the other is to be found this constant 'until'. The eschatological theme is sometimes echoed (No. 51), sometimes—and more than once—fully developed (Nos. 39, 40, 45), and it is to be found once again, like the triumphant climax of a fugue, in the final movement of the whole document (No. 93).

In other words, in this Constitution, just as in the one which deals explicitly with this very same mystery of the Church, the two aspects of this mystery, 'not of the world' and 'in this world', or, if you prefer to put it another way, transcendence and immanence, have both alike been equally proclaimed.

And so, in the light of both the one and the other, and in the light, too, of the Decree on the missionary activity of the Church, it has been made clear once and for all that when certain religious—whether men or women—stand aside from the ordinary, everyday tasks which fall to the lot of all the People of God, those who belong to the priestly hierarchy, to the laity or to the apostolic Institutes, they are not in any way absent from the work which is being done for the world within and by the Church. What it *does* mean is that, in them, what the Church has said of all religious is being put into—so to speak—maximum effect.

'No one should think that their consecration makes religious strangers to their fellow men or unprofitable citizens here on earth. Even if in some cases they have no direct contact with their contemporaries, they keep them company at a deeper level in the heart of Christ, and co-operate with them in the things of the spirit . . .' (No. 46).

In them, too, is accomplished in a special way—for this is, indeed, their 'speciality', and the one which distinguishes

them from all the other members of the People of God—
what the Constitution on the Church in the world has
thought good to repeat, from its own point of view, in a
passage which all can clearly recognise as referring to them:

'Christ was established as Lord of all by His resurrection—
the Lord to Whom all authority in heaven and on earth has
been given. He already works in the hearts of men by the
power of the Holy Spirit, and He does not merely rouse our
desire for the world to come; at the same time He stimulates,
purifies, reinforces those generous aspirations by which the
human family bends its energies to make its own life more
humane and to subdue the earth to this purpose. The gifts of
the Spirit are various. He calls some to bear witness clearly to
the desire for heaven and to keep that desire alive among
men. Others He calls to devote themselves to serving humanity here—a ministry which provides material for the kingdom of heaven. To all He brings liberation, that setting aside
self-interest and putting all earth's powers to human purposes, they may reach out towards a future in which humanity itself will become an offering acceptable to God.' [33]

Translated at Holy Cross Abbey, Stapehill.

33. N. 38. It is interesting to find, at the end of this same passage, an allusion to
the 'foretaste of the heavenly banquet', in conformity with the eschatological
terminology so dear to the monasticism of the middle ages; cf., *Un maître de la
vie spirituelle au xiie siècle, Pierre de Celle (1115-1183)*, (Paris, 1946) p. 75-81:
La prélibation du ciel; cf. *ibid.*, p. 125.—In the same way that those who are
responsible for the Church's missionary activity will be, from now on, represented
in the Congregation for the propagation of the Faith, it might be thought that
those who have the responsibility of governing the Institutes of religious life,
including those in which the life of contemplation is led, might be of use in
representing the interests, and the demands made by their vocation, of the
members of these Institutes in the Congregation of religious.

THE EXAMPLE OF CHRIST*

IN CONTEMPLATION ON THE MOUNTAIN

*Let Religious be vigilant to ensure that by them
the Church really shows forth Christ more clearly every
    day to believers and unbelievers,
whether in contemplation on the mounta..iside
or in proclaiming to the multitude the Kingdom of God,
or healing the sick and the wounded
and converting sinners to a better life,
or blessing children and doing good to all,
but always obedient to the will of the Father who sent Him.*

Lumen Gentium 46

T HE SECOND VATICAN COUNCIL on several occasions took pleasure in saying that everything done in
the realm of salvation is a participation in the work of
salvation: the continuation in the Church, the extension in its
members and in that strict sense the imitation of what began
in Jesus Christ, of what he accomplished perfectly once and
for all and which must now be shown forth and communicated to the world. So all Christians are asked to be signs, witnesses. Among them, religious are to "represent" in a special
way certain aspects of his mystery. For example, by their
voluntary poverty, they are to be the "sign" of his poverty
and to "participate"[1] in it.

* Published in *La vie spirituelle* 117 (1967) pp. 377-387.
1. *Perfectae Caritatis,* 13.

The highest activity of the Church, because it was highest in Christ, is contemplation, towards which all action is directed—as is clearly stated from the beginning of the first text promulgated by the Council, the preamble of the *Constitution on the Sacred Liturgy.* All the faithful are to embody in their lives and so "express and manifest" the mystery of Christ and the true nature of the Church by participating in his contemplation and his action.[2] All Religious without exception are reminded of the same duty, in the Decree regarding them.

And so the members of each Institute, seeking God alone and above all, should combine contemplation, which unites them to God through the mind and the heart, and apostolic love by which they strive to join in the work of redemption and extend the Kingdom of God.[3] Among them, some are "entirely given to contemplation", which they seek in "the practices appropriate to the contemplative life". A whole paragraph of the Decree *Perfectae Caritatis* recalls to them the obligations fundamental to their state, to which the renewal they have brought about in their observances and institutions should help them respond more and more fully.[4]

It was not the function of the dogmatic Constitution on the Church, *Lumen Gentium,* in the chapter devoted to Religious, to enter into these particular applications. A point is made in it, however, of giving briefly the characteristics of the main branches of Religious Institutes which express different types of charisma, of vocations, and this is done by turning to the example of Our Lord and of the various activities which he himself carried out and which Religious are to continue and represent as signs and witnesses.

Vel in monte contemplatem. . . . The enumeration of the chief activities of Christ begins by recalling his "contemplation on the mountainside." It is worth showing to what extent this brief but precise allusion is based on Scripture and

---

2. *Sacrosanctum Concilium,* 2.
3. *Perf. Carit.,* 5.
4. Ibid., 7.

Tradition. We will not consider here the prayer of Christ in general nor in all its particular instances recorded in the Gospels, but only those when he was "on the mountainside" and "in contemplation".

Scripture

In all religions, mountains had been regarded as a link between heaven and earth: the centre and image of the world, a place where the deity was met, where this world was left for his, the natural site of the temple to which he descended, and at which union with him took place. The place where all this happens is a holy mountain.[5] This symbolism and this reality occur in the Bible, where the New Testament takes up the images and ideas of the Old, particularly the "favoured mounts"[6] where God revealed himself, to Moses, to Elijah and to Elisha, and those hills on whose summit a cult was practised in his honour, where he was worshipped and sacrifice was offered to him. Jerusalem with her Temple was to be *the* mountain *par excellence*. In the Gospels and apostolic writings, she has a symbolic or geographical significance—sometimes both. Elevation, height, is the sign of a sublime mystery, of God made manifest and of his dwelling among men, and of the fulfilment of the prophetic utterances.

Moses on Horeb in Sinai had spoken with God and received the Law: the new Moses promulgates his new law in the Sermon on the Mount. The face of Moses had become radiant as a consequence of his conversation with God (Ex. 34:28): at the Transfiguration on Tabor Jesus became resplendent. On the Mount of Mystery, Jesus was tempted, beginning there the work of redemption. This work of salvation, of the reconciliation of God with humankind, was completed in his

5. See G. de Champeaux - S. Sterckx, *Introduction au monde des symboles* (La Pierre-qui-Vire, 1966) pp. 164-180.

6. See X. Léon-Dufour, "Montagne," in *Vocabulaire de théologie biblique* (Paris, 1962) col. 651-652.

person in the mountains: on the Mount of Olives, then on
Mount Calvary, he died and rose again. At his last meeting
with his disciples, on the Mount of the Ascension, he was
definitively enthroned before their eyes in his glory. And it is
on a mountain that Jerusalem, in the Book of Revelation,
appears from on high, coming down from heaven and from
God.

Now in the life of Jesus, one of his actions is specially
connected with mountains: prayer. Before the choosing of
the Twelve,

"He went out into the mountains to pray, and he spent the
whole night in prayer to God." (Lk 6:12)

After the feeding of the five thousand, he sent his disciples
on ahead and himself saw the multitude off.

"After he had seen them off, he went up into the mountains to pray." (Mk 6:46)

"He went up the mountainside by himself to pray," wrote
St Matthew (14:23) more specifically, emphasizing the solitude which he was seeking there.

Jesus "withdrew again into the mountains by himself" St
John was to say (6:15). Similarly, before questioning the
disciples about who he was and eliciting St Peter's profession of faith, "He was praying alone." (Lk 9:18)

After foretelling for the first time his Passion and the im-
minence of the Kingdom, "he took with him Peter and John
and James and went up into the mountains to pray" and "as
he prayed" the Transfiguration took place (Lk 9:28-29).
When St Peter and the two Apostles "had seen his majesty
with their own eyes" (II Pet. 1:16) they saw him at prayer.
When at his Baptism he was "at prayer" (Lk 3:2), the first
theophany, completed by that of the Transfiguration, took
place. There is a connexion between the prayer of Jesus and
the revelation of God concerning his identity and his mission.

Does that mean that he prays with only his mission in
mind, as though to prepare himself for what he is going to do

or to achieve? Is the prayer of Jesus in every case circumscribed by the action he has just performed or is about to perform, and similarly when he withdraws into solitude with his disciples, to train them? Nothing in the texts and their context dictates this interpretation. Only Lk 6:12 seems to set the solitary prayer of Jesus in juxtaposition to the choosing of the Apostles and even that is not absolutely certain and admitted by everyone, and it would not necessarily imply that Jesus regulated his prayer by his actions. St Luke moreover tells us that apart from these great moments, "he would withdraw into the wilderness and pray" (Lk 5:15). From the passages already quoted, and others (Mk 1:35; Lk 6:42), it becomes evident—and it is sometimes expressly stated—that if Jesus withdrew from time to time into solitude, it was to pray there in peace, protected from the importunity of the crowds. This outward recollection was only the expression of his intimacy with the Father, of his need to converse lovingly with him and ask his help. Nothing rules out the possibility of his thinking at that time of the next day's ministry and planning what he would do. But did he need to prepare, was he making a retreat only for that? We know that those retreats and his big retreat with his disciples in the course of his public life have a wealth of significance: the break with unbelieving Israel, adherence to the one person of the Saviour, the spiritual and eschatological nature of the Kingdom he was to found, the need for renunciation and sacrifice in order that the Kingdom might begin.[7] Let us consider here only the retreats for prayer, or the prayer which he practised in his retreats. It is has been possible to say that the prayer of Jesus as it appears in St John is "contemplative prayer",[8] this is eminently true of the times when he wished to remain alone with his Father, assenting to his will, accepting its demands in an act of utter love which received its highest

7. See X. Léon-Dufour, *Les évangiles et l'histoire de Jesus* (Paris, 1963) pp. 365-367; and "Vers l'annonce de l'Eglise: Matthieu 14, 1-16, 20," in *L'homme devant Dieu. Mélanges H. de Lubac* (Paris, 1963) I, pp. 44-49.

8. Ch. Augrain, *Témoins de l'Esprit. Aux sources bibliques de la vie consacrée* (Paris, 1966) p. 108.

expression in the prayer of the Agony on the Mount of Olives. His mission to men was included in his submission to the purpose of the Father. Obedience, even to the death of the cross, is the fruit of adoration.

Tradition

It is undoubtedly in this sense that Tradition has understood the prayer of Jesus on the mountainside. St Cyprian, the most ancient witness to write on this prayer, classed it as an act of adoration.[9] Lactantius expressed the same opinion.[10] For St Hilary[11] and St Leo the Great,[12] among others,[13] the mountain remained the site and the symbol of "retreat", of "solitude". So early a writer as Tertullian referred to the "retreat on the mountainside" in connexion with the Transfiguration,[14] and it was on this subject that Cassian handed down a whole body of teaching on the prayer of monks. If Jesus willed to go away thus into solitude, it was

9. *De dominica oratione*, 29; CSEL 13, 1, p. 288: "Ipse autem fuit secedens in solitudines adorare."

10. *Divinarum institutionum*, IV, 15, 16, CSEL 19. p. 332: "Ascendit in montem quemdam desertum, ut ibi adoraret". In the same text, Lactantius uses the expression *ibi sedebat*, thus associating the prayer of Jesus with the *sessio*. On this subject I have collected Biblical and traditional testimony in *Chances de la spiritualité occidentale* (Paris, 1966) pp. 313-328. In Lk 5, 16: "Ipse autem secedebat in desertum et orabat", certain MSS have *sedebat* as the third word; ed. Wordsworth - White, *Novum Testamentum latine* (Oxford, 1899-1918) I, p. 336.

11. *In Matthaeum*, 25, 2, PL 9, 1053: "Et cum secessisset in montem . . .'';　*secedere* and *secessus*, with *recedere* and *recessus*, are the traditional Biblical terms for a "retreat". See *Chances de la spiritualité*, p. 329-336.

12. *Sermo*, 95, 1, PL 54, −461: "Dominus . . . secessum vicini montis ascendit".

13. Cassian, *Conlatio* IX, 25, CSEL 13, p. 273; "Supplicationum formula, qua vel solus in monte secedens, vel tacite fudisse describitur"; Lactantius, *Div. Inst.* IV, 15, 20, CSEL 19, p. 334; "Fuit in montem; voluit separatim in monte orare . . ."; "Item secessurus, orandi gratia, sicut solebat, in monte orare . . .", by an anonymous Irishman of the eighth century, ed. P. David, in *Revue Benedictine*, 49 (1937) p. 76.

14. "Dominus quoque in secessu montis etiam vestimenta luce mutaverat," *De resurrectione*, LV, 10, CCSL 2, p. 1002. Tertullian uses the same expressions *in montis secessu*, in writing of the Transfiguration in *Adversus Praxean*, 14, 7, CCSL 2, p. 1117, and *Adv. Marcionem*, 4, 22, CCSL 1, p. 600.

also to urge us to imitate him,[15] find him, unite ourselves to him, pray with him.[16] And those who devoted their lives to the practice of this adoration as continuously as possible would leave the towns and the crowds, the plains and the valleys where life was easier and would take refuge in uninhabited places, on the heights. Entering the monastic life was sometimes in the days of St John Chrysostom simply "taking to the mountains".[17] A young Ethiopian girl, meeting a solitary one day on the banks of the Nile, recalled him without ceremony to his duty: "If you are a monk, go into the mountains".[18]

The Middle Ages were to continue to see in those times of Jesus' contemplative solitude the pattern of monastic life.[19] In mid-twelfth century, as in the days of Tertullian and Cassian, Carthusians and Cistercians saw a special significance in Mount Tabor, in the transforming ecstacy which, anticipating the revelation of eschatological glory, accompanied the prayer of Jesus, and in which he granted the three Apostles a share.[20] Still today good exegetes are not afraid to express themselves along the same lines.

The example of Jesus was to lead crowds of men and

15. Cassian, *Conl.,* X, 6, 4, CSEL 13, p. 292: "secessit tamen in monte solus orare, per hoc scilicet nos instruens suae secessionis exemplo, ut . . . similiter secedamus. . ." This fine passage is translated into French in E. P. Pichery's *Jean Cassien, Conférences* VIII-XVII. Sources chrétiennes (Paris, 1958) pp. 80-81, Eusebius of Emesa *De quinque panibus,* 20, "Ipse autem ad orationem ascendit, ut hortaretur et nos orare semper debere Deum", ed. E. M. Buytaert, *Eusèbe d'Emèse. Discours conservés en latin,* I, (Louvain, 1953) p. 210.

16. St Jerome, *Epist.,* 58, 4, 2, CSEL 54, p. 532, "Et Christum quaeras in solitudine, et ores solus in monte cum Iesu".

17. In *La vie parfaite,* (Turnhout, 1948) pp. 44-45, I have quoted examples.

18. *Verba seniorum* XV, 9, PL 73 p. 954.

19. "Ut soli Deo in theoria, id est in monte vacemus", Pascasius Radbertus, *Expositio in Matthaeum,* PL 120, 522. In *Etudes sur le vocabulaire monastique du Moyen Age.* Studia Anselmiana, 48 (Rome, 1961) p. 91 *et passim,* I have quoted examples.

20. Guigo the Carthusian, *Consuetudines,* LXXX, 90, 10, PL 153, 758: "De quo Scriptura refert quod, relictis turbis discipulorum, in montem solus ascenderet orare"; Amedeus of Lausanne, *Homilia,* 3, ed. G. Bavaud, *Amédée de Lausanne, Huit Homélies Mariales.* Sources chrétiennes, 72 (Paris, 1960) pp. 90-92: "Statuens nobis speculam in monte cum Moyse et Elia quatinus quod quaerimus revelata facie contemplari possimus".

women to leave the tumult which deafens human life and
dulls the sensitivity of the spiritual organism, to withdraw
into the silence of a desert or the solitude of a cloister
and to devote their life to praising God in prayer.[21]
If there is, however, one fact in the life of Jesus which may
be retained as the very symbol of contemplation, we find it
in the Synoptic Gospels: I mean the Transfiguration. Indeed
the oldest spiritual tradition has seen in that the very image
of the contemplative life—a transforming life, raising man
above the things of the senses and directing him wholly towards heaven, conforming him by degrees to God himself.[22]

Is this the special province of monks and nuns? As we have
seen, the magisterium of the Church in Council still in our
time lays an obligation on all Christians and all religious to
develop the spirit of contemplation.

But who speaks today of Tabor in Catholic Action pro-
jects? Who still speaks of seeing, hearing, touching what cannot be preached and spread abroad by any action however
zealous without having first been recognized and experienced?[23]

How can the Christian share in this experience unless he
shares in the experience of Christ? "There is", continues
Hans Urs von Balthasar, "a participation in his mystery which
is not only sacramental but contemplative."[24] There is only
one Christian contemplation, that of Jesus Christ, by which
he was continually "with the Father", in conversation with
him, in loving consent to what he willed. The Father was in
perpetual contemplation of his incarnate Son, glorious in the
likeness of man. And the Son could only look at the Father
and say yes to his will: *Abba,* Father. It is this *"Abba,* Father," which he continues in his glory to utter, or, more precisely, to be. He it is that the Spirit whom he has shed in our

21. L. de Lorenzi, "La Preghiera anima dell'evangelo" in C. Vagaggini - G.
Penco, *La preghiera nella Bibbia, nella tradizione patristica e monastica,* pp.
130-131.

22. Ch. Augrain, *Témoins de l'Esprit,* p. 109.

23. H. Urs von Balthasar, quoted by H. de Lubac, "Un temoin du Christ. H. Urs
von Balthasar," in *Pouvoir et société.* Recherches et Débats, 53 (Paris, 1966).

24. Ibid., p. 159.

hearts continues to be and to utter in his Church and in each one of us. The Christian participates in the contemplation of Jesus by looking towards him, by bringing to him all his thoughts and all his love, by reading, by pondering all that tells of his life, sets forth his teaching and transmits his mystery. This duty is common to the contemplative and the man of action.

All that we can attain of divine reality before other men, our brothers, springs from contemplation: Jesus Christ's, the Church's, our own. It is not possible to proclaim the contemplation of Jesus Christ and of the Church without participating in it oneself. . . . He who has not experienced this mystery by contemplation can never speak of it, nor even act by it. . . .[25]

"Whether in contemplation of the mountainside . . ." Where the evangelists had used the word "prayer", witnesses of ancient, mediaeval and contemporay tradition and the Second Vatican Council use the term "contemplation". It is, of course, the same reality: contemplative prayer, loving prolonged adoration, lasting at times the whole night, by which Jesus Christ, contemplator of the Father, has been the principle, the origin and the inexhaustible source of all contemplation of the Father in him and through the Spirit. He is the model for contemplatives and for that part of the contemplative life shared by all Christian living, because he was himself a contemplative, the first contemplative. He has given the example for all activity in the Church, activity involved in mission work, ministry, and, no less difficult, the work of prayer. And so the ancient writers were right in attributing to him both the contemplative and the active life because he went up the mountainside to pray and then came down to the crowds to teach.[26]

---

25. Ibid., p. 153.

26. Ps.-Jerome, In Lucam, PL 30, 571 A: "Quando orabat, ostendit theoreticam vitam; quando sedebat, ostendit actualem vitam . . . Exivit in monte orare et exivit ad turbas, ostendit theoreticam et actualem in unum . . ."; Walafrid Strabo, *Expositio in IV Evangeliis*, PL 114, 872 C: "Quando ascendebat in montem, significabat theorica, *id est contemplativa*."

They were also fond of saying that St John the Evangelist (the "theologian" in the ancient sense of the word, that is, "*the contemplative*"[27]) had been specially designated by him as an ideal for contemplatives.[28] Their prayer, like Jesus', while giving an important place to adoration, has also a missionary intention. Like his, like that of the Apostle whom he loved, like that of the Virgin Mary, it is the assent of love, the acceptance of the will of the Father, the desire, the supplication that his kingdom may come. It is the continuation of the work of him who, spending the night in prayer on the mountainside, represented, showed forth, and by that very means taught the activity of contemplation.[29] He was, as it were, the "mirror", in which the contemplative life may be seen in its perfect expression.[30]

27. See *Etudes sur le vocabulaire*, pp. 74-75.

28. Ps.-Augustine, *Sermo*, ed. A. B. Caillau- B. Saint-Yves, *G. Aurelii Augustini ... opera,* (Paris, 1842) II, 16, 7: "Christus in Ioanne formam contemplativorum proposuit"; St. Augustine, *Speculum,* 28, CSEL 12, p. 197: "Ioannes contemplativam partem magis tenuit."

29. St Isidore, *Differentiarum libri II,* 2, 134, Pl 83, 91: "Quando vero in monte orationis studio pernoctabat, vitam contemplationis significabat."

30. St Paulinus of Nola and Therasia, ed. among the epistles of St Augustine, *Epist.* 94, 6, CSEL 29, p. 503: "Ut Dominus ipse ... quasi contemplationis speculum omnibus exstiterit."

THE EXAMPLE OF CHRIST*

HE WAS RICH, YET HE MADE HIMSELF POOR

ONE OF THE DOMINANT IDEAS in the teaching of the Second Vatican Council is that every activity which the Christian practises for his salvation and that of the world is a participation in a reality first in Jesus Christ. This is particularly repeated and emphasised in the Decree *Perfectae Caritatis*, "On the suitable renewal of the Religious Life."[1] Paragraph 13 which deals with poverty seems, like all the others, highly traditional, founded on Scripture and on the interpretation given it by the saints and doctors of the great periods of the Church. It begins:

Voluntary poverty undertaken with a view to following Christ, of which it is a sign brought particularly into prominence in our time, should be carefully cultivated by religious and even, if necessary, interpreted in new ways. By it we participate in the poverty of Christ who, though he was rich, made himself a pauper for our sakes, in order to enrich us by his voluntary destitution.

For this last phrase, the notes of the text promulgated give two biblical references: 2 Cor 8:9 and Mt 8:20. The second refers to the verse in which the Lord says that "the Son of Man has nowhere to lay his head". (Mt 8:20, cf Lk 9:58). But in fact it is really the Pauline passage which the Decree recalls and quotes exactly. And indeed, it would have been difficult to choose a better text, for it gave rise among the Fathers of the Church to some of their most profound teaching. In order to speak of the mystery of Christian poverty,

---

* Published in *La vie spirituelle*, 117 (1967) pp. 501-518.
1. This has been emphasised by P. J. Beyer, "Decretum 'perfectae caritatis' Concilii Vaticani II," in *Periodica de re morali, canonica, liturgica,* 55 (1966) pp. 465-472.

they looked first, in seeking a model to imitate, not to the men around them who as in every age were poor but towards Christ, and they saw the very essence of his poverty in his condition of God voluntarily incarnate. As the heresies relating to the divinity of Christ—particularly Arianism and Nestorianism—made them pay more heed to the whole content of the redemptive Incarnation, the Fathers spoke of this as a mystery of poverty, connecting it with the verse of St Paul which Vatican II was to quote. Moreover, it was at the Council of Ephesus, where the definition of Nicea on the subject of the Incarnation was confirmed, that this teaching was expounded most explicitly. There is an admirable instance here of continuity from Council to Council.

Let us content ourselves here with a kind of patristic anthology of commentaries on 2 Cor 8:9, in their chronological order. Conclusions will subsequently suggest themselves of their own accord.

Witnesses

"You know the generosity of Our Lord Jesus Christ; he was rich, yet for your sake he became poor, that through his poverty you might become rich." So in his Second Epistle to the Corinthians (8:9), wishing to exhort his readers to give generously at a time when he was organizing the charitable collection for the benefit of the brethren in Jerusalem, St Paul gave Christ as their example. The context is practical and concrete: a matter of money to be given. Without having prepared the way beforehand, without explaining it afterwards, the Apostle gives this reminder — "You know" — of a teaching which was familiar to all his disciples and which is none other than "the whole doctrine of the Incarnation and Redemption", as Père Allo has written. And the same exegete wrote, "The best commentary on this verse is Philippians 2:5 ff: 'Have in you this same attitude which was in Christ Jesus.' The divine nature was his from the first, but he annihilated himself, assuming the nature of a slave, bearing human likeness . . . he humbled himself and in obedience accepted even death."[2] This doctrine is expounded here in the vocabulary of poverty: it treats of the "liberality", "generosity" of Jesus who was "rich" and who because of us became "poor," and "needy".[3]

What comments would this passage suggest to the Fathers of the Church? In the third century Origen showed that this richness of Christ was his glory as the Son of God, and that it was manifested in his Passion.[4] He did not emphasize the point. It fell to the great writers of the fourth and fifth centuries to elaborate a wider doctrine on this subject. That was the period when the dogma of the equality of the Father and the Son and the divinity of the Son were in question. The great champions who struggled for the truth expounded the mystery of the Incarnation in terms of 2 Cor 8:9. First in time was St Hilary (died about 367) who applied to Christ verses of the Psalms which speak of poverty: *But I am poor and needy. O God hasten to my aid* (Ps 70:5). He saw in this a prophecy of the Passion of Jesus who was stripped of everything to the point of dying on the Cross, but whom the Father raised up.[5] He emphasized this further when writing on Ps. 140:12: *I know the Lord will give their due to the needy and justice to the downtrodden.* The Lord is poor as regards his manhood. According to the Apostle, he made himself poor to make us rich, he who, from among all the things in the world, had nothing but his body. And in the cause of salvation, he willed to be born of a virgin, destitute. Lord of the heavens, he possessed neither money nor field nor flock.[6] Then St Hilary named those who, following his example, made themselves poor of their own free will to the

2. E.-B. Allo, *Seconde Epître aux Corinthiens.* Coll. Etudes bibliques (Paris, 1937) p. 217.

3. The Vulgate here has the words *egenus* (for which many ancient Latin versions give *pauper*) and *inopia*.

4. *In cantica canticorum* III, 25; ed. Baehrens, *Origenes Werke,* VIII (Leipzig, 1925) p. 106.

5. *In Ps.* 69, 5, CSEL 22, p. 344.

6. *In Ps.* 139, 13, CSEL 22, p. 788.

point of participating in his Passion, to the point of martyrdom.

In the East, St Ephrem (died 373) applied 2 Cor 8:9 to the
equality of the Father and the Son and to the humiliation of
the Son.[7] St Basil referred to this same verse in *discussing*
Psalm 34:6: *This poor man called, and the Lord paid heed to
him,* an admirable passage which connected the voluntary
character of the poverty of those wishing to follow Christ
with Jesus' own example.

> Poverty is not always praiseworthy, but only that [poverty]
> which is freely embraced in accordance with the evangelical
> counsel. Indeed there are many who, while they are poor in
> means, in their desire are among the most avaricious. Desti-
> tution does not save those, but rather their desire con-
> demns them. It is not the needy man therefore who should
> automatically be pronounced blessed, but the man who sets
> more store by the commandment of the Lord than by the
> treasures of this world. These are the ones whom the Lord
> pronounces blessed, when he says 'Blessed are the poor in
> spirit . . . this poor man called'. By the use of the demon-
> strative, the psalmist here expresses his thought, speaking
> of the man who is poor, who is hungry and thirsty, who is
> without clothing, and all that for God. He characterizes
> 'the poor man' as 'this disciple of Christ'. This saying may
> also be applied to Christ. Being by nature rich, since all the
> possessions of the Father are his, for our sakes he made
> himself poor in order to enrich us by his poverty. For
> Christ himself has initiated every action which leads us to
> strive for blessedness, giving himself as an example to his
> disciples. Return to the Beatitudes, and having pondered on
> each one of them you will see that he prefaced his teaching
> with action. 'Blessed are the meek'. Then how are we to
> learn meekness? 'Learn of me', he says, 'for I am meek and
> lowly of heart. Blessed are the peacemakers'. Who will
> teach us the art of peace? That peacemaker himself who
> creates peace, who in one new man reconciles two, who, by
> the blood of his Cross, brought peace to heaven and earth.
> 'Blessed are the poor'. It is he who was poor and who

7. *De luctamine spiritali,* 3; ed. J. P. Assemani, *S. Ephraem Syri opera* (Rome,
1746) III, 558: "Excelsus et aequalis Pater (for *Patri*) semetipsum exinanivit."

annihilated himself in the form of a slave, in order that we might receive of his fulness, grace upon grace.[8]

Referring to the poverty of Christ after quoting 2 Cor 8:9, St Ambrose (died 397) added, "She is my inheritance, her weakness is my strength."[9] Elsewhere, he showed that one form of Christ's poverty, one of its consequences, was his ability to suffer. Commenting on the words of Psalm 69:30, *pauper et dolens,* he associated *paupertas* and *dolor.*[10] He developed his thought on this point chiefly in explaining Psalm 41:1. *Happy the man who has a concern for the helpless.* First and foremost this applies to faith in Jesus:

Happy the man who has an understanding of the need and poverty of Christ, who became poor on our account when he was rich, rich in his Kingdom, poor in the flesh, because he took upon him this flesh of the poor. For we became exceedingly poor when we lost the valuable prizes of the virtues and through the guile of the serpent were shut out of paradise, expelled from our homeland, sent into exile, stripped even of bodily clothing: what the rampart of virtue had protected before, sins afterwards denuded. If therefore he was needy and poor in the flesh he was above all needy and poor in the suffering of that flesh: for it was not in his richness but in our poverty that he suffered. Consequently, it was not the fulness of the Godhead which dwelt in him bodily, as Scripture testifies, that suffered but the flesh. Understand this, strive to attain this, hold it fast, lest it be said of you: 'he did not want to have any understanding of the beggar and the poor man' ... Understand then the poverty of Christ that you may be rich. Understand his weakness that you may receive health. Understand his Cross that you may not be put to shame. Understand his wound that you may heal your wounds. Understand his death that you may acquire everlasting life. Understand his burial that you may find resurrection.

You may say: 'How could Christ be rich in poverty?' Although my understanding may fail, yet the support of the sacred texts does not. There the Apostle said: 'the Lord

8. *In Ps.* 33, 7, PG 29, 361.
9. *In Lucam II,* 41, CSEL 32, p. 64.
10. *In Ps.* 35, 3-4, CSEL 64, pp. 51-52.

Jesus became poor, although he was rich, in order that you might become rich through his need'. What then is this poverty that enriches? Let us consider it, let us ponder this venerable mystery. What can be purer or what simpler? It is not the steeping of a person in the blood of a bull, as the pagan sacrifices are said to be. The sinner is not bathed in the gore of goats and rams (for it is not so that he is purified, for the flesh is washed but the sin is not washed away). But Scripture says 'water shall well up with joy from the springs of salvation' and a celestial table is prepared before your eyes, a marvellous, intoxicating cup. These are the riches of simplicity, in which lies the precious poverty of Christ. There is also a right poverty of actions of which the Lord said, 'Blessed are the poor in spirit', and in the psalms we find that the Lord shall save those of a humble spirit. There is in modest resources a poverty which brings abundance, if faith abounds. Thus the Apostle says, 'and the depth of their poverty became abundance in the riches of their simplicity.[11]

It is to be expected that St Augustine (died 430) should frequently have quoted 2 Cor 8:9. In a whole series of passages, he connected this verse with the prologue of St John (1:3-14) which says that "all things were made by him" and that "the Word was made flesh". Such is the paradox of Christ; "rich in his Godhead, poor in his manhood."[12] "Rich as he was, he took on mortal flesh in the womb of the Virgin," and all the circumstances marking the poverty of his childhood were consequences of that first poverty of the Incarnation.[13] This is equal moreover to all the sufferings of his Passion.[14] Elsewhere St Augustine related 2 Cor. 8:9 to the passage in the Epistle to the Philippians (2 Phil 6-8) in which St Paul speaks of the self-emptying of Christ, God as he was, whose poverty consisted basically in becoming a man. Obedience, even to the death of the cross, was the expression

11. *In Ps.* 40, 4-5, ibid., pp. 231-233; *Sermo* 36, 3-5, CCSL 41, pp. 435-437.
12. *Sermo* 124, 4, PL 38, 686; *Sermo* 36, 3, CCSL 41, pp. 435-436; *Sermo* 14, 9, CCSL 41, p. 190.
13. *Sermo* 23, 9, 6, PL 38, 1129.
14. *Sermo* 14, 10, CCSL 41, p. 191.

and manifestation of this fundamental impoverishment.[15] Finally, St Augustine liked to illustrate this paradox of Christ rich and poor by quoting those same passages of St Paul in connection with the psalms which speak of poverty, need, suffering. It was also a favorite saying of his that "to have a concern for the poor and needy" is first and foremost to have faith, and to preserve an accurate faith in the mystery of the Incarnation of this poor man *par excellence,* the Son of God made man.[16]

This faith was made explicit and defended at the Council of Ephesus in 431. It was shown there that:

The Word, become flesh by an act of God's will and become man, was not abandoned by his divinity. It was not, in fact, to lose his power and his glory that, being rich, he had made himself poor, but in order to accept death for us, he the righteous for us sinners, so as to be able to present us as an offering to God, put to death in the flesh and restored to life by the Spirit.[17]

Speaking of the beatitudes and quoting Philippians 2:5-7, St Gregory of Nyssa added:

What could be poorer in God than the form of a slave? What humbler in the King of all things than to enter of his own free will into communion with our beggarly nature? King of kings, Lord of Lords . . . pure and unspotted, he bears the stains of our human nature and, going through all our poverty, he even goes so far as to experience death. See the measure of voluntary poverty: life tastes of death. . . . Let this example be for you the measure of humility.[18]

The records of the Council preserve an excellent speech delivered on Christmas Day by Theodotus, Bishop of Ankara.

15. *Enarratio in Ps. 68,* s. 1, 4, CCSL 39, 904-905; *Sermo 41,* 7, CCSL 41, p. 501.

16. *In Ps. 40,* 1, 1-2, CCSL 38, p. 448-449; *In Ps. 68,* s. 1, 4, CCSL 39, p. 905. Elsewhere, St Augustine connected 2 Cor. 8, 9 with Col. 2, 3: *In quo sunt omnes thesauri sapientiae et scientiae abscoditi;* ed. Morin, *Sermo post Maurinos reperti,* Denis XV, 4 (Rome, 1930) p. 77.

17. *Gesta,* ed. Schwartz, *Acta Conciliorum Oecumenicorum,* I, 3 (Berlin-Leipzig, 1929), p. 67.

18. Ibid., p. 73.

It contains long passages dealing with this mystery of the Word Incarnate which are worth reproducing.

The Lord of all comes in the form of a slave. Clad in poverty, he is born of a poor maiden. All around is poor, that without clamor man might strive after salvation. For if he had been born in honor and had come clad in great wealth, unbelievers would say that it was abundance of wealth that had changed the world. If he had chosen the mighty city of Rome, they would think that the power of its citizens had changed the world. If he had been the son of an emperor, they would think that power was effective. If he had been the son of a legislator, they would think that his laws were effective. But what did he do? He chose all that is poor and vile, all that is ordinary and generally unknown, that it might be known that divinity alone had transformed the face of the earth. Wherefore he chose a poor little mother, an even poorer fatherland, and he did without possessions.

And this the manger teaches you. As there was no bed in which the Lord might be laid, they put him in a manger, and the lack of necessities became the good tidings of the prophet. If he was put in a manger, it was in order that he might proclaim that he would become food even for the unreasoning. For the Word and Son of God draws to himself the rich and the poor, the eloquent and the inarticulate, as he lives in poverty and lies in a manger. Behold therefore how want came to the prophetic and how poverty shows that he who for our sakes become poor is accessible to all. For no one has held back from Christ by awe of ostentatious wealth, none has been prevented by the splendor of power from coming to him; but he appeared poor and ordinary, offering himself to all for their salvation. For in the manger, the Word of God is shown forth by means of the body, that those who reason and those who do not might be able to participate in this food of salvation. And I think the prophet proclaimed this of old, telling the mystery of this manger. 'The ox knows his owner and the ass his master, but Israel has not acknowledged me and my people have not known me'. (Is. 3:1). Next, he who although rich, became poor for our sakes makes it easy for all to grasp the salvation that comes from the Word of God. This is what the great St Paul meant when he said, 'he was rich, yet for your sake he became poor, that through his poverty you might become rich.' And who is it who was rich, and how was he rich, and in what way did he become poor for our sakes? Let those tell us who separate the man from the Word and, by separating the two natures, divide what is one, say that Christ is two. Tell me then, who was it that, though he was rich, became poor with my poverty? Surely it was not this man who appeared, whom you separate from divinity? But he never became rich, for he was poor, born of poor parents. Who was it then who was rich, and in what was he rich, who became poor for us? It is God who enriches the creature. Therefore God himself became poor, taking on himself the poverty of him who was born, for he was rich in his divinity, and for our sakes he became poor. And you cannot say that the man became rich, who is poor both by his nature and by his lack of money, nor that he who is rich by the majesty of his divinity became poor, unless you attribute to him what is human. That is why the Apostle, associating the glory of his divinity with the suffering of his humanity, and neither by word or by thought dividing what is one, declares that one and the same [person] is rich in his divinity and became poor through his suffering. He is one thing in himself, another through what he suffered for our sakes. Now if he who is rich in his divinity became poor in human poverty, how should he not have suffered everything else, since he willed by his goodness once and for all to become man.

Let that be enough. But do you look at that poor little dwelling of him who makes heaven rich, see the manger of him who sits upon the cherubim, see the swaddling bands of him who encloses the sea with lands. Contemplate his poverty here below, his riches on high. For in this poverty itself, the riches of his divinity are revealed to us. The star declares him to be poor and draws the gentiles to the manger of the poor man but the angels joyfully proclaim him to the poor shepherds, singing of the riches of his divinity.[19]

Finally, another great witness of this heroic defence of the

19. Schwartz, p. 157-158, according to the *Collectio Casinensis*, with reference to other editions.

unity in Christ of divinity and humanity, St Cyril of Alexandria (died 444), who played such an important part in the Council of Ephesus, also expounded his thoughts from time to time on the subject of the mystery of poverty expressed by St Paul in 2 Cor 8:9: *He was rich, and he became poor for us.*

> Let us investigate who this is who was rich and how he became poor . . . He who as God is rich, identified himself with us in poverty. How then did he become poor? . . . He did not lay aside his own nature and transform himself into natural man, for he remained what he was, that is, God. Then where are we to see the humiliation of poverty? Simply in the fact that he wishes to honor a man like us, as Nestorius asserts? How then did he become poor? In this, that being God by nature and the Son of God the Father, he was born according to the flesh, of the seed of David. He accepted the limitations of a slave, that is of mankind, he who is in the form of God and of the Father, he through whom and in whom everything exists, the author of all creation, and having become man, he was not ashamed of his human limitations. How would he, who did not refuse to make himself like us, cast aside the very things by which it was possible to see that he had truly become like us? . . . If we set him apart from human attributes we cannot be distinguished from those who, not only rob him of his flesh, as though it were possible, but do not believe in divine Scripture, and completely destroy the mystery of the Incarnation, the salvation of the world, hope, and the Resurrection. But it may perhaps be said that this is belittling God the Word, and that it is quite unworthy for him to weep, to fear death, to shrink before the chalice, to be a high priest. And indeed I too will say that all this is belittling for the supreme divine nature and for his glory. But it is in these humiliations that we contemplate the poverty which he willingly embraced for us. The lower the depth of the annihilation appears to you, the more you should wonder at the love of the Son for us.[20]

Theodoret of Cyprus, another great defender of the faith of

---

20. *Apologeticus contra Theodoretum,* VIII, PG 76, 440-441.

Ephesus (died before 466) spoke in his commentary on 2 Cor
8:9 of the "extreme poverty" by which the Saviour obtains
all his riches for us.[21] Hesychius of Jerusalem (died after 451)
also showed with reference to the same Pauline verse, that
the Son of God, in making himself man, became for our sakes
not only poor but "an alien, for although he came unto his
own, his own did not receive him".[22] Later, from the sixth
century on, this verse was again quoted and briefly expounded at times in connection with belief in the Incarnation. St
Fulgentius (died 533) said that the Son of God became poor
by entering into time.[23] Cassiodorus applied to Christ the
saying in Psalm 48:2, *simul in unum dives et pauper.*[24] His
friend Epiphanius the Scholastic recalled that his richness is
his divinity, his poverty his humanity.[25] The theme was
echoed by St Gregory the Great (died 604),[26] by Paul the
Deacon, his biographer (died 799), [27] by St John Damascene
(died about 749),[28] and by the author of an anonymous
sermon,[29] but without great emphasis. Development of the
idea to any considerable extent had to await St Bernard in
the twelfth century.

Rich as he was, he became poor for our sakes. He came
down from the unspeakable riches of heaven and, coming
into the world, he did not even wish to possess the minor
riches of earth. He came in poverty that no sooner was he
born than he was laid in a manger, because there was no
room for him at the inn. Who does not know furthermore
that the Son of Man had no place to lay his head? Now
how could the man who with him reaches that point seek
the riches of the world? And it is really a great illusion, a
supreme illusion, to want to become rich, this vile earth-

21. *Interpretatio epistolae II ad Corinthos* VIII, 9, PG 82, 424-425.
22. *In Leviticum* VI, PG 93, 1090 A.
23. *Sermo* 2, 4, PL 65, 727.
24. *In Ps. 48,* 2, PL 70, 341-342.
25. *Codex encyclicis Leonis imperatoris,* 31, ed. Schwartz, *Acta* 1, 5, p. 59.
26. *Moralia,* XX, 69, PL 76, 670.
27. *Vita S. Gregorii Magni,* III, PL 75, 43.
28. *In II Cor. 8, 9,* PG 95, 747.
29. Ps.-Hildefonsus, *Sermo,* X, PL 96, 275 B.

worm for whom the God of majesty and the Lord of hosts
willed to become poor.[30]

The concept of Christian poverty formed by the Fathers of
the Church sprang from a consideration of the mystery of the
Incarnate Word. In him they saw before all else what might
be called a poverty of nature or of existence, of which the
poverty of fact was a consequence. Poverty of nature was
identified with annihilation, the *kenosis,* the impoverishment
which, for the Word, consisted in becoming man.[31] *And the
Word was made flesh. . . . But he annihilated himself, assuming the nature of a slave, bearing human likeness, revealed in
human shape. . . .* These verses of St John (1:14) and St Paul
(Phil. 2:7) are quoted to illustrate this reality: being made
flesh, the Word does not only unite himself personally with
the nature of a man, mind and body, but he who is without sin
enters into the condition of sinful humanity, and of his own
free will becomes one with it. It is this human nature of ours
that is poor, needy: this indeed is "our poverty". This he
assumed, with this he unites himself, with this he identifies
himself. He became poor in becoming like us. In him—since
he was and remains the Word—it is really God who became
poor, not only his humanity. The latter, as the defenders of
the dogma of two natures in one person reiterate, is inseparable from his divinity. The poverty of Christ is the freely
willed poverty of God himself. It consists first of all in the
fact of the Incarnation willed "for our sakes" (*propter nos*)
through love.

The poverty of fact, that is the sum of the marks of poverty which distinguished his life, is a consequense and a sign of
the poverty of nature. It is because he became first of all a

---

30. *De resurrectione,* III, 1, PL 183, 289.

31. The difficulty in translating the verb used by St Paul at the beginning of
Phil. 2, 7, is well known. The Jerusalem Bible, which I quote, says "he emptied
himself" [French: "il s'aneantit"—translator's note]. Others prefer "He stripped
himself", with M. Dhainant, "Les abaissements volontaires et l'exaltation du
Christ. Philippiens 2, 6-11", in *Bible et vie chrétienne,* 71, (Sept.-Oct. 1966) p.
48. He adds: "The verb *kenoun* in fact means: to empty, exhaust, reduce to
nothing."

poor wretch (*pauper homo*)[32] that he was also a poor man. The destitution which marked his childhood and his public life, when he "had no place to lay his head", was simultaneously the consequence and proof of that redemptive Incarnation and of the universal love for which he had willed it. He had become the man of all men, even of those utterly devoid of material or intellectual resources. Theodotus of Ankara emphasised this point. Jesus became an ordinary, a common man (*communis apparuit et pauper*).[33] The poverty of the Word become man becomes the poverty of the man Jesus. He was fully aware of it, he accepted all the consequences of it. And it was this voluntary renunciation of the riches of his divinity that led him through obedience to all the suffering of his life and his Passion, even to death and death on the Cross. This poverty of nature was made a reality painfully from day to day: we have noted that poverty and suffering are linked by the Fathers of the Church when they speak of him, as they had been by the Psalmists when they prophesied concerning him. Increasingly, from Gregory the Great onwards and all through the Middle Ages, these inward, one might almost say psychological, aspects of this poverty in

32. Ps.-Hildefonsus, *Sermo* X, PL 96, 275 B: "Non solum homo pro nobis, verum etiam pauper homo fieri dignatus est."

33. See the text quoted above, p. . Compare the well-phrased expressions of a theologian of today, Fr M-J. Nicolas OP, on the subject of what the Logos "assumed of the human": "Not everything, but the most important part, what makes you a man . . . in the commonest condition, that which is most like every other because the least distinguished by any privilege: he is poor, the work he does is manual, elementary. He is of the people, of that which constitutes the mass of humanity. He obeys. In his public life, he will also give an example to the masters and leaders of men. But he is first and foremost one of those who make up the mass and the common run . . . The Logos willed to become an absolutely "ordinary" man, in whom was expressed only human nature as it is expressed everywhere and in every situation." "Les Mystères de la vie cachée du Christ et les hommes de l'histoire", in H. Bouessé-J.-J. Latour, *Problems actuels de christologie* (Bruges: Desclée de Brouwer, 1965) p. 87. And farther on (pp. 94-95): "Is there not . . . a wonderful application of the idea of the *poverty* of Christ in the realm of science to be attempted? In his earthly condition, Christ despised earthly goods. He did not wish to be rich nor to be active elsewhere than in the realm of the kingdom of God. Could we not say the same of his learning? Voluntary self-limitation by a pure and exclusive consecration to his mission, through poverty with regard to what is not properly the kingdom of God".

[Translated]

Christ are emphasised, his patience and his humility, and the outward circumstances which made these virtues visible.[34] The great defenders of the faith at the time of the controversies of the fourth and fifth centuries by no means despised these data. For them the fundamental fact was not that Jesus lived in poverty but, first and foremost, that he renounced by the Incarnation the riches of his divinity.

As St Paul says in 2 Cor 8:9, he did it only to make us partakers of his riches. His voluntary impoverishment was entirely subsidiary to his work of redemption, his death and victory over death, and his resurrection. This paradox of Christ at once poor and rich, of which the Apostle speaks, is none other than the Paschal mystery. The death of Christ is the efficacious sign, the sacrament, of the voluntary poverty by which he became man. His resurrection is the sacrament of his riches; he is glorified in the Spirit by the power of God. His human nature now participates fully and openly, no longer in a hidden way, in the riches of his divinity in order that we may benefit by it. Poverty is equalled only by liberality: "You know the generosity of Our Lord Jesus Christ: he was rich, yet for your sake he made himself poor, so that through his poverty you might become rich". All this became a reality first in him: the humanity which he enriched is first of all that which he assumed. One is reminded of the admirable words of Bérulle:

The humanity of the Son of God, the human nature of the Son of God, has a kind of need of the Son of God of which we know nothing: it is deprived of the person and as it feels a kind of destitution of God, also it has a capacity for God, for the person of the Son of God, of which we know nothing (for we have our person) and this capacity is fulfilled by the hypostatic union, so that as this nature is more destitute, so also it is more fulfilled. [35]

34. In a book on *L'idee de la royauté du Christ au Moyen Age,* (Paris, 1959) pp. 37-39 ("La contoverse sur la pauvreté"), I have given a few pointers on this subject.

35. Berulle (unpublished), quoted in the first instance by R. Bellamare, and reproduced from him by M. Nedoncelle, "Le moi du Christ et le moi des hommes à la lumiere de la réciprocité des consciences," in *Problems actuels de christologie,* p. 226.

How are we to participate in this mystery? By faith, by the Sacraments and by imitation. By faith in Christ God and man. This is difficult, and it is necessary that it be accurate. So the Fathers of the Church had no fear of giving the faithful very precise teaching on this point, teaching which may appear today too technical, too "theological," but which is necessary if we want to overcome the difficulty of believing so paradoxical a truth, and if we want to penetrate below the disconcerting outward appearances which marked the life of Jesus. There is not practice of morality without knowledge of dogma. If our role consists in sharing in a mystery, we must know what that mystery is.

By the Sacraments together with faith, we come into contact with the Paschal mystery. We have seen that, when the opportunity occurred, the Fathers recalled this fact to mind. Finally, as Christ imitated us in our poverty to make us sharers in the riches of his divinity and in his glorification, we ought to imitate his poverty. As he accepted all the painful consequences of the poor human nature which he had taken for our sake, we must accept for him and offer to the Father with him all the difficulties attendant on our condition as men, as members of a humanity marked by sin.

Here we have all the depth of human experience and all the suffering which it bears with it and which our asceticism must assume. As we have seen, the Fathers of the Church applied to Christ those psalms whose authors declared themselves at once plunged, almost submerged, in intense misery, yet filled with confidence in God. They certainly did not see in these passages simply literary clichés, impersonal formulae intended for liturgical use. They thought that the Prophets and the Psalmists had, so to speak, anticipated that experience of the human condition which was to attain its supreme clarity in Jesus Christ. Before all else, we should freely will this poverty inherent in our nature, which we should accept in an act of love for God which will make us participate in that act of love for man by which God in the Incarnate Word saved us. St Basil, among others, said this: The beatitude of poverty can only be voluntary in the Christian as it was in Christ.[36] It cannot be simply destitution endured with muttering, envy, or rebellion. The further one goes in this way of voluntary renunciation—which includes not just destitution but all forms of mortification—the more one imitates the voluntary poverty of Christ, and the better one is fitted to share in his riches. Theodoret of Cyrus showed long ago the voluntary character of the practice of asceticism and of the monastic life.[37] Similarly, the Second Vatican Council strongly urged religious to weigh all the demands made by the state of renunciation which they have desired to embrace. In dealing with poverty the Council, coming down to particular applications, did well to recall this great dogmatic truth upon which all practice should be based: Christ is the perfect model of sharing. he kept nothing; he gave all his riches. Our only riches is his divinity.

36. Quoted above, pp. 58-9.
37. *In Ps. 118*, 108, PG 80, p. 1855.

TRADITION

BAPTISM AND PROFESSION

THE GENESIS AND EVOLUTION OF THE

CONSECRATED LIFE*

HESE FEW REFLECTIONS make no claim either to present a theological exposition of the subject or even to analyse or assess the material of tradition, but simply to establish it to offer it as food for reflection. Within these limits, several dangers which must immediately be pointed out cannot be entirely avoided. First, to recall a past which was rich and complex demands elaborations or definitions with no immediate practical application, but the presentation even if arid will nevertheless be useful in understanding the problem. Moreover, as is always the case when a long evolution, particularly in the realm of ideas, has to be summarized, there will have to be simplication and a proportionate risk of distortion. Furthermore, we will touch upon questions not all of which have received clear and unequivocal answers from scholars. The consequence will inevitably be an element of conjecture and approximation of which one must be aware. Much work remains to be undertaken or carried further. And all that will be said will be borrowed from conclusions already established or glimpsed by those engaged in research: nothing but a compilation will be found here, making no claim to original thought.[1]

* Published in *Cahiers de la Revue Diocésaine de Tournai, nᵒ·7. Consécration baptismale et vocation religieuse* (Tournai, 1967).

1. For the parts dealing with ancient monasticism in the East, I am indebted to the vast and generous erudition of my colleague Dom J. Gribomont, to whom I express my thanks.

At least, the simple statement of historical variations should help to free the field of research from theories established *a priori* and subsequently projected on to events of former periods. Moreover a continuity will be observed which will guide the mind without forcing it. Because it was at the root of many practices and concepts which now fall under the critical judgements of theologians, monasticism must be conceded a place relatively larger than the one it occupies in the religious life today. The two most important elements of our argument come at the beginning—at the emergence of the life consecrated to God under these various forms—and in our day at a time of questioning rich in its promise for a future.

In the history of the relationship between religious consecration and baptism, the facts compelled us to distinguish three great periods linked with the birth and growth of three realities of the Church: the state of virginity, monasticism, and the religious life in the forms it assumed in the relatively recent period since the twelfth and particularly the thirteenth centuries.

Virginity and Baptism

The existence during the first centuries of the Church of Christian women who lived in voluntary virginity for God is an important fact in the history of the origins of the religious life. On the beginnings few details are available. It is known that in the Graeco-Roman Christian world these virgins existed and constituted a separate and in some way sacred category. At the time of monasticism's birth, a free commitment, no doubt often distinct from baptism and thenceforth final, was an established fact. There is no evidence of an explicit commitment of the same kind concerning men, the ascetics and confessors. But the virgins' commitment served as a starting-point for later development. The idea became familiar and it was only a matter of applying it little by little to others.

According to the best and most recent historian of this problem, R. Metz, it is possible to establish that Christian women were adopting the state of religious virginity from the first and second centuries, but it is not known how they committed themselves to it nor how they lived.[2] Among other designations in the third century, that of *virgines sacrae* began to be applied to them: a significant expression, for the epithet *sacra* implies, it seems, a ceremony of official consecration. This ceremony was attested only in the third century.[3] It is not known what it was but it certainly included a real vow, that is, a promise made to God to practise perfect continence.[4] From the fourth century virgins of this kind became more numerous. Certain of them began to live in community. Among them there were some who entered upon this state through a liturgical ceremony during which a bishop sanctioned their vow of virginity.[5] From that time on, the expression *consecrari* was used in this connection in Gaul and the sign, the special habit of this sacred state, was the veil, in conformity with an ancient tradition by which in the civilisations of the Mediterranean world women were veiled because of the respect due them (a veil which survives in Islam and in the Carmels because St Theresa borrowed it from practices inherited from Andalusian Muslims of her day).[6] In the sixth century, St Gregory the Great used the expression *virgines sacrae* or *sacratae* and *consecratio*;[7] the term *religiosa* was found in Gaul in the sixth century.[8]

In the ideas propounded on consecrated virginity and in the rite which sanctioned it where it existed, the sacrament con-

2. R. Metz, *La consécration des vierges dans l'Eglise romaine* (Paris, 1954) p. 48. See also Th. Camelot, *Virgines Christi* (Paris, 1944).

3. Metz, p. 54.

4. Ibid., p. 60.

5. Ibid., p. 67.

6. R. Metz, "Les vierges chrétiennes en Gaule au IVe siècle", in *S. Martin et son temps* (Rome, 1961) p. 124.

7. R. Metz, *La consécration des vierges*, p. 88. See also A. Blaise, *Le vocabulaire latin des principaux thèmes liturgiques* (Turnhout: Brepols, 1966) pp. 514-516.

8. R. Metz, *La consécration des vierges*, p. 93.

nected with this state and this ceremony was not baptism but another, of which R. Metz writes, "Its rites were borrowed from the marriage ceremony and they were applied to the consecration of virgins. Thus the ceremony by which virgins embraced their new state had eventually every appearance of marriage."[9] This idea of spiritual marriage with Christ was frequently formulated by the Fathers of the Church in texts which have been incorporated in the collections of canonical writings, in the Decretum of Gratian, and in juridical and theological traditions through the centuries. It has been extended to all religious profession, including that of male religious, affirming the character of irrevocable commitment undertaken publicly in the presence of the Church (*in facie ecclesiae*), as happens also in the indissoluble contract constituting marriage.[10] We know that even til our day the consecration of virgins and ceremonies of religious profession have retained traces of the marriage rite.

The principal feasts on which the consecration of virgins took place were the Epiphany—when the adoration of the Magi, the Baptism of Christ, and the wedding at Cana were commemorated—and Easter, whose mystery had a baptismal reality sometimes represented by nuptial symbolism.[11] St Ambrose declared: "This is the feast of Easter: in the whole world the mysteries of baptism are celebrated and consecrated virgins receive the veil." So this was a custom practised everywhere (*in toto orbe*).[12] "When the virgin received the

---

9. Ibid., p. 123.
10. Examples are quoted or referred to in R. Molitor, *Religiose iuris capita selecta* (Ratisbon, 1909) pp. 13, 26, 45. The four first examples, in particular the third, "Exercise of the espousals and consecration", appear in the edition of St Gertrude's *Exercises* that has been published in the Sources Chrétiennes (Paris, 1967). See also A. Blaise, *Le vocabulaire latin,* p. 515, an allusion to the symbolism of the ring which so many religious still wear, among them the brothers of Taizé.
11. J. Hild, *Dimache et vie pascale* (Paris, 1949) pp. 142-146.
12. *Exhortatio virginitatis* VII, PL 16, 364, quoted with commentary by R. Metz, *La consécration des vierges,* p. 128.

veil on Easter Day, she would make her entrance into the Church, in some places at least in the midst of neophytes clad in white and bearing tapers."[13] Even then, the symbolism was sometimes not baptismal but nuptial and eucharistic. "Do you remember," says the anonymous author of the *De lapsu Susannae,* "the holy day of the resurrection of the Lord, during which you offered yourself at the altar to receive there the veil? . . . In the midst of the lights of the neophytes, of the new members clad in the white of the heavenly kingdom, you advanced like a queen, to be married to the King."[14] Furthermore, [says Metz], "it is highly probable that after the homily, the virgin was asked to renew before the assembled community the vow which she had made privately some time previously."[15]

Certainly in the Roman rite at this period and in this first form of the religious life (which is what the state of consecrated virginity was), no special connection can be seen between the consecration to God and baptism. The analogy was rather with marriage. If it had a link with baptism, this was because it occurred at the Feast of Easter, which contained reminders of baptism, but of the Eucharist and spiritual marriage as well. The reference to baptism was secondary and indirect.

Be that as it may, to the East in the Syriac Church and no doubt at a very early date in certain Greek Churches, baptism—of adults, obviously—was given on condition of committing oneself to virginity or of suspending conjugal relations. Marriage was respected, and considered legitimate but confined to the state of the catechumen. Probably there were always practical adjustments. But the Acts of Thomas, Paul and other texts are evidence of such an idea. On this score there was a real connection between celibacy and baptism.

---

13. R. Metz, *La consécration,* p. 129.
14. Ibid., p. 130, n. 21.
15. Ibid., p. 131.

Monasticism and Baptism

In considering this question we must distinguish two periods coming before and after the emergence of the idea that profession is a second baptism

1. Before the Idea of Profession as Baptism.

No theory can be discerned on the relationship of baptism and commitment to the monastic life in the third and fourth centuries. But two very important facts need to be noted. The first is that baptism came late, that is, was administered to adults. Consequently it implied a change of life, a conscious, willed *conversio*. It had for the one who received it in those conditions and on that condition its full meaning. The second fact to note is that the choice of the monastic life coincided more or less with this baptism. This appeared, as we would say today, in different sectors of monasticism.

In the monastic asceticism of Syria-Cappadocia, for bishops and Doctors like Basil, Gregory Nazianzus and others, and for a goodly number of their disciples, commitment to baptism coincided exactly with the choice of the ascetic and celibate life. Baptism in these cases was as it were accelerated, anticipated, when the decision to receive it and to bestow it before the end of a normally long period as a catechumen was made. It always gave a very clear option however, Churchmen did not compel anyone to remain celibate after baptism whereas the preceding generation, that of the Eustathians, was certainly stricter, particularly as regards poverty, demanding a break with the social order. In the circles of these Doctors of monasticism and of those who thought like them, there was a close link between baptism and a radically evangelical life. The Long Rule VIII of St Basil demanded that he who follows Christ renounce goods, kindred, himself, and carry his Cross. And it comments:

> This commandment extends to many things. . . . Indeed, we renounce above all the devil [an allusion to Baptism] and the passions of the flesh. . . . And what is even more

necessary [but is this connected equally closely with Baptism?] he who strips off the old man . . . renounces himself. . . . But he also renounces the affections of the world which can obstruct the goal of true religion [an almost technical designation of the ascetical research for God]. So that *perfect* renunciation (ἡ τελεια απόταγῆ) consists in *apatheia* [the idea is here expressed in different terms]; . . . yet it begins with setting aside external things: wealth, false honour . . . ".[16] It is somewhat difficult to express exactly the connections and differences of degree in this text and it is even more difficult in the first edition —that of the minor Ascetikon preserved in Latin and in Syriac whose texts differ greatly from one another and from the present Greek. But it is certain that in it monastic renunciation is considered a consequence of baptismal renunciation.

In the eremitical life of Egypt no special emphasis either on baptism or on profession was discernible. Asceticism was the chief concern. In the Pachomian coenobitic life, no theoretical problem was raised but certain facts are significant.[17] A chapter of the *Life*, which is missing in the Greek, tells how a catechumen brother died at Thousons before Pachomius could arrive to baptize him; Pachomius, however, saw the angels who had secretly conferred baptism upon him.[18] One may conjecture over this account but it certainly implies a doctrine of baptism of desire, not visible but ecclesiastical, that is valid in the Church, and more spiritual even than visible baptism. Perhaps there would have been an element of contrast between this view and that of the local clergy which would doubtless explain why the text was omitted from the Greek.[19] What follows explains that baptism was normally given to catechumens (without any clear indication as to

16. PG 31, 936.
17. L. Th. Lefort, *Les vies coptes de S. Pachôme et de ses premiers successeurs* (Louvain, 1943) p. 83, 1.20, 28; F. Halkin, *S. Pachomii vitae graecae* (Brussels, 1932) p. 4, 1.11-16.
18. L. Th. Lefort, *Les vies coptes*, p. 141.
19. F. Halkin. *S. Pachomii vitae*, 1.27-29.

whether Pachomius or the bishop officiated) on the occasion
of the annual solemn Easter reunion of all the Pachomian
monks. So for a certain number of monks baptism was quite
closely connected with their vocation and their concept of
monks. Is it possible to state precisely what this connection
was? In referring to entry into the community, the texts
speak of rebirth and regeneration.[20] This can only mean the
rebirth of baptism and the commitments it involves: fulfilling
the law of God which consists essentially in loving God and
one's neighbour and is expressed in concrete terms in all the
other commandments which express God's will. The monastic vocation was identified for those who received it with
their Christian vocation, a fact which naturally did not exclude other Christians from living according to their baptismal promises outside the monastic state. But it seems that
the admission to this state did not involve, at least in the
early days of Pachomian monasticism, any special "profession". The "contract" made with God by the baptismal
promises was enough. This was equally true of the consecrated
virgins for whom Pachomius offered to God the same prayer
as for monks. In short, what Dom Gribomont wrote of the
ascetic groups called "sons and daughters of the Pact" around
St Ephrem in Syria and Aphraate in Persia is equally true of
this Egyptian monasticism: "This pact is in no way a contract
binding them voluntarily among themselves, neither can any
analogy be seen with our vows, a spontaneous and gratuitous
commitment. The covenant with God was quite simply the
fulfilment of the covenant of Abraham, the baptismal promise."[21]

For the West we possess a significant text, one which in its
essentials is close to those of the East. In consists of Chapters
two and three of the Life of St Martin by Sulpicius Severus.

20. For what follows, Fr A. Veilleux OCSO has been kind enough to give me
access to his still unpublished thesis on St Pachomius and to let me draw material
from it. I am much indebted to him. [A. Vielleux, *La liturgie dans le cénobitisme
parchomien au quatrième siècle*. Studia Anselimiana, 57 (Rome: Herder, 1968)].

21. J. Gribomont, "Le monachisme au sein de l'Eglise en Syrie et en
Cappadoce", in *Studia Monastica*, 7 (1965) p. 7-24.

We know that this biographer very probably felt that he was perfectly entitled to rearrange the narrative and take liberties in the matter of chronology.[22] After taking into account all these literary and historical problems, the fact still remains that the document establishes a very close connection between the monastic vocation of Martin and his baptism:

> At the age of ten, in spite of his parents, he took refuge in a church and asked to be admitted there as a catechumen. Soon, marvellous to relate, he turned entirely to the work of God. At twelve, he was going into the desert, and would have fulfilled his ambition, had the weakness of youth not put an obstacle in his way. Nevertheless, his mind always dwelling on monks' cells or on the Church, he pondered while yet a child the plan which he was to put into effect later in devoting himself to God. But an edict of the emperors having laid down that all the sons of veterans were to be enlisted in the militia, he was handed over by his father, who was hostile to these actions which were to ensure his happinesss. . . . For about three years, before receiving baptism, Martin was under arms, but he remained free from the vices by which men of this type are usually ensnared . . . although not yet regenerated in Christ. But he presented himself, as it were, a candidate for baptism, and that by good works: helping the sick, giving aid to the unfortunate, feeding the poor, clothing the naked, keeping nothing but his daily bread out of his pay. From then on, he was not deaf to the Gospel lessons: he took no thought for the morrow.[23]

It was as a catechumen that he shared his cloak with the beggar who subsequently revealed himself to him as Christ. When he was eighteen, he flew to be baptized. Yet he did not immediately give up his military service. . . . For about two years after receiving Baptism, he remained a soldier, but in name only . . . [24]

22. On these problems, see J. Fontaine, "Vérité et fiction dans la chronologie de la Vita Martini" in *Saint Martin et son temps. Mémorial du XVIᵉ centenaire des débuts du monachisme en Gaule, 361-1961.* Studia Anselmiana, 46 (Rome: Herder, 1961) pp. 198-224 *passim.*

23. French translation by P. Monceaux, *S. Martin, Récits de Sulpice Sévère* (Paris, 1927) p. 75-77.

24. Ibid., p. 78-79.

Thus the idea of commitment to the monastic life and of Baptism presented themselves to Martin as inseparable even in his early years. "A pious image? " wondered an historian. Rather, an early development—as has been noted in the cases of other great saints. We could refer to childhood memories recalled by St Teresa of Avila in her *Life.*[25] And how can one fail also to be reminded of St Theresa of the Child Jesus? What matters in such cases is the realization by certain Christians that baptism demands that they fulfill its obligations to the point of separating themselves from the world to consecrate their lives to the service of God alone.

Is Profession a Second Baptism?

The moment that the idea expressed in this question makes its appearance, we must distinguish two periods, the early stages and the later developments.

The first period comes in the fourth and fifth centuries and is marked by several events, whose results were to affect subsequent development.

The first of these was the Messalian controversy.[26] In Syria ascetics appeared who were given the name of Messalians, or Euchites, that is "Pray-ers" who, partly under the influence of certain Manichaean movements, tended at times towards ideas which would first appear among the Pelagians and subsequently among the Quietists. They thought deeply about baptism and the way it combines asceticism and prayer to purify the heart of sin to the very roots. They were accused of detracting from the value of baptism and of pronouncing it useless, and no doubt they were thinking of the external rite in particular as inadequate while they emphasised the experience of the corrupt heart and of the spiritual joy which springs from prayer and not from the sacrament alone. And so they met opposition. Mark the Hermit wrote a treatise on baptism against them. Are the Messalians at the root of the

25. J. Fontaine, "Verité et fiction," p. 224-225.

26. Outline in H. Rahner, in LThK 7 (1962), 319-320; details in J. Gribomont, "Le monachisme au IVe siècle en Asie Mineure; de Gangres au Messalianisme," in *Studia Patristica,* 2 (Berlin, 1957) p. 400-415, and "De Instituto Christiano et le Messalianisme de Gregoire de Nysse," ibid., 5, p. 312-322.

idea that profession is a second baptism, necessary to complete the first, to renew it and to reinforce its efficacy? This opinion has been put forward[27] and contested.[28] The fact remains that their ideas and the opposition they met contributed to the historical environment in which other views appeared and developed.

A second important event was the identification of martyrdom with the monastic life on the one hand and with baptism on the other. As a result the second aspect in particular appeared with some regularity in spiritual writings. From the third century on Clement of Alexandria, Tertullian, and Origen made reference to the martyrdom of virginity,[29] of renunciation, of perfect charity, of asceticism.[30] It was natural that the same idea should be applied to monasticism—as happened in the *Life* of St Anthony and other texts,[31] and also in the world of St Pachomius and his disciples.[32] The comparison hung particularly on the freely accepted suffering inherent both in martyrdom and in the life of the monk. Later in Irish monasticism, "white martyrdom"—renunciation of the world—was distinguished from "red"—giving up one's life for Christ or spending it in missionary effort—and finally "green"—*peregrinatio* or voluntary exile. In every case, it hung on purifying the heart by the gift of self and by mortification.[33]

A third important event in the evolution with which we are concerned was the spread of *paedo-baptism*, that is, baptism conferred on children. This occurred in a society which was theoretically Christian and in which consequently the baptized Christian no longer had the same need to set himself

27. J. Leroy, "S. Theodore Studite", in *Théologie de la vie monastique* (Paris, 1963) p. 431 n. 60.

28. B. Neunheuser, "Mönchsgelubde als zweite Taufe und unser theologisches Wissen", in *Leben aus der Taufe, Liturgie und Mönchtum* 33-34 (Maria-Laach, 1963-1964) p. 63, n. 7.

29. E. E. Malone, "The Monk and the Martyr", in *Antonius Magnus Eremita,* (Rome, 1956) p. 201-205. Numerous medieval texts are quoted by G. Venes, "La spiritualità del martirio nel medio evo", in *Vita monastica,* 20 (1966) p. 74-88.

30. Malone, p. 206-210.

31. Ibid., p. 210-220.

32. Ibid., p. 222-224.

33. Ibid., p. 224-228.

quite so definitely as thitherto over against the world in so
far as the "world" designated a state of human society which
was not Christian and which more often than not persecuted
the Church more or less violently. This fact seems to have
diminished considerably the psychological importance of
baptism. Baptism was not even a memory, having been received before the dawn of the retentive faculty, and it could
no longer compel a conversion in the same way, that is a
change of life which had been willed after deliberation during
the catechumenate. And yet texts survived from Scripture,
the Fathers, and the liturgies which were written when baptism had been given to consenting adults. Men were perhaps
led in some monastic circles to emphasize profession with an
exaggeration which the literature has not entirely cast off and
monastic commitment recovered some of the importance
baptismal commitment had lost.

Finally, a fourth event, this time literary, made its impact
when St Jerome spoke of the monastic life as a *"second
baptism"*. He too was no doubt giving expression to the idea,
which we have seen was traditional and universal, that entry
into the monastic life renewed the baptismal renunciation of
the devil and all his works. It gives an even fuller participation in the consecration which flows down on the Christian
from Christ when he receives the baptism of water or the
baptism of blood. But in two of his epistles, Jerome explicitly identified "second Baptism" with the monastic life. He
meant simply that, being a life of penitence and in that sense
a daily, continual martyrdom, it had the same effects as the
state of penitence or martyrdom voluntarily embraced. Like
them, it was a total renunciation of Satan and sin.[34] The
exact meaning of St Jerome's statements, in which there is as
in everything he writes an element of rhetoric, is therefore
determined by two important facts. First, it was less a question of the act by which the monastic was embraced than of
the state itself, as when one speaks of the profession of a
doctor or a carpenter. Secondly, this state was identified with

---

34. Texts and bibliography in P. Antin, "S. Jérôme", in *Théologie de la vie
monastique*, p. 198.

baptism and then with penitence or, if you like, it was a baptism of penitence. Indeed, it had been said for some time that penitence was in a certain sense a second baptism, enabling us to obtain pardon for the sins committed after the first baptism had washed away those previously committed.

These ideas, inherited from the fourth and fifth centuries, developed particularly from the sixth century on.

One of the first events to be singled out from this period is the gradual appearance of the profession rite, a ceremony, which would grow as time went on, built around the promise, the commitment—in short what has since been called the profession, or the making of vows.

The second event: Towards the middle of the seventh century the expression "second baptism" was applied for the first time to profession, no longer regarded as a state of life but as the act of commitment, surrounded thereafter by formal ritual.[35] Ideas concerning profession and the religious life go back both in the East and the West to these developments and were added to previous tradition.

In the East two figures emerge: Denis [the Pseudo-Areopagite] and Theodore the Studite. The first, at the end of the fifth or the beginning of the sixth century, developed a beautiful and elaborate theory giving liturgical rites an important place. He established the analogies between the "sacraments" by which the neophyte is admitted to baptism and the new monk to his state of life, but he also pointed out the differences. The baptized and the monk are situated on the same line, so to speak, but at different states.[36] The monk does not belong to the priestly hierarchy but he is, in the line of personal sanctification, an intermediate between the holy people and the ministry which sanctifies them:

> Whereas the life of the baptised is divine and holy, that of the monks is a most perfect life. It is aimed at a greater

35. The phrase appears in the *Paenitentiale* of Theodore, Archbishop of Canterbury († 698), PL 99, 928. The ritual was to exercise a great influence on the whole subsequent development. See F. Vandenbroucke, "La profession, second baptême", in *La vie spirituelle,* 76 (1947) p. 255.

36. R. Roques, "Eléments pour une théologie de l'état monastique selon Denys l'Aréopagite", in *Théologie de la vie monastique*, p. 289.

perfection, it is aimed at the greatest perfection, one which
has succeeded in eliminating all division and in bringing
everything together into unity."[37]
"The baptismal liturgy clearly suggested that the poles
between which the effort of the monk extends are those of
the Good and the Best (or Perfect)."[38]
"Monastic consecration confers a dignity and a rank in the
hierarchy above that of Baptism. Hence the monk's obligation to see life in different way, in a more perfect way than
the merely baptised Christian. Many a secular activity is
henceforth forbidden him. . . . Although united to that of
the Church, his life can no longer be the same as that of the
people of God.[39]

Basically, Ps.- Denis did no more than incorporate into a
theory of the Church and the "orders" which constitute its
hierarchy the traditional idea that monastic commitment is a
more fundamental, more uncompromising application of the
commitments of baptism.

With St Theodore the Studite, at the end of the eighth
century and beginning of the ninth, we find another step in
the development of tradition, the seeing in the monastic life
of a means of doing penance and obtaining the remission of
sins.

In view of the fact that the baptism of water and the spirit
has been made ineffectual through our wickedness, there
has come about, by the great goodness of God, the second
baptism of penitence.[40]

The profession by which one committed himself to this state
was not however presen:ed as a consecration of quasi-
sacramental character. Remission of sin was promised but the
result was not considered certain. It was only a hope, a sort
of very strong presumption, but one which was not absolute.
All this is merely traditional.

In the West, the evolution took place in several stages
which should be distinguished: monastic tradition, the reflec-

37. Ibid., p. 294.
38. Ibid., p. 295.
39. Ibid., p. 312-317.
40. J. Leroy, "S. Théodore Studite" in *Théologie de la vie monastique*, p. 431.

tion of scholasticism, problems posed by modern theologians, and re-orientation given by the Second Vatican Council.

In monastic custom, commitment was generally made during the sacrifice of the Lord, after the offertory at a Mass normally celebrated, if he was a priest, by the abbot who received the profession. The newly professed made his communion, as did the whole community on that day. For three days the professed "went up for the offertory and the peace".[41] In this way a link with the Eucharist was gradually established. Nevertheless, it was the analogy with baptism which occupied an increasingly important position in the development of the ceremony. This arose from several causes: first and foremost from the tendency which developed in medieval monastic life applying to the life what was valid for the whole Church. This phenomenon has been perfectly described by H. de Lubac in connection with the interpretation of Scripture:

> Whereas spiritual understanding consisted above all in the transition from the Old Testament to the New, that is, in access to the Christian faith, it was going to consist increasingly, at the heart of a believing society in which faith coexisted with secular ways of life, in illustrating the *conversio morum*, the transition from the sinful to the virtuous life, from the mediocre to the spiritual life, or more precisely, in many cases, from the 'world' to 'religion'. Then it would describe the progress of the monastic life: and the stages of contemplation, through which the monk faithful to his cell passed, would underline the progress made in the knowledge of Scripture. *Nova et Vetera.*[42]

We witness a shift of the same kind from that reality of the Church which is baptism to that event in monastic life which is profession. The idea of their similarity spread and found

---

41. The rites are described, for example, in E. Martène, *De antiquis ecclesiae ritibus,* V, 4, (Venice, 1783) p. 225-230. In A. Blaise, "Le vocabulaire latin", p. 516, 10, a phrase is quoted of the Leonine Sacramentary which associates, with reference to nuns, "the oblation of their person with that of the sacrifice".

42. H. de Lubac, *Exégèse médiévale,* (Paris, 1959) I, p. 571.

expression in both texts and ceremonies. A famous saying compared the garment of the neophyte and the habit received by the novice and was handed down and elaborated. Their effects were considered identical: illumination by the Spirit and remission of sins.[43] Similarly the consecration of the monk was likened to the ordination of the priest in a fragment falsely attributed to St Gregory the Great which was to pass into canonical collections, into the *Decretum* of Gratian, and which was frequently quoted by St Thomas Aquinas and others.[44] In point of fact the comparison with baptism, as with the priesthood, had in the context no further significance than the suggestion of participation in the Paschal mystery. Nevertheless the development of the ceremonies surrounding profession were derived increasingly from those of baptism and they tended to improve upon the natural similarity existing between them. The commentaries on the Rule of St Benedict written by Hildemar and Smaragdus in the ninth century contributed to this without, however, expounding any precise theory on the connection between the two ceremonies.[45]

At this point it is enough to quote two witnesses to the concepts born of this development, St Peter Damian and St Bernard. Damian, in the ninth century, saw in the "entry into the monastic life [as] an act of penance and expiation, the natural complement to baptism." Better still, as de Lubac has already observed, "the convert is no longer a man come from error to truth, from paganism or Judaism to the Gospel: he is the man who has renounced the world for the cloister. Thus the Christian life seems to find its true conclusion, its most complete expression, only in the cloister."[46] Peter Damian showed that baptism does not regenerate unless it inaugurates a new way of life and he passed resolutely to a strictly

---

43. Under the title "Textes sur la profession comme second baptême," in *Analecta monastica*, 2 (Rome, 1953) p. 136-139, I have given quotations.

44. Ibid., p. 137-138. In *Temoins de la spiritualité occidentale*, (Paris, 1965) p. 221-23, I have presented the testimony of Lanfranc, St Anselm and their disciples.

45. See F. Vandenbroucke, "La profession second baptême", p. 255.

46. G. Miccoli, "Théologie de la vie monastique chez Pierre Damien", in *Théologie de la vie monastique*, p. 470.

monastic interpretation. The person called to it should not refuse "to gain the summits of contemplation, to follow the most logical path of the Christian life, which consists in leaving the world and giving oneself to Christ, a path which baptism itself presupposes."[47] Here again there was a continuity between baptism and profession as regards renunciation, and so penitence. Nothing here is new to the tradition.

The same is true of St Bernard in the twelfth century. He is placed in the perspective of a Christian society where infant baptism was the universal practice. If therefore no personal cooperation was asked of the baptised, this was because he had to be purified not from personal sins but solely from original sin. He did not have to effect a return of his will since he had not yet exercised it in any direction. The position of the adult sinner is quite different: he can only recover union with Christ by means of the consent of his will to the grace which invites it, a consent which implies a sinful renunciation of all that gave the sinful man reason for living. In attributing to repentance and to personal asceticism a purifying function analogous to that of Baptism, Bernard does not, however, commit the monk to a way of holiness distinct from the sacramental way of the ordinary believers. If the sacrament of baptism does not demand conversion at the time, impossible for an infant, it nevertheless makes the demand of new life in the future. From that point, conversion has a living, continuous relationship with baptism; it is only the free ratification by man under the impulse of grace of that first commitment. Bernard does not labor the point but what he says about it is enough to show that, for him, the connection is self-evident. 'He who goes to a stricter life,' he writes, 'testifies in this way his faithfulness not only to the promises of his profession but to those of his baptism.' From this point the monastic life appeared as fundamentally dependent on the sacramental order.[48]

47. Ibid., p. 471.
48. P. Deseille, "Théologie de la vie monastique selon S. Bernard", in *Théologie de la vie monastique*, p. 516-517.

Religious Life and Baptism

In the course of the twelfth century, non-monastic forms of religious life made their appearance: military orders, Knights Hospitallers, Canons Regular. They became increasingly numerous and diverse, joined by mendicants in the thirteenth century, Jesuits and congregations of clerks regular in the sixteenth century, and innumerable foundations with an apostolic or charitable aim made from the seventeenth century onwards. All these institutions have this in common: to the sole purpose in entering the monastic state—conversion, purification of heart, the quest for God in the fellowship of prayer, penitence and charity with the whole Church—they added a second purpose, the work of the apostolate or help for one's neighbour. This is an important difference and one regarded as essential by some who go so far as to say that monks are not religious and that their life is not one species in the category "religious life".[49]

Be that as it may, the literature of spirituality remained to a great extent what the fathers of the Church or the monastic authors had written, or else it was still influenced by them. The progressive diversification of institutions therefore went hand in hand with a certain continuity in the way men saw the questions. Problems arising from monasticism were applied afresh to the new religious orders. This was legitimate up to a point, and one cannot omit mention of it. First Pius III and then Vatican II recalled that the origin of all religious life is the experience of the monks first attested and developed theologically in the East.[50] This gives a continued relevance to the living transmission of the Church's past.

49. In a study of "Le renouveau de la vie religieuse", in the *Revue diocésaine de Tournai,* 22 (1967) pp. 398-420, and further on, pp. 168-169, I have set out these problems.

50. Pius XII, "Allocution to the members of the Congress of Oriental Studies (April 1958)" published in *Il monachesimo orientale.* Orientalia christiana analecta, 153 (Rome, 1958) p. 13-14, and in Acta ApS (1958) p. 285: "Eastern monasticism . . . is the origin of the other forms of Christian monasticism, and its influence . . . is to be found to a greater or lesser degree in all the great religious orders." (Vatican II, *Decree on Oecumenism,* n. 15).

Perhaps at this point one should say what it is that the
monastic tradition brings to the whole body of life under
the counsels, exactly what the patristic tradition brings to
Christian thought. The Fathers knew no forms of the
ascetic life other than the monastic. It is utterly impossible
to take it out of their teaching as a whole. If the study of
the Fathers is believed at the present time by theologians
and laymen to be a necessary return to sources, the same
applies to the study of the ascetic tradition of the monks.
That is to state its importance in Christendom. Undoubtedly there is a danger of setting up a monastic spirituality in miniature but there is an opposite danger equally
real, that of not taking into account what is essential in the
spiritual experience of monasticism and should be present
in every form of life under the counsels. The ancient monks
are the "fathers" of the ascetic tradition. It is not a question of finding an alternative but of receiving their teaching
with the freedom of mind which a different historical context gives—not to mention the different emphasis of an-
thropology and particularly of man living in society.[51]

Meanwhile another factor emerges. In scholastic theology,
particularly from the twelfth century on, what had at first
been felt as vital experiences tended to be expressed in terms
of abstract problems. Intellectual exploration, which was
indeed legitimate, resulted in an effort to formulate clear
ideas about realities which remained shrouded in a veil of
mystery. The possible result could have been a kind of debas-
ing of spiritual themes to the level of rational speculation.
The final overall result was an advance, thanks to the balance
which men of God like St Thomas Aquinas were able to
maintain. Certain false problems were however engendered,
some of which clutter up the philosophic field almost to our
day. It is to this new phase of development that we must now
turn.

The relationship between profession and baptism, and the
effects of baptism, were discussed in the Schools, as several
scholastic *quaestiones* testify. In the course of these it was

51. G. Lafont, "Les voies de la sainteté dans le peuple de Dieu", in *L'Eglise en
marche*. Cahiers de la Pierre-qui-vire (Bruges: Desclée de Brouwer, 1964) p.
192-193.

asked "whether he who enters Religion receives a plenary indulgence for his sins and their penalty;"[52] "whether he who makes his profession in the Religious life in a state of charity is by that same fact exempt from sin and its penalty, so that, if he dies at that moment, he goes directly to heaven;"[53] "whether he who makes his profession is free from the penalties for sin which he had incurred."[54] These propositions show clearly enough that this second baptism was seen in the light of penance. And it was chiefly in this light that St Thomas considered it, placing it however in a wider perspective. For him, profession was not a purely juridical formula with purely human results; neither was it purely a symbol or a sacrament. By it the professed was marked, chosen, devoted permanently to the service of God and so cut off from all purely secular activity. The solemn consecration which inaugurated the religious state was therefore a spiritual not a sacramental consecration. The religious vow thus appeared as one of the most important sacramentals and as such, without conferring sanctifying grace by the performance of the rite (*ex opere operato*), had certain effects upon the man who yielded himself to it (*ex opere operantis*). If therefore religious profession "sanctified" the Religious, it did so by virtue of the sentiments of faith and charity inherent in every genuinely supernatural work. The religious vows were for the Religious the pledge of actual graces which all his life long would help him overcome whatever hindered the full flowering of the grace of baptism and confirmation in him, to accentuate the influence of the characteristics of those sacraments which in the Thomist doctrine were the first stages, the first "capacities", for the worship and confession of God. Profession was the pledge of actual graces which would make of the Religious a perfect Christian, that is, a true worshipper and

---

52. P. Glorieux, *La littérature quodlibétique* II (Paris, 1935) p. 248-9.

53. Ibid., p. 275, 16.

54. Ibid., p. 285-26. The problem considered from this point of view was the subject of a very well documented study by R. Collette, O. Cist., *Religiosae professionis valor satisfactorius* (Liege, 1887) to which Vandenbroucke, "La profession comme second baptême," p. 250, recognises his great debt.

confessor in spirit and in truth. This is what was called "the grace of Profession", which is not without a certain similarity to the sacramental grace of some sacraments, ordination or marriage, for example. Profession is a sacramental intended to consumate the sacramental grace of baptism and confirmation.

To say therefore that Profession is a spiritual blessing, a sacramental, is to emphasise its *opus operantis* character. The fact is worth underlining. Seen from this point of view, independent of forms and ritual actions, profession is a work of merit. As such it procures some additional effects: the increase of sanctifying grace[55] and the remission *quoad culpam* of venial sins.[56]

There remains the satisfactory effect of profession. In his commentary on the IVth book of the *Sentences,* St Thomas indicated expressly that the analogy of profession with baptism was undoubtedly founded on the suppression of satisfaction for sins. By having consecrated his will to God, the religious has already made full satisfaction for all sin. His will has been fixed on God rather than on all the created things which he could have given for alms for his sins or simply for their penalty. The Religious Life moreover, is the satisfactory penance *par excellence.*[57] In the *Summa* he taught that entry into the Religious Life procured the remission of all sins. For if one could make satisfaction for sins by means of a few alms, how much more should the total consecration of oneself to the service of God by entry into the Religious Life be regarded as a sufficient satisfaction. It was therefore a reasonable opinion (*rationabiliter dici potest*) that by entry into religion the monk obtains the remission of all his sins. "And so we read in the lives of the Fathers that those who enter the Religious Life receive the same grace as the baptised."[58]

55. Aquinas, *Summa* Ia, IIae, q. 114, a.8.
56. IIa, q. 87, a.3.
57. *IV Sent., dist.* 4, q.3, a.3, *ad* 3. Cf *Qdlb.* 3, q. 5, a.15.
58. *Summa* IIa IIae, q. 189, a.3, *ad* 3.

"But it must be admitted that doubt remains over the thought of St Thomas. The conclusion of his demonstration speaks of the 'remission of all sins'. Is it a matter of the remission of their 'guilt'? One might think so, judging by the expression. The context however suggests that it is a matter of works of satisfaction, among which profession takes first place. It seems to us therefore that St Thomas speaks here solely of the 'remission of penalties due for sins'."[59]

The Fifteenth Century Onward

Modern problems began to appear in the fifteenth century. They were raised partly by the precursors of the Reformation reacting against a certain misuse of words and ideas, certain deviations or exaggerations of thought for which the theologians of decadent scholasticism were no doubt responsible. Against Wycliff, who attributed to monks the idea that all sin was effaced by entry into the religious life, Thomas de Waldon (died 1431) recalled necessary distinctions. He went back to identifying profession with martyrdom with the renunciation of everything for the love of Christ, as St Jerome had previously done.[60] In the following century, Cajetan introduced fresh distinctions still intended to reduce the analogy between baptism and profession.

He wondered whether the novice making his Profession in a state of mortal sin could obtain full remission for it after contrition, without sacramental confession. He believed the answer to be at least doubtful. No, because profession does not imprint on the soul an indelible character, as does baptism, which will have its sanctifying effect when the obstacle is removed. Yes, because after contrition he is able in all truth to make his profession before God. But he added that, to his mind, this was no longer making his profession (a transitory act), and finally came to a negative conclusion. One may see the advance Cajetan achieved in sweeping away not only the remission of original sin but of mortal sins. He brought perfect daylight to the subject.

59. F. Vandenbroucke, "La profession comme second baptême", p. 256-259.
60. Ibid., p. 259.

Profession only allows guilt for venial sins—let us remember the Thomist doctrine of their remission by any work activated by grace, one of which is profession made in the religious sentiments which should always accompany it. The penalty is a satisfaction which is extended to every sin, mortal or venial.[61]

In the sixteenth century, Robert Bellarmine emphasised the same point.[62] And yet a certain type of pious literature has maintained, without making the necessary definitions and distinctions, almost to our day the idea that profession has, at least as far as the forgiveness of sins, the same effects as baptism. Theologians like P. Mennessier,[63] Dom F. Vandenbroucke,[64] and very recently P. Régamey,[65] have been obliged in our day to correct this idea. The most recent study published by Régamey[66]—too fine and concentrated a work to permit me to give a resumé—brings our attention back to the original and essential theme of which the real spiritual tradition had never lost sight: paschal and eschatological commitment, the break with the "world" in the Johannine sense of the word,[67] fruitful and, in that sense, espoused virginity,[68] and continuous martyrdom.[69]

Finally Dom G. Lafont, reflecting a few years ago on the constitution *Lumen gentium,* had the distinction of showing that the hesitations, ambiguities, and badly framed questions which could formerly be explained as following an ecclesiology too deeply marked by recent controversies, could now be avoided, thanks to the teaching of Vatican II on the call of

---

61. Ibid., p. 259-260.

62. Ibid., p. 260 n. 33.

63. P. Messessier, "Donation à Dieu et voeux de religion", in *La vie spirituelle, Suppl.* 49 (1936) pp. 277-301.

64. Ibid., p. 260-263

65. "La consécration religieuse, aujourd'hui contestée", in *Supplement de la vie spirituelle* (Nov., 1965) p. 385-427, and "La consécration religiuse", in *Vie consacrée* (1966), pp. 266-294 and pp. 339-359.

66. *La consécration religieuse,* p. 274.

67. Ibid., p. 274-275, 340, 351.

68. Ibid., p. 288-290.

69. Ibid., p. 356 n° 2.

all Christians to holiness. The Religious Life is only a means, albeit a "special means",[70] of progressing towards the fulfilment of this universal vocation. And Dom Lafont was also to recall the "appeal of martyrdom",[71] to emphasise the element of mystery in the traditional conception of virginity, which treats chastity as a virtue,[72] as "interior purity", a certain "renunciation of the world" expressing "dying to the world, [and] characteristic of the condition of every Christian by the very fact of his baptism."[73]

It is not therefore a question of distinguishing

"between two sanctities but between two states of life within the framework of a common pursuit of sanctity."[74]

"When this has been said, it must be admitted that, in general, the adoption of the life of the counsels presupposes a greater love because one usually reflects more deeply before embracing it and because the election of such a life is supernatural."[75]

"The state of life according to the counsels is in more profound harmony with the essence of the Christian condition. It develops to the highest degree, even in its mode of being, the hope of glory given at baptism. . . ."[76]

With this exposition of Dom Lafont—and there are others, in particular P. Martelet, who could be quoted—we have reached the contemporary phase in the history of the problem before us and the threshold of its future development. It will therefore suffice now to draw a few rapid conclusions from this recollection of the past.

Religious Consecration and the Grace of the Sacraments

Whatever elaborations theologians might make on the subject, history puts before us uncontestable facts among which a genuine continuity exists.

---

70. G. Lafont, "Les voies de la sainteté dans le peuple de Dieu", p. 183.
71. Ibid., p. 168.
72. Ibid., p. 185.
73. Ibid., p. 187.
74. Ibid., p. 208.
75. Ibid., p. 198.
76. Ibid., p. 200.

In the first place the Religious Life—whatever designations and forms have clothed it—has almost always and everywhere been set in relation to what might be called the "sacramental order" or "sacramental world". This expression is used here deliberately in order to avoid the association of the Religious Life exclusively with one special sacrament. We have seen it was associated in the course of the centuries first with marriage, whose grace it realises in a state of fruitful virginity; then with penance, of which it is a continual accomplishment; then with the Eucharist, like which it implies self-oblation; and, more rarely, comparisons with confirmation and ordination have not been wanting. At the source of all these sacraments is the first of them, baptism; it too is therefore inevitably at the source of the Religious Life and it is understandable that baptism should frequently have been associated with it. The religious vows and the life which ensues appeared as the extension of baptism. Is Profession however "another baptism" in a sense different from that by which it was considered a second penance or another marriage? We touch here upon a problem raised by the concept of sacramental grace.[77] Without resolving it, history, by the wealth and variety of aspects which brings out, gives reason to believe that religious profession was not considered as belonging strictly to the order of the sacraments themselves. Because it is, in another order of reality, a way of living out all the grace of the Paschal mystery, with the desire of living it out to the full, it is comparable with the sacraments (and baptism foremost among them) which make participation in it possible.

Be that as it may, the analogy with penance, because it is the most constantly attested, deserves emphasis. Entry into the monastic life was considered, in spiritual writings as in many legislative texts, an outstanding form of public penance. At profession, as at baptism and in the rites of penance, Satan was renounced and a treaty made with God under which the practice of severe mortification was undertaken.

77. See J. M. R. Tillard, "La notion de X grâce sacramentelle" in *Verbum caro,* 80 (1966) p. 28-41.

As a sign of this obligation, stricter than that assumed at baptism, a new name was received. Thus one of the means, and the most excellent, which a Christian had at his disposal for obtaining the forgiveness of his transgressions was to become a monk and to persevere in that state. It may be seen that the effort demanded of the penitent coming to the monastery was sufficient to remove all significance from the question whether profession acted, like baptism, *ex opere operato*. Its efficacy arose from the fact that it was one of the forms assumed by the act of penance which theologians call satisfaction. It even surpassed in this sense (in the opinion of St Thomas) all other forms of public penance. Indeed it conferred upon the practice of mortification a semi-official character which made profession a solemn act.[78]

Finally it must be said that, according to tradition, "profession", the act of making "vows", is itself only the occasion of this grace to the extent that it is an introduction into a permanent state of life. What sanctifies and, in a sense attested by history, consecrates is the whole existence of the religious. Profession is the oblation of one's self to God and the imitation of the oblation which Jesus Christ in his Passion made of himself. In view of this the entire life of the religious should assume a character of sacrifice and of expiation, which connects it as closely with baptism as with penance. It is a new direction given to a whole subsequent life.[79]

Let us conclude with a quotation of St Bernard which will sum up all the fruits of tradition while respecting the mystery in which it remains enveloped and the study of which stems from the analysis of the theologians:

How does it happen that the monastic discipline, a penitential institution, should of all others have earned the prerogative of being called a second baptism? I think because of the perfect renunciation of the world and the singular excellence of the spiritual life, for by these this state of life is raised above all the others ... It forms once

78. In *La vie parfaite* (Paris, 1948) p. 133-141 ("Le baptême des pénitents") I have quoted commentary texts to this effect.

79. Under the title "Professione religiosa secondo battesimo", in *Vita religiosa* (1967) p. 3-9, I have emphasised aspects which are only suggested here.

more in man the image of God, conforming us to Christ, as does baptism. We are in a sense baptized for a second time since, in this state of life, we mortify our earthly members and we put on Christ anew: we are grafted anew into the resemblance of his death. But as in baptism we are plucked out of the kingdom of darkness and transferred to the kingdom of eternal light, so in the second regeneration we leave the darkness, not now only of original sin, but of many of our actual misdeeds, and we enter the light of our virtues, renewing in ourselves the saying of the Apostle: 'The night is far spent, the day is at hand'.[80]

80. *De praecepto et dispensatione,* 54, ed. *S. Bernardi opera,* III (Rome, 1963) p. 289; quotation at the end from Rom. 13, 12.

CONTEMPORARY WITNESS TO THE
THEOLOGY OF MONASTICISM *

THE SECOND VATICAN COUNCIL has spoken concerning the contemplative life and monasticism. It has not only laid down directives of a practical order for them, it has gone further still and stated a doctrine which makes it possible for us to locate them in the mystery of the Church. The main points of this teaching have already been assembled.[1] But, during the Council and after it, other voices have made themselves heard on the same problem, and these have brought to our attention both the line of thought taken by the ordinary magisterium of the Pope and the way in which the *sensus fidelium* reacts to this.

As I have been asked to bring together this twofold witness, I shall confine my enquiry to the precise point at which it comes under the jurisdiction of theology. I shall not deal with questions of an institutional nature hinging on canon law.

It goes without saying that there is no question here of delivering either a eulogy or a critique of the monastic institution. Rather, my intention is to examine it because it constitutes a sort of extreme case in the religious life. It is for this reason that it arouses interest far beyond the circle of its own members, while it, in turn, certainly has lessons to learn from those who do not belong within its membership, but have nevertheless the right to remind monasticism of its role and responsibilities.

---

* Published in *Gregorianum,* 48(1967) 49-76; in English in *Cistercian Studies,* 2 (1967) 189-204. Parts appeared in Italian in *Vita contemplativa et monachesimo* (Sorrente, 1967)3-12,29-31.

1. See above, chapter one.

99

The Witness of Paul VI

Recent Popes have not failed, in the exercise of their ordinary magisterium, to speak out about the contemplative life and monasticism, their object and their place in the Church. In full continuity with them, Paul VI speaks on this subject whenever an occasion arises for doing so. He is happy to seize upon such occasions, and even, it would seem, goes out of his way to create them. This arises, no doubt, both from personal inclination and from a desire to give sound teaching on the subject to all, whether monks or not. But while there is continuity, it is also noticeable that there is an increasing precision in his statements. Never perhaps has any Pope, at least in recent times, been so outspoken in encouraging monks, and, one might add, so exacting in their regard.[2] We shall be in a better position to judge this when we have examined the relevant documents. At this time of clarifying ideas and of determining tasks proper to each member or each group of members of the Church, everything seems to indicate that the Supreme Pastor wishes to remind the monastic order of its specific role — a role which is, in this sense, limited and therefore insufficient, yet at the same time unique and irreplaceable.

As early as 24 October 1964, when he was speaking to the Benedictines at Monte Cassino, Paul VI used these forceful words:

> The Church and the world, for different yet convergent reasons, need Saint Benedict to withdraw from the ecclesial and social community and to draw about him the protective wrappings of solitude and silence. . . .
> We shall not say any more now about the function which the monk, the man who has been restored to himself, is able to fulfill, not only with regard to the Church (about which we have spoken) but also with regard to the world. He has left the world, yet he remains bound to it by new relationships which his very separation has produced: rela-

2. The texts have been assembled by A. Piel , *Les moines dans l'Eglise. Textes des Souverains Pontifes* (Paris: Cerf, 1964).

tionships of contrast, of admiration, of example, of the possibility of trustful and confidential intercourse and brotherly help. We simply state that this relationship exists, and that it increases in importance the more the world is in need of the monastic virtues and realizes that they are not its own but are preserved for it and offered to it by the monks in their monastery.... [3]

Then, just at the close of the Council, in the very session in which the *Pastoral Constitution on the Church in the World of Today* was promulgated, Paul VI canonized a Lebanese hermit of whom hardly anything is known, for he said nothing, wrote nothing, and did nothing remarkable:

After the recent beatification of Jacques Berthier, a Jesuit missionary and martyr, we are happy today to preside at the beatification of a monk supremely dedicated to contemplation. At the close of this Council, when so many of the faithful are busying themselves, and rightly so, with what the Church ought to do to hasten the coming of the Kingdom of Jesus, how opportune it is that the holy monk of Annaya should be brought to the fore to remind us of the indispensable role of prayer, of the hidden virtues, and of mortification. To apostolic works the Church must join centres of contemplative life, from which praise and intercession rise up to God as a sweet perfume ... [4]

But it was especially in a discourse pronounced after the Council, namely on 1 October 1966, when the Pope was speaking to the Benedictine Abbots in Congress, that he gave expression to the full extent of his thought concerning the monastic life. The text of this discourse, while comparatively brief, is nevertheless packed with meaning. Doubtless it surprised more than one listener by the energy of its expressions. Without dwelling on the more special directives which the Holy Father pronounced on certain points — on the

---

3. Text in *Acta Apostolicae Sedis,* December 1964, p. 983-989.
4. Text in *Acta Apostolicae Sedis,* January 1966, p. 64-65. In the preface to his biography of P. Charbel, M. Hayek wrote: 'Charbel Makhlouf did nothing sensational that would attract attention to him or merit his being recorded in human annals'. *Le chemin du désert: Le Père Charbel, moine d'Orient, 1829-1898* (Le Puy-Lyon, 1950) p. 14.

subject of the institutional structure of monasticism, for example — let us confine ourselves solely to his ideas concerning monasticism in itself and its place in the Church.

After a very brief introduction, as if he were in a hurry to get to the essentials, the Pope began by telling monks, in the person of their Abbots, what they really are: '*Monachi vos estis; homines videlicet singulares . . .*' The official French translation renders this by 'Vous êtes moines, c'est-à-dire des hommes à vocation speciale' (You are monks; that is to say, men with a special vocation). The Italian translation renders this latter expression by the words 'uomini singolari. . . .' But in such profound text why should we not think that the word *singularis* has the strong and powerful meaning which it has received from long traditional usage, and according to which it is equivalent of *monachus*: the man who lives *alone* because he has voluntarily broken away from 'the ecclesial and social community', the man who has 'withdrawn' from it, to use the expression which the Pope himself used at Monte Cassino, and who has, in this sense, separated himself from the world, the man who has become a 'solitary'.[5] The Pope then goes on to comment on the expression *homines singulares* from this point of view. We notice that he uses the terms *se segregari, solitudo, discedere, silentium.* Then he enlarges upon the phrase *soli Deo* (occupied with God alone) which St Gregory the Great applied to St Benedict. According to this monks are to be defined as 'seekers of God', men who are 'wholly given up to the presence of God', to 'conversation with Him'. And the Holy Father concludes this paragraph with a delicate allusion, poetically expressed, to the role of monks as 'watchers' wholly intent upon the world that is to come — that world which they both wait for and proclaim. The text is as follows[6] :

5. In *Etudes sur le vocabulaire monastique du moyan âge*, Studia Anselmiana, 48 (1961), p. 165, for the words *singulares, singularitas, singulariter,* I have indicated these texts.

6. Text in *Acta,* November 1966, p. 884-889. The official French translation weakens more than one of the Pope's statements. To the example already given (*homines singulares*) can be added the following: *Aeterni Dei estis investigatores,* which the official translation renders by: 'Vous cherchez Dieu'.

You are monks, that is to say, men with a special vocation, who have withdrawn, in one way or another from the secular environment of human society, in order to take refuge in a solitude that is not simply exterior but also interior because it entails a life of recollection. You are men of silence and prayer, and, imitating the example of your Founder and Patriarch who 'desired to please God alone' (St Gregory, *Dialogues,* 2, 1), each of you has retired within himself, content solely with the riches of the spirit. You seek God. This choice has been the touchstone of your vocation; as your Holy Rule puts it: 'ascertain if he [the novice] is truly seeking God' (*Rule of St Benedict,* ch. 58). You are men consecrated to the study of the divine Presence and to the art of God, conversing in an effable way with Christ and God; you are experts in the knowledge of things invisible, which are the most true and most real of all. This is the reason why We would wish to listen to you, to you who keep watch in the twilight of this present life and proclaim the dawn which is to rise for the faithful.[7]

The paragraph which follows this one speaks even more emphatically. Here the Pope purely and simply equates the profession of the religious life in the form 'proper' to monks, and especially to Benedictine monks, since it is to them that he is speaking, with the 'contemplative life'. Speaking to Abbots, all of whom are, in fact, priests, he begins by reminding them of what the *Dogmatic Constitution on the Church* teaches about the necessity of uniting prayer with action and

---

7. Monachi vos estis: homines videlicet estis singulares, qui a profana vos conversatione quoddamodo segregantes, in solitudinem non tantum exteriorem, sed etiam interiorem, id est in supernarum rerum meditationem discessistis. Homines estis silentio et precationi addicti; atque propterea unusquisque vestrum, non secus atque Patriarcha idemque legifer Pater vester, 'soli Deo placere desiderans' (S. Greg. *Dial.* II, 1), se ad se revocavit, in animi dumtaxat divitiis acquiescens. Aeterni Dei ,estis investigatores; atque ad norman huius electionis vocatio vestra probata est, sicut vestra regula statuit: 'si revera Deum quaerit' (Chap. 58). Quam ob rem vos totos sive divinae praesentiae cognoscendae, sive arti inenerrabili cumque Deo colloquendi addixistis; ita ut in rebus invisibilibus, quae omnium verissimae et praesentissimae sunt, bene versati facti sitis. Hanc ob causam vos audire vellemus: vos dicimus, qui huius vitae veluti crepusculo vigilatis, et auroram praenuntiatis, quae omnes manet christifideles.

of making action spring from contemplation itself. Then he 'transfers', that is to say, applies to Benedictines what the *Decree on the Renewal and Adaptation of the Religious Life* has to say on the subject of institutes wholly dedicated to the contemplative life. The Pope precedes his quotation from the *Decree* by two expressions which are full of meaning. He speaks of those followers of Christ who dwell 'in silence' and 'hearken' to his word. We think of Mary who 'sitting at the Lord's feet, heard his word', while Martha was 'busy with many things' — *sedens secus pedes Domini audiebat verbum illius* (Lk. 10:39). By this the Holy Father means to say that he want to 'confirm and sanction' the value of this form of life and its 'office' or function (*munus*) in the service of the universal Church:

But it is not possible for us at this moment to keep silent and for you to speak. Content yourselves with hearing us acknowledge the special character of your profession as contemplative religious, and be assured of the esteem, respect and confidence which you enjoy in our mind and heart. We spontaneously address to you the words which the Council reserves in the first place for priests — for such you also are: 'Their praise lives on in the Church of God. Praying and offering sacrifice, in virtue of their office, for their own people and for the entire People of God, realizing what they do, and reproducing in themselves the holiness of the things they handle . . . nourishing their activity on the plenitude of contemplation, to the delight of the whole Church of God' (*Lumen Gentium*, no, 41).
To you we repeat the words of praise that the *Decree on the Renewal and Adaptation of the Religious Life* addresses to those followers of Christ who dwell in silence and hearken to his words. The Council says: 'Institutes which are totally devoted to contemplation must continue to play their wonderful role in the Mystical Body of Christ, in which *all members do not have the same office* (Rom. 12:4), their members giving all their time to God alone in silence and solitude, praying continuously and willingly doing penance. They offer to God an outstanding sacrifice of praise, making God's people resplendent with the rich

fruits of holiness; they stir it by their example and give it growth by the hidden fruitfulness of their apostolate . . .'. (Chapt. 7)

We desire in this way to confirm the value, the eminent value of your calling, and in consequence the role which you have to fulfil, whether in the personal religious life of the faithful, or in the spiritual life of Christian communities, or finally in the complex and harmonious framework of that life which animates the Church under the action of the Holy Spirit.[8]

After these considerations which are, so to speak, of an ecclesiological order, the Pope turns to the question of the primary activity of monks namely that of contemplation. He does not hesitate to use this word twice more in this paragraph, as well as the expression 'to contemplate' and 'contemplative life', citing the latter from one of the admirable questions in which St Thomas develops his theology of the 'states of life'. Paul VI is here echoing the Prologue of the *Constitution on the Sacred Liturgy,* in which the contemplative character of the Church's public prayer is clearly enunciated:

8. Sed se fieri non potest, ut hoc temporis momento Nos sileamus, vos autem loquamini, satis tamen vobis sit novisse, Nos probare professionem vestram Religiosorum propriam, qui vitae contemplativae sunt addicti, ad testanda vobis gratiam, observantiam, fiduciam, quibus vos prosequimur. Nos namque ad vos ea verba libenter adhibemus, quae Concilium Vaticanum secundum praesertim ad sacerdotes, quales vos estis, convertit: 'Quorum laus est in Ecclesia Dei. Pro plebe sua et toto Populo Dei ex officio precantes et sacrificium offerentes, agnoscendo quod agunt et imitando quod tractant . . . , ex abundantia contemplationis actionem suam nutriendo et fovendo, in oblectamentum totius Ecclesiae Der'. (*Lumen gentium, no. 41)*

Ac eam laudem in vos transferimus, quam Decretum de accomodata renovatione vita religiosae silentibus Christi sectatoribus et auditoribus tribuit: "Instituta quae integre ad contemplationem ordinantur, ita ut eorum sodales in solitudine ac silentio in 'assidua prece et alacri poenitentia soli Deo vacent, in corpore Christi mystco, in quo omnia membra non eundem actum habent (Rom 12:4) . . . , praeclaram partem semper retinent. Deo enim eximium laudis sacrificium offerunt, populum Dei sanctitatis uberrimis fructibus collustrant atque exemplo movent, necnon arcana fecunditate apostoloca dilatant. Ita Ecclesiae decus exstant et caelestium scatebra gratiarum" (Chap. 7).

Hoc modo confirmare volumus dignitatem, immo excellentiam religiosae vestrae vivendi formae, atque etiam muneris, quod ad ipsam spectat sive in singulorum christifidelium pietate, sive in spirituali vita communitatis christianae, sive in vario et concinno contextu vitalis vigoris, quo Ecclesia Dei a Spiritu Sancto animatur."

It is of the essence of the Church that she be both human and divine, visible and yet invisibly endowed, eager to act and yet intent on contemplation, present in this world and yet not at home in it. She is all these things in such a way that in her the human is directed by and subordinated to the divine, the visible likewise to the invisible, action to contemplation, and this present world to that city yet to come, which we seek (cf. Heb. 13:14).[9]

Monks ought to bring fully into being and proclaim by their example the contemplative character of the liturgy and the necessity of uniting it with personal prayer. The text reads:

To contemplate, that is to say, to draw ever closer to God in mind and heart, is to a certain extent the concern of all Christians, since all ought by means of prayer to bring into play the highest faculties of their spirit, namely, reflection and love. We cannot conceive of an act of worship which would not draw its essential element from the personal effort of the one who prays. This personal effort can be said to be directed to contemplation, and it would be quite wrong to dispense a person who takes part in the Divine Office from making it, as some seem to want to do, as if this exercise, because it is performed in community, could excuse anyone from bringing his personal cooperation to it. It would be as if belonging to a choir were considered a reason for excusing the individual artists from uniting their own voices with those of the others. You well know to what extent this personal effort towards contemplation is required and supported by the liturgy, and you will recall the memorable words of the encyclical *Mediator Dei*: 'Far from stifling the inward sentiments of Christians, the liturgy, on the contrary, fosters them and helps them to develop'. And what is true for all the faithful worthy of the name, you in particular achieve to the fullest extent and in the most exemplary way, so that in your case the beauty of the contemplative life reveals itself in all its splendor (cf. St Thomas, *Summa. Theologia*, 11a 11ae, Q. 180, A. 2, *ad 3um*), and it spurs on the whole people of God to seek *those things which are above* (Col. 3:2) and to yield them-

9. *Prooemium*, no. 2. Cited from *La Maison-Dieu* 76 (1963) p. 37.

selves to the fruitful and fascinating attraction of your art of praying.[10]

After prayer, work. Paul VI spoke of the apostolic function proper to monks, the function which is their very own — *vestrum apostolicum munus*. This is determined by the contemplative orientation which we have just pointed out: *Hoc sane modo . . . agnoscitur*. It consists in part, but only in part, in undertaking certain forms of work of a pastoral or cultural character, provided these are in conformity with the monastic vocation. The expression which the Pope uses here — *nonnulla opera* — recalls that used in the paragraph of the decree *Perfectae Caritatis* (no. 9) concerning monks: *sive aliqua opera*. In this connection, the Holy Father, though without dwelling on the subject, makes a brief mention, a reminder (*recolere*) of the schools and missions entrusted to monks. But he adds that monks are men 'wholly or principally dedicated to prayer and to the ascetical life, and it is this dedication which should mark the whole of their apostolate and be the sign by which they are to be recognised: *Hoc sane modo . . . agnoscitur*. Then, in thoroughly traditional language, the Pope goes on to describe this life led in quiet and obscurity: *tranquillam quasi atque umbratilem vitam* — a life tranquil and hidden. The first of these marks has often been

10. Contemplari, hoc est ad Deum tendere cogitando atque amando, tale opus est, quod ad omnes quodammodo pertinet; omnes enim, cum Deo preces fundunt, nobiliores animi facultates exercere debent, nempe facultates meditandi et amandi. Nullo modo actus divini cultus intelligi potest, qui non secumferat necessarium nisus ipsius hominis orantis; a quo nisu, ad contemplationem spectante, perperam quidam eos eximendos esse putant, qui actionem liturgicam participant, quasi actio liturgica, utpote communitaria, eximere posset fidelem a propria ponenda socia opera, haud secus ac si in canentium choro singuli cantores eximerentur a munere suam vocem cum aliorum vocibus coniungendi. Ceterum probe vobis in comperto est, quantopere sacra Liturgia postulet atque foveat illam animi contentionem, quae fidelem orantem ad contemplationem conducit; ac probe meministis verba illa Litterarum Encyclicarum *Mediator Dei*, quae semper sunt recolenda: "Tantum abest ut sacra Liturgia intimos singulorum christianorum sensus reprimat, ut eos potius idcirca refoveat atque instimulet" (*Acta Aps* 99 (1947), p. 567). Quod autem proprium officium est cuiusvis veri nominis christifidelis, id ipsum vos plene atque in exemplum ad effectum deducitis; ita ut per vos magis magisque resplendeat illa vitae contemplativae pulchritudo (*Summa Theol.* IIa IIae, Q. 180, a. 2, and 3) quae impellit Populum Dei universum ad quaerenda 'quae sursum sunt' (Col. 3 : 2) et ad salutarem eamque allicentem vim percipiendam vestrae artis orandi.

attributed to the monastic life.[11] So for that matter has the
second,[12] and it has been used repeatedly by Popes since Pius
XI, and now by the Council in the paragraph of the decree
Perfectae Caritatis which deals with the monastic life. The
word *consistere* is to be noted here. It calls to mind the
whole vocabulary of *sessio* and of 'residence' in solitude.
There is in fact a new insistence on solitude here.[13] The
whole idea is that of a presence, a sign, a mark, a secret
fascination, a source of radiance, rather than on that of a
direct activity in a number of different fields.

In this way your apostolic function is duly and rightly
recognized. It flows not only from the exercise of certain
works of a pastoral or cultural character which are in
harmony with your vocation (and here it is especially fitting to remind ourselves of the Benedictine motto *Ora et
labora,* and of the schools which you direct and the missions entrusted to your care). It flows also from the fact
that your life is exclusively or at least principally consecrated to prayer and asceticism. In a world such as ours
which is unmindful of God and lives far away from him, a
world which is indifferent to him and even denies his existence, you give your witness, the witness of men who are
austere yet full of humanity, living in a spirit of tranquillity
and recollectedness in your monasteries, where you exercise on others a sort of secret and holy fascination. You
have your Rule to support you, which says: *Ubique credi-
must divinam esse praesentiam* (We believe that the Divine
Presence is everywhere). And your presence becomes a sign
of God's presence among men. You sing God's praises, but
who listens to you? You celebrate the holy mysteries, but
who pays any attention to you? It may seem that you are
neither rightly understood nor properly valued by others.
Your very solitude seems to put you beneath notice. But
this is not so. Some at least have noticed; some at least have

11. Texts referred to are in *Etudes sur le vocabulaire, p. 165,* Index, for the
words *tranquillus* and *tranquillitas*; and in *Otia monastica, Etudes sur le vocabulaire de la contemplation au moyen âge,* Studia Anselmiana 51 (Rome, 1963) p.
187, Index.
12. In *Chances de la spiritualité occidentale* (Paris: Cerf, 1966) pp. 279-280, I
have brought together the texts.
13. Texts in *Chances de la spiritualité,* pp. 313-328.

seen that you have lit a fire. Some at least have discovered the light with warmth that radiate from your cloisters; there are some at least who stop, observe, and reflect. For the world of today your life serves as a reminder of higher things. It provokes men to reflection, and this can often be for them a source of salvation and renewal. But on one condition — that your monastic life be perfect in every respect, as the venerable Rule so wisely drawn up for it by St Benedict intends it to be.... [14]

Let us take note, in the final exhortation, of the kind of activities to which the Holy Father asks the Benedictines to devote themselves: the study of Holy Scripture and Church History, the publication of books of spirituality 'full of the fruit of the experience of the things of God' and 'capable of providing solid spiritual nourishment'; hospitality and ecumencial dialogue. Here we see a perfect consistency between these practical directives and the principles laid down at the beginning. It is evident that the Pope, with every word weighed, wished to give clear teaching to all Benedictines, teaching which, while given to one monastic institute, would also serve to extend and give precision to what the Council had said

14. Hoc sane modum vestrum apostolicum munus iure merito agnoscitur; quod non solum ex nonnullis operibus constat vocationi vestrae consentaneis, quae ad pastorale ministerium et ad animi culturam spectant—hic peculiari modo recolere placet illud Benedictinorum monachorum insigne 'ora et labora', nec non scholas et sacros missiones moderationi vestrae concreditas—sed etiam ex quod unice vil praecipue vos orationi et asceticae vitae addicti estis. Revera in ea hominum societate—ut ob plures rationes nostra est—quae Deum ignorat, quae a Deo seiuncta est, quae Deum neglegit, quae Deum esse negat, vos tranquillam quasi atque umbratilem vitam degentes, austeri atque humanitate pleni, in monasteriis vestris consistitis, quasi ad homines sacra quadam arcana fascinatione alliciendos. Vestra regula fulcimini, quae haec habet: *Ubique credimus divinam esse praesentiam.* Praesentia vestra veluti signum et indicium est praesentiae Dei inter homines. Cantatis; qui vos audit? Sacra celebratis; quis ad vos animum intendit? Vos videmini ad aliis haud recte intellegi atque aestimari; solitudo vitam vestram deprimere videtur. Sed non ita est. Sunt qui animadvertant, vos ignem accendisse; sunt qui intelligant e claustris vestris lucem et calorem radiari; sunt qui gradum sistant, aspiciant, meditentur. Vos hominum huius aetatis mentem ad excelsa erigitis. Initium quoddam eorum meditationi praebetis, quod saepe eos ad salutem atque ad novas suscipiendas vires conducit. Id tamen hoc tantum pacto fieri potest, ut scilicet vita vestra, monachorum ratione instituta, omni ex parte perfecta sit. Perfecta in vivendi modo, vetustissima lex, a Sancto Benedicto condita, sapienter descripsit. . . .

with regard to monasticism as a whole. The decree *Perfectae Caritatis* had established a distinction between 'institutes of wholly contemplative life' and the 'monastic institution'. Here we have an authentic interpretation, which, as least as far as Benedictines are concerned, reduces this distinction to a minimum. Here we can glimpse an indication of the *sensus Ecclesiae*, the mind of the Church.

The Holy Father expressed his thoughts on the contemplative life on yet another occasion, shortly after the Council, in a long allocution to the Camaldolese Nuns on the Aventine in Rome.[15] In the opening sentence, the Holy Father took up the problem that was occupying his mind, that of the place proper to each state of life in the mystery of the Church: 'Your courageous and heroic act of withdrawal from the world and from the social community, that act which goes under the name of *enclosure*, keeps you confined here . . . But your enclosure is not a prison; it does not cut you off from the communion of Holy Church'. Once again, we shall confine ourselves to quoting some of the vigorous statements by which the Pope situates the contemplative life in the mystery of the Church:

> Our first word to you will be on the subject of your relation to the Church. Looking at things from the outside, one would say that you are cut off from the main body; you are not in the procession; you take no part in the assemblies; you stand apart; you are recluses . . . But this material, external, social reclusion does not separate you from the Church . . . The Church turns her eyes towards you who have dedicated yourselves to this way of life in order to engage in constant dialogue with the Lord, in order to be able to hear his voice more clearly, and to be able to express our poor human voice to him with greater purity and intensity. You have made this close harmony between heaven and earth the sole preoccupation of your life. While the world is pursuing its material ends, you contemplatives are content to let your souls be absorbed in God. So then the Church sees in you the highest expression of herself. You are in a certain way, at the summit.

15. The Italian text was published in *Vita monastica*, 20 (1966) p. 67-72. A French translation appeared in *Lettre de Ligugé*, 119 (Sept.-Oct., 1966) p. 3-7.

For what does the Church desire to do in this world but unite souls with God, to make it possible for them to say 'Our Father' and to engage in dialogue with God? What does the Church wish to do but create in every soul this aptitude for listening to the word of God? For you must realize that our salvation proceeds entirely from this fact of listening to the Word . . .

The Church sees contemplative souls as those who fulfil her programme — fulfil it partially, of course, but in the highest possible way. You are at the summit of the religious life which the Church desires to foster among men. . . .

After this, the Pope four separate times takes up the idea of 'talking with God' by which contemplatives, in their own persons, put the world in dialogue with its Lord. He alludes to the dialogue which took place on the mountain of Transfiguration (and we can hardly fail to remember that Cassian made this event the starting point for his teaching on the prayer of monks)[16]. The idea that the contemplative life is the form, the expression, the supreme realization of everything towards which the mystery of the Church tends, confirms the views expressed in the same direction by some of the most discerning theologians of our day. The insistence on the necessity of 'listening to the word of God' is found, as we have seen, in the Pope's discourse to the Abbots. In short, there is complete continuity between these two instructions of Pope Paul VI on the subject of the position of the contemplative life and monasticism in the Church. To be sure, the allocution to the Camaldolese was addressed to contemplative nuns, among whom there is even a recluse to whom the Holy Father was please to make an allusion. But just as reclusion is an extreme case—exceptional, rare, but legitimate — in the eremitical life, so monastic life in its totality is being considered throughout all these texts as an extreme case in the life of the Church. It is, says the Holy

---

16. *Conlatio X, De oratione, 6,* Nicene & Post-Nicene Fathers, Second Series, Vol. XI, chap. vi, p. 403.

Father, a 'partial' form of the Church's life but it is 'the highest'.

Finally Paul VI stated the position of the monastic life in the Church still more precisely and clearly when, on 29 October 1966, he addressed a long allocution to the Benedictine abbesses of Italy, in the course of which he distinctly emphasized the importance of this audience and its character, 'perhaps unique in history'. As he had already done when addressing the abbots, he quoted in its entirety paragraph 7 of *Perfectae Caritatis* concerning institutes totally devoted to the contemplative life, showing thereby that in its essentials the life of nuns does not differ from that of monks. On this occasion, as with the Camaldolese on the Aventine, he laid stress on enclosure. The teaching which he gave this time confirmed what he had previously said and shed light on two accepted principles: union with the universal Church, and yet within that Church, a specific role, different from the roles undertaken by others. The Holy Father speaks of a 'function' which is 'distinct' and even 'specialized'. Here we shall just pick out two passages where these ideas are formulated most concisely[17]:

> Not only is a place conceded to you in the Catholic Church, but you have, as the Council states, a function in it. You are not separated from the great communion of the Family of Christ, though you are specialists. And your special function is no less useful and constructive for the Church and for the whole of society today than it has been in the past. You preserve and affirm values whose need is felt more than ever today and you know very well what these are: the supreme and exclusive search for God in solitude and silence, poor and humble work, everything that gives to life the character of unceasing prayer, of a *sacrificium laudis* celebrated in common and consummated in common, in an atmosphere of fraternal and joyful charity....
> Your monastic vocation requires solitude and enclosure. But you should never consider yourselves for that reason isolated and cut off from fellowship with the universal Church. You are not cut off, we say, from communion

17. Text in *Acta ApS* December 1966, p. 1155-1162.

with the Church. But you do hold a distinct place in it, in order to enable you to realize the special aim of your religious life . . . .

With regard to the way in which the charity of nuns makes itself effective in the world that surrounds them, the Holy Father speaks not of activity nor of the apostolate but of 'radiance', of 'irradiation', of the 'spectacle of contemplative consecration', of a 'diaphanous emanation of peace, of joy, of holiness'. This idea of 'irradiation' is to be found in several contemporary writers on the monastic life.

Christian Witness

The Actuality of Contemplation

The contemplative monastic life of which the present Pope loves to speak can be understood only if we situate it within a wider reality, that of contemplation understood in the broad and rich sense which tradition and the common language of the Church have given to this word. In proportion as activity and work in all their forms have not only developed in our times but have also become the subject of reflection for thoughtful men, so too their necessary complement, 'the activity of contemplation', has emerged into the full light of day. Many testimonies to this effect could be gathered from among recent authors—for example, from a philosopher like Jean Lacroix[18], or from a theologian such as Romano Guardi-

---

18. "However noble it may be, work is but a preparation for contemplating what one cannot give oneself by oneself. Beyond laborious activity, even if it be lodged in the depth of the spirit, there is the activity of contemplation, without which the former would have no meaning . . . The danger of a cult of pure work would be to take the position that man can find his last end in this world and that the transformation of this world by his labour suffices to make him happy", *Socialisme?* (Paris, 1945) p. 59. Along the same line, *ibid.*, p. 89, and in numerous parallel passages in the work of the same philosopher: "Travail et contemplation," in *Le sens du dialogue* (Neuchâtel, 1944) pp. 83-85; "La notion du travail," in *XXIXes journées universitaires* (Lyon, 1952: Supplement to *Cahiers universitaires catholiques,* but 1952) p. 25; "La promotion du travail dans la pensée et la civilisation modernes," in *Reflexions sur le travail, Lumière et vie* 20 (1955) p. 18; "Philosophie du travail," in *Travail et condition humaine,* Semaine des intellectuels catholiques 1962 (Paris, 1963) p. 29.

ni[19]. Father de Lubac has recently assembled some remarkable passages from the writings of one of the clearest thinkers of our time, Hans Urs von Balthasar, stressing 'contemplative participation in the mystery of Christ':

All that we can attest to other men, our brothers, about the divine reality is derived from contemplation — the contemplation of Jesus Christ, that of the Church and that of ourselves. We cannot speak in a telling and effective way about the contemplation of Jesus Christ and of the Church unless we ourselves share in this . . . But who ever speaks of Tabor nowadays in the programmes of Catholic Action? Who ever speaks of seeing, of understanding, of touching something which cannot be preached or propagated by any activity, no matter how zealous it may be, unless it has first been recognized and experienced? Who ever speaks of indescribable peace of that eternity which lies beyond all our struggles here below? Or who ever tells of the unutterable weakness and powerlessness of Crucified Love, whose 'emptying of himself' to the point of becoming 'sin and a curse' has brought into the world all power and salvation for the Church and mankind? Anyone who has not experienced this mystery through contemplation will never be able to talk about it nor even act in accordance with it, without feeling himself affected by a sort of embarrassment and bad conscience, unless the naïvete springing from some fundamentally worldly involvement has already masked this bad conscience.[20]

'We are living in a time of spiritual aridity. The vital balance between action and contemplation has been disrupted in favour of action, and that means to its detriment as well. Balthasar wants to re-establish the balance between them. All this work has a contemplative dimension, and that, more than anything else, is what gives it its depth and savor'.[21]

---

19. In particular in *Unterscheidung des Christlichen* (Mainz, 1963); on the importance of recollection and solitude (*Einsamkeit, Einsamsein*), of the contemplative attitude (*kontemplative Haltung*) in the era of 'mechanization', pp. 96-100, 229-237, 244-259.

20. H. De Lubac "Un témoin du Christ: Hans Urs von Balthasar," in *Pouvoir et société*. Recherches et débats, 53 (1966) pp. 133-159.

21. *Ibid.*, p. 152.

The Prior of Taizé, on his side, eulogizes contemplation in some pages whose opening lines set the tone:

In the interior life a communication is set up between the Christian and Christ. This personal relationship, renewed through prayer, meditation, and communion in the Body and Blood of Christ, leads to apprehension of the presence of God in contemplation.[22]

Contemplation is then an actuality for the present day. But there have always been two ways of tending towards it — the one in the world, the other in the cloister. In Paris, on 21 April 1966, at the end of the communication with which he brought UNESCO's session in homage of the Council to a close, Maritain declared:

And while I am on the subject, why should I not express everything I am thinking. The thing that gives us real ground for hope is the fact that there is today an awakening — invisible in itself no doubt and yet discernible by many signs — an awakening, I do not say in the mass of men but in certain souls, and these less rare than one might be led to believe — an awakening of this life of contemplative prayer and union with God which is the hidden spring from which love is pouring out through a thousand channels and which supports and sustains the work of men dedicated to apostolic action as well as those who give themselves to the temporal activities which are necessary to keep this world from perishing. Did Paul VI not say, in the discourse of 7 December 1965, with which he closed the Council, that contemplation is the most perfect form of human activity and serves as the scale against which, in the pyramid of human acts, the individual worth of those acts is measured, each according to its kind? An invisible constellation of souls dedicated to the contemplative life in the world and at the very heart of the world is, I say, our ultimate reason for hoping.[23]

22. Roger Schultz, *Vivre l'aujourd'hui de Dieu,* (Taizé 1961) pp. 52-61 (extracts in *Spiritualité protestante,* Edition du Soleil levant (Namur, 1965) pp. 184-186. [Eng. transl. *This Day Belongs to God* (London: Faith Press, 1961) and *Living Today for God* (Baltimore: Helicon, 1962)].
23. Text in *Informations catholiques internationales,* May 15, 1966, p. 36.

Philosophy has become the interpreter of a reality which has never been lacking to the Church — the contemplative life led in the world, *in domibus propriis,* as the ancient texts used to say. This is being spoken of anew today because we are discovering, as in the days of St Melania in the fourth century or in those of St Catherine of Siena in the fourteenth, that, though difficult, it is very fruitful.

The Cloistered Contemplative Life

Alongside the way of life of those who have sought and attained contemplative prayer in the midst of the world, the Church has always given approval—and we know that she continues to give approval—to those men and women who, with the same object in view, withdraw from the world. In their case, too, there is no lack of testimony. When it comes from theologians, this testimony tends to locate the cloistered or monastic contemplative life squarely within the Church with particular regard to the relationship which it establishes between God and the world. On this point, too, Hans Urs von Balthasar has written some penetrating and courageous pages, of which it will be sufficient here to give a few brief extracts:

It is incumbent on the Church to safeguard contemplative vocations as the apple of her eye. For such they truly are, according to the affirmations of Origen and other Fathers. They have need in their cloisters of choice spiritual direction. The office of spiritual father or director of souls in contemplative cloisters cannot be entrusted to any elderly or retired priest who happens to be available. It is the duty of the teaching Church to foster recruitment for contemplative monasteries. Preaching at liturgical celebrations must unceasingly explain and commend the meaning and urgency of this vocation both for the Church and for the world . . .[24].

In this context, von Balthasar mentions the leisure of contemplation, the *otium* or *vacatio* (leisure or freedom from cares) that it presupposes and which makes contemplation

---

24. *Sponsa Virgo* (Einsiedeln, 1961) p. 386.

possible and is 'the very act that constitutes the Church, the activity to which she is called in her entirety.'[25] Similarly it is in the context of leisure and free time that Father Karl Rahner has made some striking observations concerning the legitimacy 'of persons whom society allows to follow a contemplative life even though, economically speaking, they may not be considered as particularly productive':

> It is hard to see why the State should subsidize a profession which seeks to discover the very last species of ants and yet does not subsidize the Carmelite who risks the adventure of mystical contemplation and makes love for God the whole of her existence. [26]

Thinkers and Men of Action

It may be objected that although it is taken from theologians of note, this testimony which we have presented dates from before the Council. But how does the matter stand now that the *Constitution on the Church in the Modern World* has acclaimed what we have come to call 'openness to the world', so much so that some people are now preaching 'conversion to the world'? The answer to this question is furnished by the replies received to a questionnaire sent out in view of the forthcoming Congress of Benedictine Abbots in the spring of 1966 to a number of very different personalities. Fifty-six of these answers have been collected in a volume called *Points de vue actuels sur la vie monastique* and published at Montserrat in September of the same year. This volume contains declarations on the monastic life from very different Christian personalities: pastors, theologians, historians, philosophers, clerical and lay members of the Catholic, Orthodox and Reformed Churches. They thus present a good cross-section of up-to-the-moment opinion. Naturally, they offer a good number of suggestions of a practical order and of an individual character concerning the *aggiornamento* of the structures and observances of monasticism, and it is noteworthy that there is a real convergence of opinions on many

25. Ibid., p. 382. This text is quoted in *Chances de la spiritualité,* pp. 372-373.
26. "Theologische Bemerkungen zum Problem der Freizeit," in *Schriften zur Theologie,* IV (1960) p. 481.

of these points. But in conformity with the object of our enquiry, we shall present here only what has to do with the place of monasticism in the Church.

The first fact that stands out is the practical unanimity of the answers, not only in recognizing the contemplative character of the monastic life but also in speaking of it in the terms of traditional vocabulary. We are dealing with 'the contemplative life in the Church' (H. Batiffol, p. 45). Benedictines essentially vowed to the contemplative life' (J. Maritain, p. 196). 'We must continue to hold fast to the traditionally expression *contemplative life*' (P. R. Régamey, p. 240). Some replies speak of a 'life of prayer and contemplation' (N. Chadwick, p. 59), of a 'vocation to contemplation and prayer' (H. R. Weber, p. 310). These ideas and this vocabulary are accepted by a great number. [27] Mgr. B. Gantin cites paragraphs 7 and 9 of *Perfectae Caritatis* (p. 112-113); the late Mgr. M. Larrain stresses the 'pre-eminence (*prevalencia*) of contemplation' (p. 188-190), and P. Régamey the 'distinctly *contemplative* objective' and 'strongly contemplative exigency' (p. 240-241). Some theological nuances are introduced on the subject of this vocabulary by Father J. M. De Garganta, who also mentions the legitimacy of the eremitical vocation (p. 115-124); M. A. Guillaumont (p. 139) and Father M. J. Le Guillou (p. 151) likewise argue in favor of it. Useful distinctions are also given by Father K. V. Truhlar (p. 269, 272-278), while Canon G. Thils recalls the ambiguity which this terminology had in the early eays (p. 251). Mgr. E. D'Souza sees in the contemplative presence which monasticism makes possible a compensation, a remedy for 'the heresy of good works' which, he declares, 'is already very widespread and has already done serious damage to the spiritual structure in our country [India]' (p. 83).

Those who do not employ the vocabulary of contemplation and the contemplative life use equivalent expressions: 'spiri-

27. H. Camara, p. 51; P. Th. Camelot, p. 54; Ph. Delhaye, p. 76; A. Guillaumont, p. 139; G. Huyghe, p. 169; H. I. Marrou, p. 204; J. Orlandis, 204; J.-M. R. Tillard, p. 263; cf. 256; P. Trembellas, p. 267, cf. 266; R. Velez de Piedrahita, p. 282, cf. 283; A. Vergote, p. 290, cf. 287, 289; P. K. Christou employs the equivalent in Greek of the word contemplative: "théorique", p. 66.

tual recollection and Christian fathoming' (H. F. von Campenhausen, p. 58), 'spirit of adoration' (P. Evdokimov, p. 104), 'sacrifice of time' and 'ministry of prayer' (L. Génicot, p. 126-127), 'primacy of adoration' (B. Häring, p. 155), 'stable centres of prayer . . . of repose, of silence, of recollection' (A. M. Henry, p. 160-162), 'house of silence, of prayer, of peace' (J. Leclercq, p. 193), 'concentration on prayer and on the study of the divine realities' (Chr. Mohrmann, p. 211). 'Largely because of this close tie between the monastery and the world, the Eastern Church has been able to become conspicuously a praying Church' (A. Kniazeff, p. 174).

Several of those who replied to the questionnaire did not hesitate to draw a number of clear-cut consequences from this concept of monasticism as contemplative. 'As for the activity of monks outside the abbey in parish work, preaching, directing Catholic Action groups and the like, it does not in itself appear to be in conformity with the contemplative life' (H. Crouzel, p. 73). 'The sole activity of the monk ought to be prayer in the form of the Divine Office, the reading of Scripture, and private prayer' (M. J. Le Guillou p, 147). 'We do not expect that monasticism will necessarily take up works of the active apostolate' (A. Fernandes, p. 109). With regard to the obstacle to monastic vitality which is set up by the exercise of ministries outside the house, Father J. M. Garganta requires that we be 'absolutely sincere' (p. 123).

The problem of the priesthood of monks is bound up with the problem of the apostolate. Almost all of those who touched on this did so in order to come out against it: 'A man does not enter a monastery in order to become a priest . . . The monastic order has been diverted from its objective by being made into a priestly order' (Jacques Leclercq, p. 192). 'We must at any price return to what is called *lay monasticism*. The clerical overpopulation of monasteries is not merely a practical but a theological problem' (J. M. R. Tillard, p. 261). 'Only so many should be ordained as the monastery needs for the administration of the sacraments' (J. C. Guy, p. 154). The following contributors expressed themselves similarly in favour of this 'declericalized monasticism':

A. Guillaumont (p. 139), G. Huyghe (p. 169), E. von Ivanka (p. 171), H. I. Marrou (p. 205), G. Ramsey (p. 234), M. Schmaus (p. 249), L. M. J. Verheijen (p. 296), H. Vorgrimler (p. 301), H. R. Weber (p. 310-311). Ph. Delhaye not only emphasized that monks should not be priests but that they should not be clerics either (p. 80-81). One isolated voice was that of J. M. De Garganta who favored 'clerical monasteries' such as now exist in the West but would like to see monasteries provided for laymen (p. 122).[28]

In short, these replies, taken as a whole, establish the fact that there is a reaction against 'the danger of failing to make a distinction between the different members of the Mystical Body' (J. Orlandis, p. 219), and in favor of 'the clear differentiation' between the various organs of the Body of Christ (P. R. Régamey, p. 240). Monasticism is viewed as a sort of extreme form of Christian life, without alloy, without additions, 'without equivocation' (I. Hausherr, p. 159); not more perfect, but more radical, and more exclusive in its realization. 'The monk is the religious *par excellence*' (J. Orlandis, p. 217). 'The monk is the religious *sine addito*' (G. Huyghe, p. 164). 'May the time not have come for restoring to the religious life, and notably to the monastic life, its specific character by making *religious* and *monk* the synonym for the Christian who, in order to follow the ways of perfection, does not believe that he is obliged to become a priest? ' (Ph. Delhaye, p. 80). Moreover, and this follows precisely because they are excluded from the specialized tasks of the active apostolic ministry, monks are expected to give to

28. In my article in *Gregorianum* 47 (1966) p. 511, I called attention (note 26) to the rejection of an amendment to the *Decree on the Pastoral Function of Bishops* in a context which could lead one to think that this amendment applied to No. 13 of the Decree, whereas it refers to No. 9. A rather long amendment relative (in so many words) to the monastic priesthood (No. 32 c, p. 101) had been proposed and it too had been thrown out. In both cases, contrary to what my text would lead one to think, both these amendments were rejected, not because they were contrary to the doctrine of the priesthood, but because they were elaborations that were unnecessary in view of the principle *congrua congruis* laid down at the beginning of the Decree. This having been said, the basic difficulties remain, and witnesses here quoted confirm the fact. One could wish that they might be made the subject of undisturbed researches by theologians who would be at the same time historians.

the world only the great essential forms of Christian witness and to the Church only the form of service that is essentially their — those of the wholly interior, relatively hidden but transparent diffusion of the *vita apostolica,* according to the mind of the Middle Ages' (H. U. von Balthasar, p. 41); of giving example—and this is the point on which dwell the Protestants (K. Barth, p. 43; J. Bosc, p. 49; R. H. Esnault, p. 97) and the Orthodox (P. Evdokimov, p. 104; A. Kniazeff, p. 173; P. K. Unistou, p. 66); of eschatology (M. D. Chenu, p. 63; M. Larrain, p. 187; J. Orlandis, p. 217; R. Pannikar, p. 221; M. Rubio, p. 246; M. Schmaus, p. 248; and of the forms of service and edification of the People of God (H. Roux, p. 244) compatible with retirement from the world, openness and availability to men (Y. Congar, p. 68); 'intercession, pastoral liturgy, spiritual retreats, diaconate, theological research, teaching' (H. Roux, p. 244); contribution to the implanting of the Church in each culture, 'truly Indian' to the people of India (L. J. Raymond, p. 237); 'ecumenical encounters' (O. Meinardus, p. 209; H. R. Weber, p. 306). Here again an isolated voice was raised, that of H. Musurillo: 'It seems scandalous, when there are so many men and women to be aided, cared for, and taught, and so many children to be educated in the ways of Christian virtue, that a religious should let himself be absorbed in futile introspection or in the fulfilment of tasks which have little usefulness for himself and for society at large' (p. 215).

The testimonies contained in the Montserrat volume which we have just passed under review also include many valuable observations which reveal, on the whole, a fair measure of agreement on matters such as simplicity, work, poverty, observances, 'monastic theology—of which ecclesial theology has great need in order that it may be well balanced, faced as it is with a certain pragmatism, whether spiritual or apostolic' (M. D. Chenu, p. 64)—and on many other points. These points which we have been able to indicate only briefly are often given historical, speculative, or doctrinal development which make this collection a veritable gold-mine in which monks and others will need to delve. Several Protestants acknowledge that the difficulties raised agains the monastic and religious life by the Reformers no longer have the same significance in our day that they had originally (J. Bosc, p. 48-49; H. von Campenhausen, p. 58; R. Esnault, p. 96; H. R. Weber, p. 406), although H. Roux shows how deeply seated the problem is (p. 242-243). We hope that this hasty review, superficial though it necessarily is, will be sufficient to make those interested in the question want to study the volume itself.

Since the Council: A Canonist

Finally, to these testimonies given by thinkers and men of action involved in theological reflection on pastoral ministry, we can add that of a specialist in problems concerning the religious life in the particular field of canon law, P. J. Beyer, S.J., Vice-Dean of the faculty of Canon Law at the Gregorian University. Commenting the on the decree *Perfectae Caritatis*, he began by acknowledging and regretting that, taken as a whole, it is inspired by, or in any event makes use of, a terminology which is too much marked by monasticism. Now this fact is not due to the personal influence of monks, for they numbered only three among the forty-six members making up the Commission which prepared the text.[29] Rather it is the reflection of the kind of spiritual formation received by many clerics. Father Beyer asked insistently that henceforward a clearer distinction be made between what is specific to each of the three principal forms of consecrated life —monastic life, apostolic life, secular institutes.[30] What then is to be singled out as peculiar to monks? After reminding us that, according to the Decree, 'whether it be by its contemplation or by its apostolic works, the religious life is a sign of the love of God in the Church', Father Beyer showed that one and the same charity is differently exercised in the various states of life: 'In the monastic life this charity is directed solely towards God, and by assiduous prayer and self-obla-

29. "Decretum *Perfectae caritatis* Concilii Vaticani II," in *Periodica de re canonica, liturgica* 55 (1966) p. 432-433.
30. P. 457, 471, 472.

tion it is diffused in a mysterious way for the benefit of the Church and the salvation of the world. In the apostolic life this charity seeks God in all that it does, through the fulfilment of a ministry undertaken out of love for Him, loving Him in all men and all men in him, in conformity with his most holy will'. In secular institutes, both these forms of charity are exercised within the context of life in the world.[31]

The author offered the following ideas on the first of these three kinds of life: 'Monks are men of God who devote their entire existence to the imitation of Christ in prayer and contemplation on the mountain top. According to the ancient doctrine and practice of the Church, this life dedicated to contemplation calls for silence, solitude, austerity, assiduous contemplation of the divine mysteries, manual labour which allows the monks to support themselves and promotes good health...' This way of life is realized by those who live under an abbot as well as by hermits. But if you are looking for the *true* monk, then 'those who do not live this solitary, silent and austere life ordered to the contemplation of the divine mysteries cannot be called monks'.[32] Father Beyer also thinks that one of the merits of *Perfectae Caritatis* is that it 'restricts the apostolate of monks to an apostolic activity carried on within the enclosure of the monastery'.[33] He commented at some length on these ideas, indicated certain consequences flowing from them 'in the institutional domain',[34] and reminded us that the decree *Ad Gentes* (On the Missionary Activity of the Church) No. 40 calls for the establishment in mission lands of institutes of the contemplative life conceived in this way. Father Beyer even quoted in its entirety a document which may well become a classic and which it is only right on this account to reproduce here. It is the declaration of the Superiors of the monasteries of Africa, assembled in congress at Bouaké in 1964:

31. P. 471, 484.
32. P. 473.
33. P. 474, 475-476.
34. P. 477-481.

The Superiors of the monasteries of Africa, gathered together in fraternal assembly, have taken note of their unanimous desire to present to Africans a monastic life open to their own genius and at the same time in conformity with the place of monasticism in the Church and with its traditional ideal.

This ideal, as it has been lived since its origin on African soil, is that of a humble and hidden life, entirely directed towards the search for God. Aiming at the perfect realization of evangelical charity through an effective separation from the world and a common life of the brethren, 'forming but one heart and one soul', the monastery will be a witness to the demands of the kingdom of God and to His presence among men. Through prayer, penance and work, the monk joins himself intimately to Christ's sacrifice and cooperates in His adoration and redemptive work. Through poverty according to the Beatitudes, which awakens in him a desire for the eternal realities on whose account he has left everything behind, he helps to hasten the coming of the kingdom.

The primary goal of monastic foundations in Africa is to allow those African souls who feel drawn to it by the Spirit to realize the contemplative ideal in a state of life consecrated by the Church, and thus to bring about its firm establishment in their native land.

Since the monastic life represents a state of humility in the Church, it does not of itself tend to prepare its members for hierarchical functions: its goal normally excludes all pastoral offices. The monks in no way intend to be unconcerned about the influence which monasteries, through their life of prayer and charity, exercise upon the surrounding population. The traditional practice of hospitality allows them to take care of the spiritual and corporal needs of those who come to them in search of peace, help and encouragement without prejudice to the essential conditions of silence and recollection, without which an authentic monastic life cannot flourish.[35]

35. P. 469-470. This text, which has been published several times in various languages, was quoted recently in English by C. Peifer, *Monastic Spirituality* (New York, 1966) p. 375-376.

The Problem of Monastic Prayer

We have seen that the magisterium and the testimonies of those who concern themselves with reflection on the theology of the monastic life recognize that in it primacy goes to prayer. Can we go further in the inquiry and ask what place this prayer holds among all the forms of prayer that are practised in the Church? For here as in all other fields the prescriptions of liturgical law must be governed by theological principles. However, on this point, contrary to what was true in the preceding cases, the monastic authors quoted in the following pages should be understood not as witnesses to their own religious experience or formation but as theologians and historians.

We must begin by making clear what monastic prayer is *not*. It is not of its nature choral prayer, for the simple reason that the hermit (who is certainly a monk) does not pray in choir. Father Beyer, who emphasizes this point, felt impelled to write: 'It is an error to think and to claim that the monk exists for the choir'.[36] He demonstrated that the expression *cultus divinus* in the paragraph of *Perfectae Caritatis* concerning institutes of the contemplative life cannot be taken to mean purely and simply 'the choral office, defined at the end of paragraph 9 as an essential element of conventual and canonical institutes'.[37] Dom A. Verheul also declared unequivocally: 'Monastic communities are not in principle—but solely in fact, in virtue of juridical definitions—communities of clerks regular'.[38]

36. *Art. cit.,* p. 475. This error had already been pointed out some time ago; cf. *Gregorianum* 47 (1966) p. 506, No. 19. Fr Beyer ascribes to the Rule of St Benedict the aphorism 'propter Deum monachum' which, as a matter of fact, does not appear in the text in just so many words; but equivalents are to be found in it, especially the expression concerning the first criterion for the admission of a candidate to the monastic life: 'si revera Deum quaerit'.

37. *Ibid.*

38. "Liturgie et vie monastique aujourd'hui," in *Liturgie et monastères*, I (1966) p. 43.

The fact nevertheless remains that choral prayer has its place in the life of cenobites, and it is for this reason especially but not exclusively that the question can be raised concerning its place among forms of prayer in the Church. A general principle for its solution has been indicated by the Constitution on the Sacred Liturgy: public worship ought to be the outward sign of the Church's faith, the cultic expression of the work of salvation effected in her by Christ. This requires that 'liturgical signs be situated at a level that makes them models of worship for the world of today'. The liturgical prayer of monks does not escape this law.[39]

Another aspect of the problem raised here concerns what has been called 'prayer in the name of the Church'. One authority pre-eminently acquainted with ancient monasticism, Dom Eligius Dekkers, has felt able to make his own conclusions reached on this subject by Father Karl Rahner[40]: 'the sole fact of its being prescribed or regulated by the Church does not confer on a particular form of prayer a dignity, a value *sui generis*'.[41] We now possess on the question of this deputation by the Church a clear-sighted work by Dom G. Lafont in which he strives 'to seek the origin and the meaning of the deputation itself, in order to see if it must be retained'.[42] It will suffice here to present the essentials of his conclusions:

> Only a thorough historical inquiry would permit us to reestablish the complete theological framework within which lies the idea that the Divine Office is principally the business of 'priests and others deputed to this work by institution of the Church'. Some soundings that I have made lead me to think that the controversies at the time of the Reformation had no little influence on the systematization of this doctrine. This tenet must in fact have been elaborated

39. D. A. Verheul, *ibid.,* pp. 36-37, points out the practical applications of this principle.

40. "Thesen über das Gebet 'im Namen der Kirche," in *Zeitschrift für katholische Theologie* 83 (1961) pp. 307-324.

41. D. E. Dekkers *"La prière du moine: prière liturgique ou prière privée? "* in *Liturgie et monastères,* I, p. 48.

42. *Liturgie et ministères dans les communautés baptismales,* photocopied prior to its publication, (La Pierre-qui-vire, 1965) p. 8, note 9.

so as to resist the pressure of the attacks levelled against the
privilege of those whom Johannes Brenz calls in his pictur-
esque language the *sacrificuli* and *fraterculi.* Problems such
as: who are the ministers of the canonical hours and what
language is to be used in their celebration, and especially
what is the impetratory or meritorious significance of such
prayer — all these have been matters for polemics since the
day Luther published his *De abroganda Missa.* In any case I
do not think I am wrong in suggesting that deputation to
the Office was first definitively formulated in the *De oratione publica Ecclesiae* of Suarez, and that this text provides the explicit or implicit basic reference for all discussion on this subject.[43]

After explaining Suarez's teaching at some length, Dom
Lafont continues:

I would like to emphasize the congruity of this doctrine
which rests entirely on a precise concept of the universal
Church as a totality and as a pontifical monarchy. In such a
perspective, the idea of delegation to public prayer is absolutely necessary, and on the other hand this universal type
of delegation confers on that prayer a title which surpasses
any other title in the prayer of the Church. As a matter of
fact, these titles, whatever they may be, only give the right
to participate in the concrete prayer of some particular
community. But this community is only one small part of
the universal Church. In this case therefore it is through the
part that one has access to the whole, whereas one who is
deputed by the Sovereign Pontiff prays directly in the
name of the entire universal Church. In the end, such delegation comes to surpass even the ministerial priesthood . . .
Delegation and obligation are after all two notions that
tend to overlap each other. In practice we regard as being
deputed by the Holy See the whole body of those who, by
virtue of juridical custom or of approved religious rules, are
bound *sub gravi* to the recitation of the Office. The intervention of this notion of obligation, which Suarez energet-
ically affirms to be of ecclesiastical and not of divine origi-
ne, ends up, according to the theory of deputation, in putting the whole question of the doctrine of the Divine Office

43. *Ibid.,* p. 9.

on the juridical plane of pontifical law. There is no question of course of contesting the eminently religious views and the genuine piety which are manifest in these pages. But my purpose has led me to study them rather from the point of view of how they have affected teaching concerning the Divine Office. It can now be seen that such a doctrine does exist and that it is thoroughly consistent with the type of ecclesiology on which it is based.

We do not find in this work of Suarez any assertion concerning Latin, nor any declaration to the effect that the Roman liturgy has primacy over all others, being the liturgy of the universal Church. Nevertheless it is clear that the idea of Latin as the language of the Church and the tendency towards a Romanizing of the liturgy are within the logic of the position we have been studying. In any case, insofar as our present purpose is concerned, we observe that the idea of deputation, conceived in this way, does not allow any place for laymen in the prayer of the canonical Hours. Since they are not deputed to it by the Roman Pontiff, they have no active part in the office, at least insofar as this is accomplished in the name of the universal Church. Thus we can understand how the curious reversal of values which we observe today came about. Instead of public prayer being considered primarily as the praise of God offered up by the whole People of God — and quite apart from the idea that its priests act in the place of those of the Christian people who are hindered by secular occupations from taking part in the Office — the prayer of the canonical Hours is considered in this perspective as the prayer proper to priests and to those delegated to it by the Church, apart also from the fact that laymen may come and join in. It could not therefore be considered as a liturgy of all the baptized . . .

Liturgists and canonists have somewhat lost sight of the dogmatic theses that govern the edifice: the ecclesiology of totality in the Church and the universal authority of the Head of the Church. On the contrary, they have abundantly retained and developed the canonical features of its structure. These latter have so far become common currency that they in their turn have contributed to a sort of theology of the liturgy out of which we are far from having found our way. I simply line up a certain number of themes, not in order to deny them in an over-simplified way but in order to ask that they be submitted to fair critical examination. Even in recent works it is common to find writers basing the superiority of the liturgy on the fact that it is the *official* prayer of the Church. The mere juxtaposition of these two words is surely strange when one comes to weigh their meaning. In the same perspective one would easily be led to attribute to liturgical prayer a sort of *ex opere operato* effectiveness, whatever the actual dispositions of those who are performing it *hic et nunc*. Perhaps this is the source of the current renascence of the controversy over the relative merits of liturgy and contemplation . . . In short, we are confronted with a whole diffuse and lively mentality, springing (though perhaps no one is quite aware of it) from a certain type of ecclesiology. But what if the Council should direct us towards a different theology of the Church (and the Constitution on the Liturgy already does so)? [44]

After this critical examination of the recent idea of 'liturgical prayer', Dom Lafont goes on to lay foundations for a concept that is more traditional and more in conformity with the orientations given by the Council, and he concludes this part of his study as follows:

To sum up what we have just said, I would propose to define liturgical prayer, first of all, from the standpoint of the *Word*. It is the truly authentic expression, within the concrete framework of time and space, of the mystery of Jesus Christ in its twofold aspect as gift of God and faithful response of mankind to its Creator. In the Church it is the language suitable for the function of praise and intercession essential to the exercise of the priesthood of Jesus Christ. And it belongs to the ministry of the Word in the Church to safeguard this language for the People of God not only free from error but also ever nearer the truth of salvation and the condition of men .[45]

---

44. *Ibid.*, pp. 12-13.
45. *Ibid.*, p. 18. This conception is in conformity with the one at which Fr. K. Rahner arrived in the article summarized by D. E. Dekkers, "La prière du moine," p. 48.

Finally, the writer comes to the application of these principles to the monastic life:

> The liturgical *cursus* described by St Benedict in his Rule . . . is an instance of a liturgy composed by a layman for laymen dedicated to the perfect life. It is a liturgy which freely draws its inspiration from *cursus* already existing in the Church, and it is offered to monks with the modest suggestion that they are free to improve on it or alter it if their heart prompts them to do so.[46]

He concludes:

> It is permissible to hope that monks themselves will approach the problem with breadth of mind and a sense of their monastic tradition. The question is not one of suppressing Prime but of seeking to restore to liturgical prayer its rightful place in a life essentially orientated to prayer pure and simple.[47]

A Case of Progressive Differentiation

The testimonies presented in the foregoing study are, of twofold interest. On the one hand they reveal a real unity on many principal questions and their consequences while on the other they enable us to situate in a general way certain isolated, and sometimes singular, points of view. It is normal that, in the full ferment of the period immediately following the Council when 'here and there a certain restlessness reveals itself like the foam in the wake of a great ship',[48] startling ideas should be put forward. These ideas are sometimes highly intelligent and for that reason impressive but they are nevertheless out of line with and foreign to tradition, in the true meaning of the word and not in the sense of a mere identification with the past, and foreign too to the meaning of the monastic life, to that kind of sensitivity to the super-

---

46. *Ibid.*, p. 19, note 24.
47. H. De Lubac, "Un témoin du Christ," (see note 20 above), p. 156.
48. J. Orlandis in *Points de vue actuels sur la vie monastique* (Montserrat, 1966) p. 219.

natural which the Holy Spirit, in this matter as in others, preserves in the Church. It is understandable moreover that some declarations concerning primary monastic values may be clothed in a form which some would judge to be too absolute. These are reactions against the danger of seeing things essential and permanent called into question, even if only in isolated instances and with reference to accessory and transitory elements. With regard to this, the Pope in his pastoral teaching and the *consensus fidelium* join together in attesting that monasticism, just like the other organs of the Body of Christ, ought to progress in the direction of acquiring a keener awareness of its own specific function. In this reaffirmed unity in the same Spirit, the diversity of charisms within the Church would stand out more clearly. Equivocation, ambiguity, and confusion over tasks, which may have been brought about through particular historical circumstances, ought not necessarily be allowed to continue if they are not found to correspond to the inner demands of each vocation and to the needs of the various institutes in which they are struggling to find fulfilment. Moreover, it is to be hoped that new canonical legislation will recognize and respect the diversity of charisms and institutes, and will aid each to fulfil the end proper to itself. One single *ius de religiosis,* one undifferentiated law common to all religious institutes, would not satisfy this requirement, and the particular law making up the Constitutions proper to each institute would not be sufficient either unless norms are also established which are appropriate to groups characterized by a common goal. Contemplatives, missionaries, and members of secular institutes constitute for example distinct groups of this sort. There must exist in the Church a *ius monasticum* which permits the determination of conditions to which a monastic institute ought to correspond and the fundamental observances which all such ought to accept.

We are making our way towards a progressive differentiation that runs counter to that 'danger of indifferentiation'[49] which previous epochs have not always avoided. At the same

---

49. J. Orlandis, *ibid.,* p. 217.

time, monasticism stands out as one of the elements of the ecclesial organism in whose health, vitality and right functioning the hierarchy and the faithful have an interest. Spontaneously, without premeditation and without being subjected to propaganda, the People of God recognize their concern in this sort of 'pilot Christian life', in this 'extreme case', in this advanced post, this sign of the Christian life. We have reached the point when people are saying that 'the monastic life is the quintessence of the religious state.[50] It is consoling to note that the central idea of monasticism as a life apart — a life of attention to God alone and of waiting for God in prayer and asceticism — does not have to be adapted or modified but simply strengthened, purified, liberated — one might even dare to say disencumbered — from the excrescences that have accumulated in the course of history. This imposes upon monks a responsibility. They need clear-sightedness and courage to accomplish in a new epoch and in a new way, and under forms yet to be discovered, a task which always exists in the Church. It is to be hoped that they will do nothing to justify the apprehension recently expressed by a nun: 'I fear that we lack imagination — at least we contemplatives'.

Postscript

While these pages were being printed, His Holiness Paul VI again spoke about the monastic life in a discourse addressed to the Major Superiors of the Religious Orders and Congregations of Italy, the text of which was published in the *Osservatore Romano* on 19 November 1966. In it he called to mind the value of monasticism in itself, independent of the priesthood, and suggested the canonical possibility of such monasticism sanctioned from now on by the decree *Perfectae Caritatis,* No. 15. In it he further declared that the ordination for many centuries of the greater number of monks has not been

50. In *Fallait-il un concile?* , special number of *La vie spirituelle* 65 (Oct.-Nov. 1966), p. 276.

a deviation; that the norm for the advancement of monks to the priesthood ought not to be based on the needs of the interior or exterior ministry of the monastery; that monasticism has been associated with the priesthood in people's minds because of the harmony existing between religious and priestly consecration. Regarding this latter question, he referred to an article entitled "Contemplation et sacerdoce," in *Angelicum* 42 (1966). Finally, he affirmed that, while the Council in *Presbyterorum Ordinis* insists on the ministerial office of priests, it certainly did not intend to take away the *raison d'être* of the priesthood in the case of those monks who exercise it almost exclusively in the celebration of the Mass.

Translated by a monk of St. Joseph's Abbey, Spencer.

CONTEMPORARY OPPOSITION TO
MONASTICISM*

AN EXAMINATION OF THE DIFFICULTIES raised at the present time by the existence of monasticism, and particularly of the fundamental problem which it constitutes in itself, presupposes at the outset the acceptance of at least a general idea of what it entails. This idea should correspond to the reality without limiting it by a conceptual definition. Bearing in mind the charism peculiar to the monastic life, without confusing it with other charisms, this idea should simultaneously indicate a direction and leave a margin of flexibility for institutional expressions and forms which have ever been and remain diverse. It is difficult even to define the religious state let alone to reduce all its forms to a common denominator. An organized whole, rather than some of the elements which constitute it, or their sums results. And among the different types of religious life, the monastic life is recognized as being up to a point gratuitous, one might almost say disinterested, with regard to charitable or apostolic activities. This idea has been formulated in the ninth paragraph of the Vatican II Decree *Perfectae Caritatis* in a text which is no longer under discussion and which should be considered satisfactory. It may be that monks did not deserve the honor the Council did them in its attention. The decree did not however fail to suggest that they, like everyone else, effect a renewal.

* Published in *Nouvelle revue théologique,* 99 (1967) pp. 607-618; in Italian in *Ora et labora,* 22(1967) pp. 164-173.

The fact that such a way of life is legitimate, that it has its place in the Church where it fulfils a specialist function—in the words of Paul VI—is accepted not only by the representatives of the magisterium, but generally by witnesses to Christian thought.[1] This unanimity, however undisputed it now is, should not disguise the tasks remaining to be done in order to give solid theological justification to this widespread affirmation of the validity of the monastic life. Various commissions are presently at work studying this problem in the monastic orders, and those who are not monks also have something to say on the matter. The problem of monasticism, as it has been called, is put to monks and to others. On this point, as on the others, all is not research nor questioning. We must be able to define the field of investigation. In the realm of Christian doctrine the faith is not strictly speaking and of itself (in so far as it is a gift of God) the subject of scientific research, although theology is to a certain extent. Similarly, the value of the religious and monastic life is not effectively disputed. People are simply questioning particular ways of presenting it, or particular arguments brought forward to justify it. We may therefore aim at greater understanding without losing what a twelfth century writer called "confidence in present day monasticism" (*De fiducia nostri* temporis monachorum).[2] rum).[2]

"Monasticity"

The immediate relevance of the problem in our day is accentuated—and its study complicated—by the rapidity with which what can only be termed slogans are diffused; at a time when the broad culture of some and the specialized learning of others are balanced by the easy diffusion of commonplace ideas among the general public, which includes

1. The texts have been set out above, Ch. I. pp. 18ff and Ch. V. pp. 100ff.
2. This question of whether it is possible to maintain confidence in contemporary monasticism was already being asked in terms not dissimilar to today's at the time of the great monastic crisis of the twelfth century, in the course of which the author of the phrase quoted here took his stand in a text which I have published in *Recueil d'études sur S. Bernard*, II (Rome, 1966) p. 75; for the context, see pp. 72-73.

clergy and religious. These slogans create a jargon which consists either in inventing new terms which more often than not
end in -ism, or in reducing old words to just one of their
meanings. There is also a complete, sometimes amusing, vocabulary of "commitment", which makes people speak of the
"positive" rather than the "negative" aspects: must we not,
at all costs, "stick to what is relevant" if we want to "come
out on the positive side? " This leads us to demand that, for
the expression "mortification" (Biblical though it is) the
more modern term "vivification" be substituted. Monasticism
is one of the principal targets struck by this language. When
some idea or practice is to be discredited, it is labelled
"monastic" or, in some places, "claustral".

We know that lexicographical fashions pass quickly. Quite
recently the word and the idea "missionary" were discredited
as bound up or synonymous with colonialism, imperialism,
and politico-religious proselytism. Prominent Catholic journals took up its defence to try to rehabilitate it before it was
too late. Ten years later it was applied to the whole Church,
to everything and everyone in the Church. Now people take
pride in calling themselves missionaries, and certainly a clearer definition, even a purification of terminilogy has meanwhile emerged. Similarly today it happens that advanced
adults—monks or not—conjecture on what "the young monk
of today" thinks, or they create myths in order afterwards to
destroy them more easily. The legitimate tendency that many
religious institutes of modern foundation are showing to rid
themselves of vocabulary, customs and concepts which, created by and for monks, are not suited to the demands of their
life accentuates this. But the very fact that many of the new
terms being forged to denounce what is "monkish" or "claustral" end in "-ism" is sufficient indication that they are
frequently abstractions and purely artificial creations. Let us
retain a civilized sense, or at least humor, in these rich and
fertile years which have may be forgiven a certain glibness.

Anti-monastic slogans generally consist in applying the vocabulary of monasticism to things which are not monastic.
Some admit honestly that they use the procedure as a con-

venient means of expression. A reputable author writes: "We use indifferently the terms 'monastic spirituality', 'religious spirituality', 'transcendental spirituality': each time we mean, properly speaking, to refer to the spirituality of the 'evangelical state'."[3] Under the title monastic, all the forms of, even non-monastic, religious and clerical life are designated, as well as yet other ways of living the Christian life. Everything that is not secular (in today's sense of the word) is broadly spoken of as monastic.[4] And all the criticism raised against modern asceticism devolves on monasticism. The same procedure is applied on other spheres. Referring to Dominicans, people speak of the "monastic inquisition", although monasticism never had anything to do with it, and some have even thought that the Order of Preachers was founded merely because the monks, particularly the Cistercians, failed to intervene against the heresies of the twelfth and thirteenth centuries. The *Imitation of Christ* is severely criticized as a medieval and monastic document, whereas it was written during the Renaissance, the so-called Humanist period, by someone who was not a monk. The phrase "monastic ideal" is used in the title of a study of a seventeenth-century Capuchin although the study concerns in fact the "religious life". There is moreover only one single use of the term "monastic" in the text itself..[5] Of course, the label is good publicity.

To indicate this misuse of words, a gifted essayist has recently created the term "monasticity", in a provocative article entitled *Der Monastizismus.*[6] The author dwells particularly on the influence of "claustrality" (*Klösterlichkeit*) on the forms of political life "from the end of the Middle Ages and right up to our day . . . inside Christian regions and outside them". Because it involves hierarchy, order, discipline, uniformity, conformity, and collectivity, the cloister is seen as the model and the precursor of the factory, the barracks,

3. P. Brugnoli, *La spiritualità dei laici* (Brescia, 1965) p. 18.

4. Ibid., pp. 19-20.

5. Second de Turin, "L'emprise de l'idéal monastique sur la spiritualité des laïcs au XVIIème siècle d'après le P. Philippe d'Angoumois († 1638)" in *Revue des sciences religieuses,* 40 (1966) p. 234.

6. E. von Kuehnelt-Leddihn, "Der Monastizismus", in *Civitas,* 21 (1966) pp. 321-355.

prison, the party, and dictatorship. This "claustralization" of the secular life has engendered the "pan-monasticity" of modern times; it more or less fashioned the Reformation of that "Gothic monk", Martin Luther, and of Calvin with his *Soli Deo Gloria,* the French Revolution with its "fraternity" and other "republican virtues", Bolshevism with its Communist "cells" ("Russia" he writes, "had always had a claustral character) and Nazism, with its monasteries of young *Füehrer,* and its *Ordensburgen.* Everything involving the common life today — dormitory, refectory, silence, solitude, imposed continence, regulations, supervision—is a perversion of the "claustral" in realms for which it was not intended. Originally, claustral was synonymous with liberty: "Unamuno has compared the monk to an anarchist. . . ." One wonders whether the author, somewhat obsessed by his theme, does not tend to see "pseudo-cloisters" everywhere. He is, of course, careful not to condemn the real ones. On the contrary, he affirms that "the authentic monastic life is not an outmoded form today": it is rather, for many, a means of growth and fulfilment (*Wachstum, Erfüllung*).At least he has the merit of denouncing a misuse of terms and ideas when he affirms rightly, *Perversio optimi pessima.* If the "demonacalization" of which we are witnesses contributes to the elimination of such ambiguities or of others more subtle within the religious vocabulary, it will be a good thing. Monks will know better what is peculiar to their vocation and the others what is specifically theirs.

Other "ISMS"

It must be pointed out however that the present-day criticism of monasticism sometimes introduces fresh ambiguities when it condemns expressions which have not always had the meaning it attributes to them. I need not here recall once more all that separates the biblical theme of the "angelic life" from so-called modern "angelism", against which there is a justifiable reaction. The monastic tradition as a whole has done this, insofar as formulating the problem was possible in the past.[7] Suffice it here to quote the testimony of one person, the monk Job, in the sixth century. "They are insane, those who would prefer being angels rather than men."[8]

A further objection is sometimes raised against monasticism in the name of "witness"—as if everybody had to be a witness of everything to everybody else—and in the name of effective witness, which means witness which everybody could understand, accept, and receive as a motive for conversion. Again on this point a study of the biblical vocabulary of witness and the traditional concept of the Church would be enough to permit some distinctions. Similarly, when the idea of the contemplative life is rejected because monks are not exempt from that practice of virtues which constitutes the "active life", there is a confusion between "acts" and "states of life", and a whole semantic evolution is swept away. In order to proclaim the "value of earthly realities", there is a protest against the vocabulary of separtion, flight, and contempt for the world, whereas the same attitudes could be evoked with the Biblical words exodus, exile, desert, retreat, or with the traditional vocabulary of "detachment". As for "the world", it signifies a great many diverse realities, between which the Council has been careful to establish distinctions.[9] There are words whose meaning has developed at the same time as economic, social and cultural conditions were changing, so that they have ended up saying the opposite of what they originally meant. Unless we begin by defining the meaning that they had in the Bible and then at other periods, no dialogue is possible with our time. We are not speaking the same language. However, trying to speak for today in the idiom of today does not mean that we must deny everything that has been achieved by tradition. It merely needs to be translated and, before that, understood. *A priori* facts can be

7. See below, Ch. VII, p. 151.
8. Already quoted by M.-J. Scheeben, *Les merveillees de la grâce divine,* translated into French by A. Kerkvoorde (Paris, 1940) p. 71. On the author, see PG 86, II, 3313.
9. This right from the Prologue of *Guadium et spes,* no. 2, and elsewhere. More recently, Paul VI in his allocution to the general audience of April 5th; See *La Documentation Catholique,* 64 (Paris, 1967) 784-785.

misunderstood because the meaning of certain propositions has not been verified. Thus certain intellectuals in Europe—and they are not always Europeans—do not want any monastery founded in the Third World because everything there still needs development and they have heard that monasticism is based on contempt for the world. But it is enough to travel in Africa, Asia, or South America to discover that where there is a monastery, there is around it, and sometimes within a wide radius, material and cultural development.

Monasticism is also accused of an anti-humanism based on a dualism between the human and the divine, between what is earthly and what is heavenly, and in accordance with what is called the Platonism of the Fathers of the Church. Here again, the statement must be qualified. If the Fathers or the ancient monastic authors were mistaken, we must not hesitate to recognise the fact; but if a mass condemnation is made, how effective can it be, and on whom will it fall? There are such differences between Origen and St John Chrysostom, between St Augustine and Gregory the Great, that we have no right to take such generalizations seriously. If Platonism did exercise at times a strong influence on many Fathers or even on the Fathers as a whole (but not on all the Fathers) and through them on monastic literature, we have not, for all that, the right to speak of profane or even pagan contamination. Were the Fathers not sufficiently imbued with the spirit of the gospels—at least as well as we are—to adopt what was good in Platonism without distorting the Gospel message? Some think that the substitution in the thirteenth century of Aristotelianism for Platonism removed the thought of the time even farther from the Gospel. This is not the place to open a judicial inquiry into these two currents of thought but simply to warn against over-simplifications of which monastic spirituality, or what passes for it, would be the victim.

There are those who see in monasticism, and even more in the high value put upon virginity in the first centuries of the Church, a strong element of Manicheism. In reality it was writers with monastic learnings, such as St Augustine and St

Bernard, who struggled against Manicheism, ancient or renewed, in favor of matrimony. Furthermore, humanism,
creationism and incarnationalism are sometimes represented
as recent discoveries, whereas Christians have always realized
that man is made in the image of God, that the world was
created good and that the redeeming Incarnation provided a remedy for the sin of man. These truisms arise
from an uncritical knowledge of history, including the history of words, and a confusion between a variety of meanings.
Since St Paul there have always been "the man according to
the flesh" and "the man according to the Spirit". The flight
towards God presupposed the recognition of values in the
world which were voluntarily renounced. Do all those who
choose celibacy today flee from marriage because of the
contempt they are supposed to have for it? Do those who
opt for marriage necessarily believe that celibacy is a bad
thing?

The Real Problem

And yet, beneath these not very satisfactory questions,
there remains a genuine and profound problem, which is
worth pausing to consider. It justifies and gives usefulness to
such criticisms. There is today at times a risk, a great and a
glorious one, of adopting a humanist outlook, in which man
seems to appear in his original light, as if he had just come
unsullied from the hands of God, charged to enjoy this
world, to possess it, to inventory and use it and to consecrate
it to its Author. Faced with the danger os such a view,
monasticism vigorously affirms sin. Monasticism is of itself
the affirmation of that wound with which one must always
reckon when confronted with oneself and all creation, men
and things alike. There is a state of prudence in which, knowing both created values, good in themselves, if man has not
polluted the, and ourselves, always carnal, although become a
radically "new man" through baptism, we separate ourselves
from certain of these values, not because of them but because
of ourselves and because of the relative taint or deviation
which they may have acquired through contact with man.

The whole of history proves that after this renunciation very many values are rediscovered. The love of letters and of every form of beauty in the world has always been and remains compatible with the desire of God. But the monk is one who proclaims, and reminds everyone, that it is first necessary to pass through the narrow gate, to renounce ourselves and all things to seek the Kingdom of God. After that our liberated self will be returned with a heightened capacity to assent to all genuine values.

This said, we must recognize that Christian antiquity, and not only monasticism, may have denied value to certain created things simply because they were created and not the Creator. It also exaggerated certain flaws acquired by created things through mankind without seeing clearly enough the the good in them. For example, a certain deprecation of marriage, in practice if not in theory, is undeniable in certain witnesses of the spiritual life until quite recently. Today is there not a risk of going to the other extreme? These two possible exxaggerations must be honestly perceived if the need for the happy medium is to be seen. But must there be an average solution which is universal, when human phychology, which grace does not violate, is so diverse? Should we not rahter envisage complementary trends in harmony with what seems to be a general law in the fulfilment of God's purpose? The more advanced, the more highly perfected, an organism is, the more diverse are its components. The richness comes from their interaction and their mutual give-and-take. In the dimension of the Christian life, this unity in diversity is the sign and fruit of charity, as St Paul has so often described it.

The important point is that every man, every Christian, the representative of every healthey trend, should know that he is not the unique model. He is a partial fulfillment which the others, apparently opposed or divergent as they are, need as he needs them in order to complete the whole, in order that the organism may attain its perfect, i.e. its completed, structure and function. Each therefore has a duty to be comprehensive, to be receptive towards those who are unlike him, to help them to be themselves. And he too has the right to be respected. This duty may not at times have been recognized by the monastic trend. It is quite possible. But if it should be proved that this was so, should we not still ask ourselves whether this was not partly the result of the opposite tendency being, speculatively speaking, non-existent? It had not produced its own theory. It excels in this in our day, and a good thing too. But we must not apply its ideas to every trend without modification. Let us learn to agree with a good grace, without bitterness towards the past, that throughout the centuries there has been a human and a Christian development. Let us admit that our ancestors, whether monks or not, can no longer be our models on every point. Let us consent to be the heirs and the continuers of diverse traditions and points of view which have emerged, some more distinctly than others, in the course of the long, slow evolution thanks to which humanity and the Church in its human element are on their way towards God. If someone in the past took up the whole seat, it may be because nobody asked to share it with him. But the newcomer is not entitled to oust him completely. If only we could be content to make the journey together, sharing all we have in common. It is a good deal and vital part. If we could only be content to be enriched on the other hand by our differences, our differing ways of seeing God, the world and ourselves.

In this way the positive result of current research would be to help monks and non-monks to a better understanding of their authentic position. What seculars can still imitate in monasticism will no longer be a state of life consisting of fasts, vigils and other practices formerly recommended to all by St John Chrysostom. It will be the common ideal of complete charity towards which we are moving in different ways in the cloister and in the world. And the monks for their part may be well edified by the ardor of seculars in aiming, in their own particular way of organizing their life, at generous self-giving, together with a prayer as intimate, as intense and as continuous as possible. This implies the abandonment of such generalizations as: "the aspirations of the modern world ... What the world expects of the Christian (or of the religious) today. ..." The ancients can still teach us this respect for diversity in the pastoral field, in immediate contact with men or in the exchange of views. The whole of Book III of the *Pastoral Rule* of St Gregory the Great consists in explaining that the same advice should not be given to everyone. All the chapters, there are thirty-five of them, have at the beginning of the conclusion these words: *Aliter admonendi sunt...* [10] A single quotation from the same Doctor will characterize his attitude of charity:

> It is most important to know the great diversity of souls. Some men are of such a peace-loving nature that if they are caught up in the worry of activities they immediately succumb to it. Others, on the contrary, have such a restless nature that if they have no worries they are more worried than ever... That is why a peace-loving nature should not dissipate its energy in the exercise of immoderate labors nor a restless nature apply itself forcibly to contemplation. [11]

May I be permitted to illustrate these reflections with a contemporary example? It would be possible to follow, and it has been done, two conflicting parallels between the Rule of St Benedict and the writings of Teilhard de Chardin. One sets them in contrast, like black and white, and the whole assessment is to the obvious advantage of the man who so loved the earth and asked that it should be loved. The other shows, with equal facility, that the monastery is a special realization of that *milieu divin* of which the Jesuit dreamed. Let us beware of smiling at such comparisons: they can be fruitful, provided both sides practise moderation. But the second would certainly be the one which would best take into account the diversity of vocations, as Teilhard was so anxious to do. As Father de Lubac wrote to me one day.

The abrupt way in which the monk sets about practising detachment from the world in its present forms does not

10. PL 77, 49-121.
11. *Moralia*, VI, 57, PL 75, 761.

involve contempt for the work to be accomplished by the general run of mankind in this world and through this world, any more than the vow of chastity indicates for the Christian (as it does for the Manichean and others) contempt for or condemnation of marriage. Teilhard wanted to define a spiritual attitude which would be valid for all men, and therefore particularly for all laymen, one which implied a real fundamental detachment, without a break. His special vocation as a scientist, for one thing, drew him towards this attitude. But he was far from despising a more absolute form of detachment. Witness this text, drawn from one of his letters:

"I remember certain things which Françoise said to me—she was a Little Sister then—about the unique and beatifying importance which the *reality* of God had taken on in her life; and I felt aware that we were fundamentally much more like one another than I had hitherto believed, only she was following a path in which the realities of this world were blotted out or outstripped to a greater degree than is the case with me." It is true that what is newest in the spirituality of Teilhard is this element of interest in the increase of the earth. But the newest is not the whole story, nor even always the most important part of it. And Teilhard has none the less for all that magnified the so-called passive virtues, and the role of suffering loved, and the silent contemplation of things divine. We fail to understand him if we suppress, in his work, that which nevertheless has an important place in it.

In Praise of Nuances

This justifiable correction of misconceptions, among other things, warns us against the principal reef which must be avoided if the discussion on the monastic life is to continue to be useful: the over-simplification of complex data. We must avoid reducing it to one or some of its aspects. Moreover we must, if we wish to discuss it, find out what were and what are the facts. A simple verification of date or origin would free us from elementary mistakes. It was for instance after the great monastic period, and during the period dominated by the mendicant Orders Dominicans and Franciscans, that, with the emphasis on poverty, the contempt for the world was most widely cultivated. It was then that treatises *De contemptu mundi* proliferated. It was also at that time that angelism (in so far as it existed formerly) appeared. Witness the number of religious in those orders who were called Angel, Angela, Angelica, Angelico, Cherubim, Seraphim.[12] To monasticism may be applied the recent words of an historian:

> It is at the end of the Middle Ages that the most dubious ecclesiastical institutions were seen to appear, whose existence a clumsy apologetic tried to the bitter end but in vain to justify. It is undoubtedly there that we must look for the origin of that animosity which the modern era has so frequently nurtured against a Middle Ages which it did or would not know except in its last centuries.[13] And indeed, certain forms, institutions and concepts which weigh most heavily upon monasticism today come neither from its origins nor from its ancient tradition, but from the late Gothic. This period has been criticized by some and idealized by others who dream of restoring it. Let us retain our critical sense, our liberty of judgment and that precondition of impartiality, our humor. Nothing but detachment will help to take the heat, so to speak, out of this discussion.

Though we must not try to defend every text of the monks of old, yet we must not, in order to be up to date at all costs, say or think that we have found out everything. The historians of the future may perhaps have reason to smile at our generation. Perhaps they will find as much naiveté among certain representatives of contemporary Catholic thought as among the revolutionaries of '89 or the Romantics and the scientists of the last century. It will perhaps be written one day that the "opening up" at the time of Vatican II was not

---

12. It was in the first half of the sixteenth century, at the height of the Renaissance, that a congregation of Sisters was founded called "Angéliques", who were addressed as "Mon Angélique"; The "Angelines" were founded at the end of the sixteenth century and approved in the twentieth. See LThK I, cc. 532-533.

13. J. Châhillon, "Le Moyen Age fut'il civilisé? in *Réflexion chrétienne et monde moderne* (Paris: Desclée de Brouwer, 1966) p. 184.

even Christian because it had its origin with a philosopher who was condemned under Pius X. Yet the adoption, after a delay of fifty years, in Christian circles of today of the Bergsonian vocabulary of the "closed" and the "open" was a normal occurrence. It leads one to reflect on the criticism of the Fathers and theologians of the Middle Ages because they used terms borrowed in part from a Stoic, Neo-Platonic or Aristotelian tradition.

Another over-simplification to be eliminated is the "every-body" myth, as if, for instance, "openness to the world" means: "Everybody in the street must be open to the world in the same way." On the contrary, the Council has brought into prominence once more the texts of the New Testament which stress the variety of charisms. These charisms affect not only one's way of life, his behaviour towards the outside world, the degree of his mingling or separation. They also affect certain directions in the interior life, certain appeals to lay the stress on this or that element in the Christian voca-tion. For example, today the progress of science, technology and history is seen and appreciated, as is only right. But it is also important to recognize the sin which compromises everything, even simply from man's point of view. Is man going to fulfil himself easily on his own, to make of the earth by his own effort a kingdom where justice will reign with order, ease and prosperity? Of course man should strive with all his might in this direction. But he must not forget that he will achieve nothing without God. It is just this that the monks have traditionally felt very keenly. They have kept as their mission reminding the world of it by their very exis-tence. If in the eyes of some they seem to reveal a lack of interest in the present aeon, it is because they live turned towards eternity. This does not mean that they condemn those who have other centres of interest. And the others for their part should not make their attitude an absolute stan-dard and condemn those who look in the direction from which the Savior will come again, and indeed is already coming. Each to his own vocation in the Church. In the name of what intolerance are we to reduce everybody to one grace, when grace is multiform?

There is between monasticism and humanism an undeniable and necessary tension. Why turn it into a quarrel or an opposition? But it is a good thing for monks to be conscious of the conflict as a temptation, and in that the present criticisms are useful. It should be seen as an attack on a good which they possess but must verify, on a vocation which they have been given but must justify and in that sense earn, a test which will show them whether they are "holding firm" or "giving way". After it, those who have held firm will have a better idea of the reason, and they will live by their grace more fully and more intensely. They will perceive better the true foundation of monastic optimism as they deepen their awareness of being part of a world which is still under the sign of sin. Christians already possess values whose fulness will be given only in the hereafter. Those of them who, here and now, direct their life towards those great, ultimate and eternal things, love, praise, contemplation, proclaim them in their own way. In their daily life they anticipate, humbly by reason of sin, the most human values, which are those of the perfect man.

MONASTICISM AND ANGELISM*

A False Problem

EVERY AGE HAS ITS CATCH-PHRASES, and the study of them throws a particularly clear light on fashions of thought in theology. One of these fashions at the present moment consists in calling everything of a monastic or contemplative nature 'angelism'. The word is seldom defined, but it is commonly so used as to include under its meaning pessimism, dualism, anti-humanism or (in the current jargon) anti-incarnationalism, and Platonism. 'Platonism', in particular, becomes, in a highly simplifying way, the symbol for certain attitudes of mind which historians of philosophy must be surpirsed to find attributed to Plato or to his authentic followers. Sometimes, too, 'angelism' is applied as a definition of chastity.

To discover what 'angelism' properly refers to, one must go back to the sources of monastic tradition. In them no conflict between angelism and humanism is discovered. Generally speaking, the reference to angels does not serve the purpose of contrasting two natures, that of a pure spirit and that of corporeal beings, nor does it remove man—and the God-Man—from the conditions of time and space; its purpose is to illustrate the present state of redeemed mankind by a comparison with that of the blessed who share already fully in

* A paper read to the Ecumenical Congress on the Angels held at Mont Saint Michel in late September, 1966. Published in English in *The Downside Review*, 85 (1967) 127-137.

God's glory: angels have significance as religious signs.[1] Abstract speculation about the nature of pure spirits was chiefly developed by the Scholastics of the thirteenth centuty. Revelation and earlier tradition had little to say about it. In monasticism, as in the tradition of the Old and New Testaments and of later Judaism, and among those influenced by this literature, the function rather than the nature of the angels is important. And in our own time historians influenced by philosophies deriving from Aristotelianism raise problems which the ancients hardly touched.

Nor do we find, in the texts in which the monks spoke of the angels, the obsessive insistence on chastity which became so marked later on.[2] It is interesting to note that until the twelfth century few monks took the names of angels, but in the mendicant orders, especially among the Franciscans and the Dominicans,[3] such names and their cognates—Angela, Angeline, Angelique, Angelico—are quite common. There we find the 'Seraphic Doctor' and the 'Angelic Doctor'.

The Origin of the Medieval Tradition

In the earliest monastic writings, and in all patristic literature, even when it is not addressed to monks, many texts evoke or develop the theme of the 'angelic life'. This has nothing to

1. This has been emphasised by J. C. Didier, "Angélisme ou Perspectives Eschatologiques? " in *Mélanges de Science Religieuse* XI (1954) pp. 31-48.

2. Just like angelism, in so far as it existed, satanism, if one may so describe an obsession with demonology, developed chiefly in modern times, after what may be called the monastic age, from the thirteenth century onwards, according to R. G. Gerest, "Le Démon en son Temps, De la fin du Moyen Age au XVIe Siècle," in *Lumiére et Vie*, 78 (1966) pp. 25-30, who speaks, in this connection, of the 'moderation of the high middle ages'.

3. This results from a calculation easily made on the basis of entries in encyclopaedias referring to Christian personages in alphabetical order, for example U. Chevalier, *Répertoire des Sources historiques du Moyen Age: Bio-Bibliographie* (rpt. New York: Knaus, 1960) I, 233-327; *Dictionnaire d'Histoire et de Géographie Ecclesiastique*, III (1924) 5-76. The nuns called 'the Angelicals' were founded in the sixteenth century and approved in the seventeenth; those called 'the Angelical Franciscans' were founded in the nineteenth century and approved in the twentieth; cf. Th. K, 2 ed., I (1957) 532-33. In antiquity, the 'angelicals' were heretics, probably influenced by gnostic movements and combated by St Epiphanius, himself a monk; cf. Frank, work cited below in note 5, pp. 165-66 and 199.

do with an angelism which would, in one way or another, assimilate the nature and condition of man to that of the angels. Learned works have made this clear in the past and in our own time.[4] It should be sufficient here to recall the reaction of monastic good sense against any temptations to angelism and then to indicate the principal ideas which this sort of language was meant to illustrate.

In regard to the first point, a single text of pungent simplicity will stand for many others. It has been quoted often enough but has lost nothing of its relevance:

> John the dwarf said one day to the brother with whom he lived: 'I want to be at peace like the angels, not troubled with any kind of work and worshipping God without interruption'. And taking off his clothing he disappeared into the desert. After spending a week there he returned to his brother and knocked at the door. His brother, before opening, said: 'Who are you?'. 'It is I, John.' And his brother replied: 'John has become an angel and is no longer among men.' John kept on knocking, saying 'It is I, John'. But his brother left him to his laments.
>
> He did open to him in the end and said to him: 'If you are a man, you should find some work to do for your living; if you are an angel, why do you want to enter this cell?' And he said, repenting: 'Forgive me, my brother, for I have sinned'.[5]

This reaction of popular monasticism was embodied in monastic legislation and teaching. When Pachomius teaches monks to be 'friends of the angels', it is not at all for the sake of what has been well called a 'lazy quietism', but it implies 'an exacting activism, with the call to battle sounding continuously in one's ears'.[6] Again, St Jerome explains that, if

---

4. The two latest works in this field are those of S. Frank, ΑΓΓΕΛΙΚΟΣ ΒΙΟΣ, Munster 1964 and P. Nagel, *Die Motivierung der Askese in den alten Kirche und dér Ursprung des Mönchtums*, Berlin 1966, pp. 36-47 ("*Die Vita Angelica*").

The first form of angelic activity studied by S. Frank in the sources is devotion to the welfare of one's fellow-men "Sorge für den Mittmenschen," pp. 62-69.

5. Latin text in *PL* 73, 769 and 916; here quoted according to H. Bremond, *Les Pères du Désert* (Paris, 1927) I, p. 151, translating Pelagius, *PL* 73, 916.

6. H. Bacht, "Pakhôme et ses Disciples (IVe Siècle)," dans *Théologie de la Vie Monastique* (Paris, 1963) p. 64.

we want to unite ourselves with the angels and imitate them, we must first accept our human condition and be obedient. 'Placed on earth as we are and involved in various labors, let us do everything we can to be transformed into glory with the angels . . .' 'The angels are always watchful, ready to obey God's commands; and we must imitate by our frequent vigils the service of the angels . . .'[7] Both vigilance in ascetic practices and watching in prayer are necessary: like the martyrs and the saints in the land of the living, we must praise the Lord in purity. Theodoret, among others, insists on this 'liturgy', this worship which the monks, like the angels and the martyrs, keep up for the glory of God and for the good of the elect.[8]

The texts which speak of virginity and of chastity must be seen in the light of this general conception of ascesis and the life of prayer. These practices, like obedience and other virtues, are first of all opportunities for spiritual combat. 'Struggle in chastity and subjection until you gain the kingdom', writes Pachomius, for example. He says again, in a formula which underlines the eschatological character of the combat, 'Fight, for the time is at hand, and the days are shortened'.[9] Ephraim points out what a difference there is between angels and monks: 'The angels have received the gift of virginity without effort on their part, but you only at the end of the combat'.[10] Chastity is also a means of preparing and promoting union with God in prayer, and of returning to him, an anticipation of the heavenly condition. The Trinity itself, Gregory of Nazianzen makes bold to declare, is the source and model of all virginity, that of angels and monks.[11] Thus, in one way or another, chastity, although practised by men who are fully engaged in the present life and its struggles, is a 'preparation for the life to come', as an historian has

7. Quoted by P. Antin, "S. Jérôme," ibid., p. 196.
8. P. Canivez, "Théodoret et le Monachisme Syrien avant le Concile de C-halcédoine," ibid., pp. 253-54.
9. H. Bacht, "Pakhôme et ses Disciples," p. 64.
10. L. Leloir, "S. Ephrem, Moine et Pasteur," ibid., p. 91.
11. Quoted by J. Plagnieux, "S. Grégoire de Nazianze," ibid., p. 125: 'Prima virgo est sancta Trinitas . . . Ex illa autem angeli splendentes . . . Cum his iuncta virginitas, Deo similis, expedita semita ad Deum'.

written in regard to Theodoret. His weighty conclusion is calculated to remove all ambiguity in the matter:
'In Christ Jesus, according to the Apostle (Gal. iii, 28), there is neither male nor female. The one and only faith has been given to both men and women.' In the thought of Theodoret this text shows that, in the order of faith differences of nature are in a sense cancelled out so that all the faithful may be brought together in the unity of the divine filiation. At any rate, if Theodoret thinks that virginity allows one to live the life of the angels, this must be understood only in a figurative way. The sexes remain and the passions also. For we must be careful not to think that man is an incorporeal being: that is an heretical idea which Theodoret often denounces. If we suppose that the profession of faith and the choice of the monastic life extinguish passion to the point of abolishing the differences between the sexes in the present life, we run the risk of falling, under the holiest pretexts, into the licence which he denounces in his treatise against the heresies. There is a dialectic between man and woman, just as there is one between Pagan and Jew, and the opposition between them will be overcome only in the Kingdom of God. In our present condition it is resolved only on the level of faith. The monk, however perfect he may be, is not an angel; the possibility of sin remains for him along with his body.[12]

The Middle Ages

There is the same realism and the same insistence on eschatology in the medieval monastic writers as in the Fathers.[13] For them also the theme of the angelic life is connected with the present condition of the Church, awaiting its achievement, its perfection when the stature of the body of Christ shall have reached its fullness. So they are fond of associating this theme with that of the expectation of the prophets: Elias and his disciples, and the 'sons of the prophets' mentioned in the Old Testament, are united with the angels and imitate them by retiring into the solitude of the mountains and

12. P. Canivez, "Théodoret et le Monachisme Syrien," p. 257.
13. In *La Vie Parfaite* (Turnhout, 1948) pp. 19-56, I have quoted some texts.

devoting themselves there in community to the practices of prayer and mortification.[14] In the Gospel, St John the Baptist was called both a new Elias and a messenger of God.[15] The chant of the monks is of a prophetic character in so far as it praises God in the very words of God.[16]

The angels are models of the contemplative life as well as of the active one. They stand before God and praise him; so do the monks in their prayer. Their worship is not a liturgy which is shouted out or declaimed—it is sung, even danced. They are, so to speak, the Church's *corps de ballet*. They love the Psalms in which the whole Bible becomes prayer and, in particular, praise and Alleluia, the Paschal song *par excellence*. Isn't there a relationship between the angels and the revelation of the mystery of salvation? They knew it before we did. The two cherubim above the ark of the covenant, according to the Epistle to the Hebrews (ix, 5) the two seraphim mentioned by Isaias, facing one another and flanking the Mediator, are symbols of the 'agreement and harmony of the two Testaments, which both look to Christ'.[17] And since God spoke to men in Hebrew, some think that the angels praise God in this language, and that the Alleluia, which comes from it, is an angelic song.[18] So their relations with men are always interpreted in the light of eschatology, as regards with purpose. But they are interpreted as well in the light of the Economy as regards the way in which God has communicated himself in revealed writings and then in Christ. The angels are already in God's temple and share in those realities which eye has not seen, nor ear heard, but which God prepares for those whom he loves.[19]

They are sinless. Thus they incite man to ascesis, to the active life. They are brought to mind in the context of the conversion required by baptism, or by the monastic life, of all the virtues which that implies: not only sobriety, chastity,

14. Ibid., p. 59.
15. Ibid., p. 61.
16. Ibid., p. 65.
17. Cf. H. de Lubac, *Exégèse Médiévale*, I (Paris, 1959) pp. 325-27.
18. Ibid., II, I (Paris, 1961) p. 248.
19. Ibid., p. 249.

and voluntary poverty, but obedience and unanimity.[20] They are 'heavenly cenobites', writes Peter of Celle, *caelestes illi coenobitae,* and one has the right to depart into solitude only for the better practice of prayer and of charity.

A Witness: St Bernard

Since it is both impossible here to go over all the ground and yet unsatisfactory to confine oneself to generalities, let us take a writer who has in some sort synthesized the whole spiritual tradition of the twelfth century and influenced all his successors. He has delivered his message with so much doctrinal and literary excellence that he has been copied, read and imitated more than anyone else. St Bernard of Clairvaux has written of the angels in many places, especially in his *Sermon on Psalm 90* and in the fifth book of the *De Consideratione,* and his teaching has been expounded in definitive works which require no comment here.[21] It will be sufficient to consider the two sermons which he composed for the feast of St Michael.[22] They are short but compact. He does not speak of the legend of the Archangel's apparition (and does not even mention him by name), but of the mystery of the Angels in the Church and of the monastic life.

At the beginning of the first sermon, Bernard states the whole difference between the Angels and ourselves: they are in God's presence, and we are far from it. But their love for us abolishes all distance for they are at our service for our salvation, and the two words, 'ministry' and 'salvation', which occur in one verse of the Epistle to Hebrews concerning them, and concerning ourselves (Heb. i, 14), provide the theme for all the subsequent development (n. 1). In the second section Bernard indulges in one of those plays on biblical words at which he excels: the verb *ministrari* occurs ten times, and the noun *ministerium* thrice. And the meaning of these terms has been given by the teaching and exam-

---

20. Cf. *La Vie Parfaite,* p. 42.
21. Cf. E. Boissard, "La Doctrine des Anges chez S. Bernard," dans *S. Bernard, Théologien* (Rome, 1953) pp. 114-35.
22. Text in *PL* 183, 447-54.

ple of Christ. He whom the angels serve humbled himself like
a servant; he became the example and principle of all service.
And so, from the start, this angelology is centered on Christ,
on the mysteries of the Incarnation and of the Paschal Sacrifice performed by him who is the servitor, the minister *par
excellence* (n. 3). He offered himself, and has not ceased
thereafter to minister his flesh to us as nourishment. Thus it
is around him, in him, that angels and men find their unity.
Not without humor. Bernard quotes 'Love me, love my dog'.
Are not we the little dogs of whom the Gospel speaks who
eat the crumbs under the Master's table? The angels sit at
table with him, but we all, whatever our condition, make up
a family, a house, a city. This last image is then taken up (n.
4) and illustrated by biblical texts about Sion and Jerusalem.
The only desire of the angels is for us to share in their bliss
and to lead us to it. Bernard here uses a new biblical comparison, suggested by the Old Law and St Paul, that of the
first fruits: the Angels possess these first fruits of the perfect
praise of God; they help us on our way to it by their watch-
fulness over us and by their prayers *expectatione et expedi-
tione.*

This character of initial but imperfect eschatology, which
marks our condition and distinguishes it from theirs, determines all our moral conduct (n. 5): we have to remain worthy
of the friendship of those who already live in full intimacy
with God. What, then, are the virtues which please them
above all, the heavenly virtues which they want to find in us
and which, from this point of view, we may call angelic?
Sobriety, chastity, voluntary poverty, frequent groanings to
heaven, prayer with tears and the intention of the heart.
Preeminently the angels of peace require of us peace and
unity'. Why so? Simply, as St Bernard explains at once,
because it is for us to begin this life which will be ours in the
heavenly Jerusalem, a life of unanimity since it is a sharing in
the very being of God: *cuius participatio in idipsum.* This
formula of Ps. 121, 3, on which St Augustine had so magnifi-
cently commented,[23] and which St Bernard himself had so

23. Especially in *Enarr. in Ps. 121,* 5, CCSL 40 (1956) p. 1805.

often quoted, expounded and applied to the common life of the monastery,[24] he here takes up again. Let us be in agreement with one another, profoundly so; let us be the different members of one and the same body, in Christ. And this unity can come to us only from the Spirit sent by Christ. Jesus had spoken of the angels in connection with the scandal which does harm to those who are his (Matt. xviii, 6). What is the scandal which causes them most offence? Division, the schism which disrupts unity. All the concluding section of the first sermon is founded on the difference between life according to the Spirit of God and life according to the flesh, not (that is) between a pure spirit or even the human soul, on the one hand, and the body on the other, but between grace and sin. In all this there is nothing which is not biblical, centred on the mystery of salvation in Christ.

The second sermon also speaks of charity, this time in connection with the scandal of division and especially about the unity which should reign in a community of monks. It is not of an order different from that which should exist among all Christians, but it is more demanding and perhaps harder to achieve: hence the emphasis on 'charity', 'peace', 'fraternity', 'unity', 'unanimity'. By the love which we have for one another, the angels, whose concord and whose sharing in the divine life we have to imitate, will know that we are disciples of Christ (n. I). They love us only because of him, *Christi gratia,* and we can love him only if we love one another. Once again Bernard refers to our incipiently eschatological condition which moves towards its completion, towards the perfect harmony of the eternal city, wholly occupied in God and penetrated by the light of his glory (n. 2).

Then, in one of those very candid avowals of his—and of everyman's—wretchedness, Bernard recalls the 'interior scandal' which all of us experience.[25] 'We know it well, in everyday life. But it happens in three ways. Sometimes we have an inward simplicity, otherwise called a truly spiritual

24. *In Septuag.,* II, 3; *In Ascensione,* V, 5; *De Diversis,* I, 8.
25. Cf. "S. Bernard et L'Expérience Chrétienne," in *La Vie Spirituelle,* 1967.

intention, which can only be the effect of grace; but then our eye interferes. Our will suggests to us a less pure intention. And what is true of the eye also applies to the foot and the hand, to our actions: our own will tries to divert us from good works' (n. 3). So we must struggle. It is not easy to climb Jacob's ladder. We must learn to submit this will which is 'our own' in so far as it is opposed to God's and thus to regain simplicity. Instead of being divided, being as it were two persons, we must become unified again, united to God alone. Here Bernard quotes one of his favourite texts: 'He who adheres to God is one spirit with him' (1 Cor. vi, 17). Perfect peace is reserved for the time of bliss, of glory and of victory; here we are still in the time of struggle against temptations and scandals, a time therefore for courage and the other virtues (n. 4).

Such is the teaching which Bernard gave his monks in connection with the angels, their feast, and the texts of the Gospels which refer to them. The angelism we find there is one which is concerned wholly with the Incarnation and the Redemption and with the daily struggle by which the Christian shares in Christ's victory. The virtues which the angels teach us and help us to practise belong to the lowly condition of man who tries to live on earth a life which will make him one day worthy of heaven. The chief of them, which makes the happiness of heaven and which makes heaven of our earth, is charity, the source of all concord, peace, mutual help and fraternity. Monks know—Bernard reminds them of this 'daily experience'—what it costs to make a community, a family, *familiaris congregatio,* of their house. All this is very realistic and may seem humdrum in comparison with the sublime speculations about the angels in the works of spiritual writers of succeeding ages. Let us cheerfully accept the fact that the greatest representative of medieval monastic spirituality has no knowledge of this sort of angelism.

Elsewhere too Bernard has insisted on all the difference that exists between the condition of man in the Church and the condition of an angel: 'I too possess the Word, but in the flesh; the truth is offered to me too, but in a sacrament. An angel is fed on the richness of the wheat, on the pure grain. But I, in this time of waiting, must be content with the rind of a sacrament, with the husk of the grain, the chaff of the letter, the veil of faith.'[26] 'This one same nourishment of truth which is Christ, the Wisdom of God, is provided in one way on earth, in another in heaven. We mortal men, in our time of waiting and in the place of our exile, must eat bread in the sweat of our brow, beg for it from others in toil and labor, that is to receive it from those who know, from the sacred writings or at any rate grasp the invisible mysteries of God in his works. But the angels receive it in themselves if not of themselves in all fullness and with equal ease and enjoyment, and their whole life of beatitude comes from it. They receive from God the full teaching which is only promised, albeit with certainty, among God's other creatures to men. But men do not yet experience it in a joy which can never fail.' [27]

And yet angels and men are fellow-citizens of the same city of God, 'which is both in heaven and on earth, one part of it in exile, and the other part reigning'.[28] There is a difference and a distance between them, but there is also union, a possible resemblance and even proximity. Bernard is not afraid to say of monks: 'our order has, on earth, the greatest likeness to the angelic orders; it is the nearest to that heavenly Jerusalem which is our mother in virtue of the splendour of chastity and the ardour of charity.'[29] If, then, Bernard has no truck with 'angelism', he has an angelology: it is that of the Gospel and St Paul.

Angelism and the Angelic Life

The real purpose of the theme of the angelic life is to illustrate one aspect of the present condition of the Church and of every Christian: the part played by the movement

26. *Sup. Cant.*, 33, 3, ed. *S. Bernardi Opera*, t. I (Rome, 1957) p. 235.
27. Ibid., 53, 5, *Opera* II (Rome, 1958) pp. 98-99.
28. Ibid., 53, 6, p. 99.
29. *Apologia*, 24, *Opera* III (Rome, 1963) p. 101.

towards the fulfilment of an incipient eschatology which is realized already every day in ascesis and in prayer, in the militant life and in the contemplative life, sharing in the mystery of Christ in union with the saints of the glorious Jerusalem, with their help and, so far as we can imitate them, according to their example. When the Second Vatican Council and leading theologians of our time have reminded us of the contemplative goal of the Church, they have in doing so taken up an ancient tradition which monasticism kept alive in the Middle Ages.[30]

Angelism in a later period represents a deviation from this norm. An element of the ancient synthesis—the theme of chastity for example—was isolated from the rest and given an exaggerated importance. Nevertheless, the chastity of religious, according to Vatican II, is still valid as an eschatological sign.[31] The angels were taken as a sort of perfect example of realities whose accomplishment is yet to come. Just as St Thomas and the Scholastics tended to illustrate certain problems about human intelligence and will by referring to these realities as possessed by pure spirits, so the monks threw light on the present condition of Christians by referring to the condition of the angels, already united, totally and definitely, with the glorified Lord. Unlike vague angelism, the traditional theme of the angelic life made possible, in a way which was both practical and biblical, the evocation of the mystery of the presence of God and the mystery of the presence of his creatures with him.

30. Vatican II, *Constitution on the Church,* nn. 49-50. 'Until the Lord comes in his glory, and all the angels with him (Matt. xxv, 31), . . . some of his disciples are pilgrims on earth . . . others still are in their glory, gazing clearsighted on God himself, three and one, as he is . . . She (the Church) has joined them (the Apostles and Martyrs) to the Blessed Virgin Mary and the holy angels in her especially affectionate respect. She has piously implored the help of their intercession . . .' I have indicated some of the texts of the Council on the subject of the eschatological character of the Church in a study of "La Vie Contemplative et le Monachisme d'après Vatican II," in *Gregorianum,* 47 (1966) p. 496-516. The contemplative end which the Church pursues is proclaimed in the Proemium of the *Constitution on the Sacred Liturgy.*

31. *Const. on the Church,* n. 44; *Decree on the Renewal of the Religious Life,* n. 12.

THE FUTURE OF MONKS*

T HE SECOND CONFERENCE OF ANGLICAN
Religious at Oxford in July, 1967, chose as its theme
'The Religious Life in the World of Tomorrow', and it
had on its programme a paper on 'The Monastic Life After
the Second Vatican Council'. We have indeed the right to ask
ourselves about the future of monasticism. There are young
people in monasteries at present, and there is no reason to
suppose that they are the last generation.

But what will they be and what will they do? And in what
area will the study of this problem fall? This is complex. As
a phenomenon of the past and the present, monasticism
comes simultaneously under theology, history, and canon
law, and then, because it involves psychological and sociolo-
gical factors, under philosophy and finally missions. As for its
future, it would come under the jurisdiction of that science
of the immediate future, forecasting. In this article will be
found neither prophecies nor exact predictions, only con-
jectures based on the establishment of certain contemporary
facts which furnish material for theological interpretation.

First we must posit an idea of monasticism; then place it in
the context of the Church and the world, today and tomorrow. One of the first duties which is likely to fall on monks is
that of defining themselves and of deducing the consequences
of what they decide to be.

* Extracts from a lecture given at the Gregorian University on 16 March 1967.
Published in *Irénikon*, 40 (1967) pp. 333-353; in Italian in *Ora et labora*, 23
(1968) pp. 49-58 and 124-128.

Towards a Definition of Monasticism

We know—at least monks know—how difficult it is to define the monastic life, at least to enclose it in a single brief formula, still more so in a word or expression. It is at this point that some have given up. Others have put forward many divergent ideas. And yet, there is no reason for not looking for one which will convey the reality, however complex. An old phrase of Roman Law much quoted warns that "definitions are dangerous." But it was forged in an historical context different from ours, and only for the realm of jurisprudence. Surely the law of the Church can presuppose, even if it does not recall, ideas resulting from the analysis of realities on a different level, that of theological reflection?

One could, by simplifying it and consequently reducing it almost to a caricature, formulate a definition which would have some chance of support in the monastic world. For example: monks are a regular order but they are not religious and although their life includes none of the activities of religious, neither does it exclude them and, in fact, it permits them all. This position has been defended with further qualifications in the following way:

Monasticism is not specified by works. It only seeks to be the Christian life pursued with a kind of absoluteness. It is for this reason that the monastic life which can more easily be contemplative is not characterized by contemplation. It can be harmonized with activities, provided these activities do not become an end which determines the life. There are not monk-missionaries, monk-teachers, but there are indeed monks who teach, who live in mission lands and work there. But these monks lose the foundation of their monastic life if they so give themselves to their activities that these become even a secondary end of their life. It is evidently possible that a member of an abbey may be temporarily so absorbed by his activities that he does not for the moment remain a monk except by belonging to a monastic institute. But during such a time his monastic life suffers an eclipse—momentarily, we hope.

I believe then that it is necessary to say that the monastic life is situated prior to the division into secondary ends that characterize human life in its activities. In this the monk is again a man of oneness of life (μόνος). What characterizes him is perhaps his pursuit with an absoluteness of that which the ordinary Christian pursues less closely. It is in these terms that the Council said, 'There are men in the Church who follow the Lord more closely.' (*Lumen Gentium,* 42). Monks desire to do only this, at least as the essential note of their life. It is here that I find the doctrinal reason for not giving to monks the name 'religious'. The monk ought not to enter into a category of Christians who are characterized by their works, even if that work be contemplation. It is certainly possible that there be in the Church institutes founded for the work of contemplation. This is not true of the monks. The monk seeks only the perfect Christian life. Each age and each milieu, each culture will produce circumstances which will diversify the life of the monks. This is why they so tenaciously defend the autonomy of their monasteries. Even within a monastery there can be a whole gamut of life-forms.[1]

Should we, after such declarations, give up trying to find ideas and distinctions which would allow us to define still further? One mode of expression which is proving helpful consists in establishing a distinction between 'monastic life' and 'apostolic life'. There is another which, although perhaps less helpful, has the recommendation of a longer history. In fact, in speaking of the monastic life, ancient and medieval tradition, recent Popes, Vatican II, Paul VI and a large number of witnesses of Christian thought today have used and are using the expression 'Contemplative Life'.[2] This is a fact. Instead of deploring it, as that does not eliminate it, we would do better to understand it. It corresponds exactly to the idea of monasticism which St Gregory the Great wanted to give when, intending to commend it, he recounted the life of its most illustrious representative in the West. Recently an extremely learned study devoted to one of the last episodes

1. V. Truijen, "Are monks religious? " in *Cistercian Studies,* 2 (1967) p. 241.
2. See above, Ch. V, p. 113.

in the life of St Benedict, by an expert in Patristics, Pierre Courcelle, ended with this conclusion: "The aim of Gregory as hagiographer is to describe here, in the most concrete form, the marvellous nature of contemplation, and to present Benedict as the type of the contemplative saint."[3]

This vocabulary, like every specialized vocabulary, presents difficulties. There is a risk of its not being understood, or of its being misinterpreted by the uninitiated—one might almost dare say those who are not "in the trade", in the sense in which Dom Alexis Presse spoke of "contemplation as a craft."[4] Every branch of human knowledge has the right to create its own peculiar vocabulary and to derive it from the languages of antiquity. Today, 'econometry', 'agroclimatology', 'electronic', 'astronautic' and many other neologisms of Graeco-Latin origin are used freely but their meaning no longer has anything in common with the physics or mathematics of Pythagoras or Archimedes. Modern tradition has given them a new and legitimate meaning which is not without a certain continuity with a whole tradition of research and aspirations. Certain existing words have themselves proliferated: the science of the computer is known as 'computerization', 'optimum' gives 'to optimize' and 'optimization', and 'programme' has given birth to a whole family of 'to programme' and its derivatives: 'programmer', 'programming', 'programmization' etc. So in order to eliminate the terms 'contemplative life', it is not enough to object that they existed in some ancient civilization and had in it a meaning given them before Christianity. Neither is it enough, in order to understand them, to project on to the past the ideas which one wishes to put forward today, as happened in a short dissertation (130 pages) which was called 'Active Life and Contemplative Life: A study of the Concepts from Plato to the Present' (in fact, a public opinion pollster put the question to passersby in the street) but which, in reality, moved

3. "La vision cosmique de S. Benoît," in *Revue des études augustiniennes,* 13 (1967) p. 117.
4. Title of an article published in *Le message des moines à notre temps* (Paris, 1958) pp. 121-138.

from the present to Plato.[5]

The real difficulty does not come from the history of words. It is more serious and it was brought to light a long time ago by Gabriel Marcel: "We are today in the midst of confusion. It is almost impossible for us to avoid making a physical image of activity in a sense, imagining it as the setting in motion of a certain machine of which, basically, our body is the starter, or even the model. The ancient idea . . . according to which contemplation is the highest activity, is completely lost. . . . Moralism, in all its forms, with the belief in the almost exclusive value of works, has certainly contributed in a large measure to bringing discredit on the contemplative virtues."[6]

When a vocabulary exists legitimately, we have the right to retain it, but insofar as it presents difficulties, we have a duty to try to translate it. Paul VI has come to our help in this. To the Benedictines, in the person of their abbots and priors assembled in a Congress in 1966, he said, "You are seekers after the Eternal God."[7] *(Aeterni Dei estis investigatores.)* As early as 1964, in their common declaration at Bouake, the representatives of the African monasteries summed up this traditional designation: "This ideal . . . is that of a humble, hidden life, entirely set upon searching for God."[8] Now this terminology, which is of biblical origin and has always been maintained in the monastic life, is at present charged with a new richness, with great intellectual and human potentiality. Formerly one searched for something lost. Today a seeker is one who searches with his head and with his heart, and his qualifications are recognized, sanctioned and furthered by the whole of society. Every country has a "Centre for Research" or "Scientific Investigation". And this vocabulary may be applied to what the ancients called the 'quest for God,' *quaesitio Dei.* It suggests a reality which has its enig-

---

5. Sr E. Mason OSB, *Active Life and Contemplative Life. A Study of the Concepts from Plato to the Present* (Milwaukee: Marquette University Press, 1961).

6. *Etre et avoir* (Paris, 1935) p. 277.

7. See above, p. 103.

8. Quoted above, p. 124.

matic side, an element of mystery bound up with the very nature of the object considered and with the mode of knowing which makes possible its attainment. Thus there are men and women who specialize in the search for God and who, on these grounds, have a right to the consideration of the contemporary world; who, so to speak, dig deep into the mystery of God and who, for that reason, are taken seriously and respected. It is recognized that God should be a valid subject for study until the seeker, having found him, kneels, prays, worships, and is ready to share the discovery with others. For today, all experience belongs to everybody. The world is waiting for the diffusion of monastic experience; it must not be refused. Not that it is necessary to rush to meet the world, nor that every movement towards God should necessarily be communicated; but a movement from a centre of spiritual life should be communicable. And one of the great qualities of today's world is that this experience will be discovered in the place where it has occurred.

For everyone today who specializes understands that his discipline makes demands and that he cannot devote himself to it just anywhere. If you want to study electronics, you go to a research centre such as Saclay in France, where batteries, computors, laboratories, and other facilities—including silence and to a degree remoteness from the city—are assembled. If you want to practise winter sports, you go where there are: according to what you want to do, you find snow and ski-lifts, or else peaks, tracks and mountain huts. Similarly, if you want to give yourself to the life of prayer, it is natural to go where favorable conditions are to be found: a measure of recollection, a measure of organization in the economy and way of life. Industrialists will countenance men of prayer not staying in the world, and the latter will go away not simply to separate themselves from their kind but because, in order to carry out their programme of research, they need to be apart. The solitude should be welcoming, and it would no doubt be an exacting form of asceticism to welcome everyone who came asking for God. Men will grasp the fact that the searchers for God have their own claims. When the businessman is at his office or the research worker at his laboratory, he has no shame about making it known. Similarly, there are times when monks are at prayer. Let them be happy to pray, let them never be cut off from their sense of contemplation, which is their only wealth in today's world. Everything else can be done by other people, and often better.

Monasticism and the Modern World

We may set this renewed concept of the "search for God" in the context of an entire ancient tradition. In the Hebrew and later the Greek Bible, this expression, which has undergone a whole evolution, denoted an interior, spiritual attitude and concerned less the mind and the memory than the will: desire, zeal, prayer; encountering God in worship and intimate union, cleaving to his love in keeping his law, pouring out the heart in adoration. All this without excluding, particularly at the point in her history when Israel found herself in Greek surroundings, the application of the mind to the study of wisdom.[9] This extremely rich idea, with which the Psalms and Wisdom literature had familiarized them, St Benedict, [10] and later William de Frutharia,[11] and Elmer of Canterbury,[12] preserved, took up and developed.

Let us content ourselves here with underlining the relevance of this reality to the Church today. We are reminded of it on all sides:

Then I want to pass on and notice something that is an enormous encouragement and ground of hope . . . there is

9. G. Turbessi, "Quaerere Deum. Il tema della 'ricerca di Dio' nella S. Scrittura", in *Rivista biblica*, 10 (1962) pp. 282-296, and "Quaerere Deum. Il tema della ricerca di Dio nell'ambiente ellenistico e giudaico contemporaneo al Nuovo Testamento", in *Studiorum Paulinorum Congressus internationalis catholicus,1961* (Rome, 1963) pp. 2-16; A. Feuillet, "La recherche du Christ dans la Nouvelle Alliance . . .," in *L'homme devant Dieu. Mélanges H. de Lubac* (Paris, 1963) I, pp. 93-112.

10. *Regula*, 58, 7.

11. Witness this extract from the invocation which I published among the "Prières attribuables à Guillaume et à Jean de Fruttuaria", in *Monasteri in Alta Italia* (Turin, 1966) p. 162: "Fac me . . . ardentissimae delectationis desiderio investigare et inquirere ubi investigandus es et inquirendus."

12. See the *Excitatio mentis in inquisitionem Dei* which I published in *Analecta monastica*, 2 (Rome, 1953) pp. 110-114.

one great thing that is happening and that is the revival of
the contemplative spirit. Now we see this in the emergence
of distinctively contemplative orders of men and women
but we see it more widely than that. We see it in a revival
among Christian people of the sense that the contemplation
of God is nothing so very queer or *outre* but is a wholesome Christian thing and a very part of man's prerogative as
God's child.... I always think of contemplative prayer in
this sort of way—it's just wanting God very much.... I
want to want God . . . And if there is just that fragment of
desire before God, God takes it and accepts it and enlarges
it.... Let us thank God for the revival of the contemplative spirit.[13]

In addition, Bishop de Roo, of Victoria, Canada, said, at the
ordination to the priesthood of one of the members of the
Society of the Hermits of St John Baptist, which is not intended for the apostolic ministry, "We see in the restoration of
the eremitical life a providential and highly significant intervention. It looks as though the Holy Spirit is trying to coun-

13. Text of an address by the Archbishop of Canterbury in *Cowley Evangelist*
(July 1966) pp. 102-103. On the importance of monasticism in Orthodoxy, see
for example J. Meyendorf, *Orthodoxie et catholicité* (Paris, 1965) p. 47, or A. V.
Vedernikov's article in the *Zurnal Moskovskoj Patriarchii* (the official revue of the
Moscow Patriarchate) n⁰ 10 (October 1958). Ernst Benz had pointed out in *Geist
und Leben der Ostkirche* (Munich, 1957, 1971) "as a certain danger for Orthodoxy its liturgical isolationism and its refusal to serve the world"; and A.
Vedernikov replied: "It is not so much a question of the refusal of an active
service on the part of Orthodoxy, as the way in which she understands this
service. And much more, the way in which she understands Christian action. If in
the West it is always seen in terms of one or other outward service (missions,
instruction, ethico-social activity, etc.), in the East it involves above all training
for prayer and the path of ascetic perfecting of the personality, called in Eastern
asceticism 'spiritual action'. Consequently, the Orthodox Church places service by
prayer in the front rank of means of serving the world. It believes that liturgical
prayer for the members of the Church, living and dead, and for the whole world,
far from being secondary means of serving the world, is perhaps more important
than any outward activity. That is why, if major circumstances deprive some local
Church of the possibility of practising outward activities other than the celebration of the Divine Offices, the result is not a liturgical isolation, but rather a
widening of experience in the field of liturgical prayer. The divine office in these
cases takes on a particularly clear character of active service, laden at the same
time with graces for men and for the whole world. And this is also valid for
individual action. The spiritual action of the cenobite or the anchorite, living far
from the world, and even if he remains unknown by men, retains its value for the
whole world." (p. 80).

terbalance whatever may be too human in our apostolate of involvement in the temporal order, in the promotion and development of creation."[14] And, indeed, is it not suggestive that at the height of the post-conciliar period, articles, at times under high patronage, appear on "the relevance of the eremitical life"?[15] The eremetical is, of course, an extreme form which must remain exceptional even within the monastic life. The life of prayer lived in common is an authentic way, and the normal one for most monks.

The affirmation of the contemplative character of all monastic life should certainly not result in attributing to it a monopoly of the interior life, even of continuous prayer. It would be illusory to hurl all the others into agitated, superficial and completely worldly activism under the pretence of keeping "contemplation for the contemplatives". Moreover, facts prove that plenty of laymen, within Catholic Action or outside it, attain to a depth of contemplative sense which confounds the professionals. Even these know full well that they never see God. "He has opened my ear that I may listen to him" comments St Bernard, "not my eye that I may behold his face. . . . He is behind the lattice: he listens; he is heard, but he does not appear."[16]

It is nonetheless true that this obscure waiting and this loving attention, practised in conditions which guarantee their genuineness, mold a mentality and encourage spiritual states which the world needs to know to be possible and real. A man who knows our times well, P. Liégé, is not afraid to proclaim:

14. Extract from a sermon given at Courtenay, B. C., Canada, on 21 November 1966.

15. M. Farrell, "Attualità del' eremitismo", in *Vita religiosa* (1967) pp. 23-24 (a review directed by Fr L. Ravasi, of the Sacred Congregation of Religious). *Actualité de l'érémitisme,* title of the special number (121) of the *Lettre de Ligugé* of January 1967. M. B. Pennington OCSO, "The Structure of the Section Concerning Religious Life in the Revised Code", in *The Jurist,* 25 (1965) p. 283, mentions the Society of the Hermits of St John the Baptist and other new foundations.

16. *In Nativitate Sancti Iohanni Baptistae,* 1, 2, PL 183, 398-399 On the place of contemplatives among those who surrounded the Lord and followed in his train, there are some beautiful sentences in *In Dom. Palmarium* II, 2 and 6-7, PL 183, 257-259.

The modern mind is so molded by the technological mentality, so taken up with worldly greatness and human creatures, that it becomes apparently insensitive to all interior reality and, consequently, to a personal God. Only the witness of men who have met God, who have entered into his world of holiness; men who make visible in themselves the existence of a spiritual energy arising from a real communion with the God of holiness, can reveal to our contemporaries the realism of the great divine presence. 'God is dead,' said the unbeliever. 'It is impossible,' answers the saint, 'I meet him every day, and every morning I open my eyes again in Paradise'.[17]

The appearance of a new age of the world, the technological age, does not therefore in the least close the future of monasticism. Technological civilization is legitimately real but not exclusive. If it were considered as having the right to supremacy over every other activity of man, it would kill what is most fundamental in him: love. Love which is above all contemplation, in the broad sense which philosophers of today allow, and which is able to rally even the technician. That certain Christians, churchmen at that, will not grasp this gratuitous, apparently ineffectual, vocation would only confirm the urgency. The apostolate of monks is sometimes represented as consisting of "thinking of others" and "praying for them", which reduces it to the level of doing, of working, of that technique which needs exactly what Paul VI (quoting Bergson) called a "soul supplement".[18] If the apostolate consists also in making the truth upon which we live attractive to others, the first duty of the apostle is to live intensely what he wishes to share with all. To secure this, it is

17. Quoted by A. M. Henry, "Sens de Dieu et du péche", in *La Vie spirituelle*, 93 (1955) p. 310.
18. In *Chances de la spiritualité*, p. 369, I quoted this phrase in its context, a declaration made on 9 May 1964, at the international Colloquy on the problems of technical assistance, published in the *Documentation Catholique*, 61 (1964), p. 874. Since then, Paul VI has written in the encyclical *Populorum progressio*, n°20: "If the pursuit of development requires more and more technicians, it demands even more wise men of deep reflection, seeking a new humanism which will allow modern man to find himself, assuming the superior values of love, friendship, prayer and contemplation".

not useless for some men to separate themselves from an environment which they feel scatters the very thing which they want to gather in to themselves. That is, that unity of life which it is so difficult to let happen in us.[19] Besides, isn't the aim of every apostolate from the most implicit to the most explicit, from the most unobtrusive to the most delicate, to identify men with the situation of Jesus Christ, who is "face to face with His Father? " This interior attitude, this participation in the adoration of Christ, has a value so absolute that every man has the right to find it by the way which he judges most conducive for himself.

The fathers of the desert said this about solitaries. Laymen of today affirm it for their fellows. Madeleine Delbrel spoke thus to the Lord: "What you need to carry out your work on earth is not so much our sensational actions as a capacity for submission, a degree of surrender, a pull of blind abandonment somewhere in the crowd of men."[20] Whether this kind of presence in the world is demanded or the situation of an Edith Stein or a Simone Weil is between the soul and God, and does not come within the appraisal or the control of the public. There are established situations which are themselves affirmations. And monasticism is one of them. The accusations of dualism, neo-platonism, masochism, and heaven knows what else, may perhaps touch those within it who grant them a foothold, just as others in the world certainly yield to other deviations. But monasticism is a fact within the Church and it is not called into question by these criticisms.[21]

The future of monks after Vatican II lies perhaps in being more aware of their specific function relative to other forms of life, (those described by the Council concerning priesthood, laity, and religious apostolates) and in drawing practical conclusions. Aspirants will appear if God wills it as he has

19. See on this subject the pertinent reflexious of Irenaeus Hausherr SJ, "La théologie du monachisme chez S. Jean Climaque," in *Théologie de la vie monastique* (Paris, 1961) p. 404.

20. M. Delbrel "Joies venues de la montagne", in *Ma joie terrestre où donc es-tu? Etudes carmélitaines* (1947) p. 190.

21. On "the real problem" implied in these accusations (more of less well founded), see above, p. 142.

willed it for many centuries. Nothing in contemporary civilization leads us to believe that those who are called will
refuse. But, insofar as they are necessary, the forms of their
apostolic outreach will be determined by the position of
Christianity in the world today—and that is not what it was
twenty years ago. In short, monasticism has a future if it
perceives, and if it lives its relationship with God and with
the world from its position of physical and material exit from
the world. A Little Brother of Jesus, a diocesan priest and a
member of a secular institute are, each in his own way, "out
of the world"—as is every Christian by his baptism. For the
monk, this is simply true in a different way.

Finally, we should return briefly to the problem raised by
the development of cybernetics and their application in a
society already described as 'cybercultural', to the foresee-
able 'age of leisure' with all its 'promises' and 'threats'.[22] A
single example will recall the data

The claims of the New York Transport Workers' Unions (a
35 hour week and 30 per cent increase in wages) leads us to
believe that, in the eyes of the trade union officials, the age
of leisure is not far off. The violence of the public reaction, on the other hand, shows that they are not ready to
accept a differentiation between the traditional concepts of
work, leisure and wages. And yet, the logical conclusion
would be a situation in which higher and higher wages will
be paid for shorter and shorter work time. In the end, the
day may come when, in order to support their claims, the
workers' best weapon will be to refuse to stop working.[23]

Many already visualize the consequences:

It will be necessary to invent new roles for the mass of
those whose work will have become redundant, even if a
pensions policy or the right to a guaranteed income pre-
vents actual want. Men's outward behaviour will change

22. These words are taken from the title of an article in the *Bulletin du C. T. N.*
(Centre d'étude des conséquences générales des grandes techniques nouvelles), 38
(1966) p. 24. Under the title "Sur le role des contemplatifs dans la societé de
demain," in *Chances de la spiritualité occidentale* (Paris, 1966) pp. 354-373, I
have tackled this problem.
23. C. T. N., 37 (1966) p. 15.

considerably. We are beginning to observe the first symp-
toms of these modifications already in the United States
and elsewhere in the form of non-violent protests, in orga-
nizations like the Volunteers for Peace, in the form of
efforts to turn back on oneself.

Another observer of these same phenomena has noted that it
is not long before the question, "What am I to do with my
leisure?", turns into, "Who am I and how should I lead my
life?"[24] Someone has put forward the theory that "leisure
could nevertheless make it possible to renew contact with
nature. But, except for a minority, [men] will fail [to do so]
because they will be too well organized." And that is another
disquieting thought. "Progress today accentuates the difference between an active creative majority and a minority
which assimilates passively, without participating."[25]

Thus, as Teilhard said, "The more rational and mechanized
man becomes, the more he needs poets as the saviours and
leaven of his personality."[26] But will the conditions which
demand and permit, even at the cost of difficulties, a return
to oneself and to nature not be equally favorable to return to
God, to a contact with him? Beyond the dilemma of work or
free time, there is their conciliation, their reconciliation in a
supreme spiritual activity which confers new and higher value
on both. The contemplative life gives direction, not only in
the use of leisure, but also in a new appreciation of work.
This appreciation cannot fail to be highlighted just as, according to some forecasts (or at least in some of its forms), it
threatens to lose its importance.[27] The contemplative life
looks still further ahead. It teaches us to balance between
work and contemplation, and even the subordination of work

24. C. T. N., 36 (1966) p. 13.
25. Ibid., p. 32. "In the year 2000, thanks to automation and robot machines,
you will have 344 days' holiday a year, spent killing time in stadiums, at the
cinema, watching T.V. while you look forward with your mouth watering to the
joy of setting off for three weeks at work". Quoted by Pierre P. Defert, "Une
société en quête de repos absolu", *Etudes,* 311 (1961) p. 307, who shows that
there is more than one "publicity stunt" in this and recalls further on (p. 311)
some far from cheerful consequences.
26. Quoted in *Cahiers Pierre Teilhard de Chardin,* n°3 (Paris, 1962) p. 103.
27. See, for example, how E. Rideau, *La pensée du Père Teilhard de Chardin*
(Paris, 1965) pp. 468-472 and *passim* advances activity, prayer and work a
concept which fills that of Teilhard, which tends to be unilateral.

to contemplation. And finally it attributes to contemplation itself the character of work *par excellence*. We have heard Gabriel Marcel speak of contemplation as the highest activity, contrasting it with the semi-physical image of activity that we have today. A Carthusian wrote recently: "It is the prayer and holy restfulness of contemplation which demand the Christian's greatest effort."[28] The Fathers of the Church had already said that contemplation is the only work of Adam in Paradise. Will this not be the same in eternal Paradise? Without sweat, because without sin, our labor will be without end: it will be, *par excellence*, the *otium negotiosum*.

Monastic Solitude and the Fellowship of the Church

If monks have to be defined in order to be placed, they must be defined not only in relation to the modern world but also in relation to the modern Church. It is the same Church always, but in our time, as in every age, certain aspects of what it is are accentuated. In particular it emphasizes, more than its leaders and its members have done previously, its character as the people of God, among whom everything is communication and a sharing of the one same gift of God. Thus, paradoxically, we move, in monasticism as elsewhere, towards an increasingly specific character and even specialization, while at the same time we move towards a more conscious universality.

This is not the place to demonstrate in detail how broad movements and fundamental observances must become increasingly monastic, that is, perceived and accepted, even willed, as such. P.J. Beyer has done it with the authority given him by his knowledge of all forms of religious life and by his special sympathy for those expressions of it most remote from one another, the monastic orders and the secular institutes. On the subject of obedience, poverty and consecrated celibacy, he has made distinctions appropriate to religious of monastic, apostoloc and secular life.[29] For each of

---

28. *L'Ordre des chartreux* (Grande-Chartreuse, 1949) p. 42.
29. "Decretum 'perfectae caritatis' Concilii Vaticani II", in *Periodica de re morali,* 55 (1966), pp. 472-498; 56 (1967) pp. 4-60.

these three groups, the aim and constitutional character of their life determine the manner in which the main evangelical counsels will be put into practice, on the spiritual as well as the practical level. Certain activities practised by monks are now considered with enough historical objectivity for us to be able to mark the limits clearly. Thus an historian whom Professor Knowles has commended admitted without beating about the bush: "The monks of the Middle Ages were rarely schoolmasters in the ancient or modern sense of the word. . . . Apart from exceptional cases, they were not educators."[30] The high proportion of priests among monks is attacked from various sides.[31] As someone acutely observed, "the same man could not observe the rule of St Benedict and the pastoral Rule of St Gregory the Great."[32]

The stability of monks, similarly, does not necessarily take the same form, and should not be given the same justification as it did when St Benedict set it in the rank of those primary duties subject to a solemn promise. Juridically it still means simply belonging to a Community, to a group, rather like the enrolment which binds a person to a society on the payment of certain dues. But in the thought of St Benedict, it was already more than that, for he rightly considered the common life as a means of moving towards perfection—a means at once ascetic, theological, and mystical. Stability of place was the expression of, and the means towards, permanence in

30. "The medieval monks were rarely schoolmasters in the ancient and modern sense of that word. . . . They were not, save in rare cases, themselves educationalists . . .", Herbert B. Workman, *The Evolution of the Monastic Ideal* (1913, reprinted Boston, 1962 with a preface by D. Knowles OSB) p. 147.

31. See for example Dom B. Webb, "Monastic *aggiornamento*", in *Downside Review*, 85 (1967) pp. 1-15, and F. Petit O. Praem., "La vie Religieuse. Son histoire" in *Au seuil de la théologie*, III (Paris, 1966) p. 352. "It must be noted that clericalization through the access of monks to the priesthood and through the conversion of clerics to the religious life, has often led to a confusion of religious with regular clergy, which is dangerous, for religious consecration and sacerdotal functions are of a very different order, although they can coexist in the same people. A man is a religious in order to seek God by pursuing perfection; he is a cleric in order to work for the salvation of his brethren".

32. Lester K. Little, "Calvin's Appreciation of Gregory the Great", in *The Harvard Theological Review*, 56 (1963), p. 152. The author recalls the great difference there was in the mind of St Gregory between the life of the monk and that of the priest.

the brotherhood, in that daily cheek-by-jowl contact in which all virtues are simultaneously forged within the soul of the cenobite. There the monk becomes—if he wishes, of course—the man-in-relationship that his nature and grace mean him to be. Because the two poles of the relationship—God and neighbour—are present in the cloister, in St Benedict's eyes, he deduced that the monk should not leave it. The outside world envisaged by St Benedict was, as it was then conceived, a world "without values". Today there are too many values in the world which cannot be found in the cloister for us not to look at things differently. Not that the monk should go out more, but he must keep contact, or make contact, with those exterior values which are most definitive, most liable to lead towards God, except, obviously, if, seized by the Spirit, he is capable of going beyond everything and therefore of seeing everything and, like St Benedict at the end of his life, "gathering it up" in God. That is already eternity.[33] Stability for the hermit is now being fixed not in a human environment but in the simple spiritual converse which he carries on and which can lead him back to the very heart of the world.

Forms which separation from the world formerly took could be renewed. There have always been country monasteries and urban monasteries. The problems raised today by urbanization, by traffic tie-ups on the outskirts of large towns, can bring in unrehearsed elements. Must a monastery necessarily be in a forest or, if it is situated in a town, surrounded by vast and expensive green spaces which will be a guarantee of solitude and recollection? Isn't it possible to dream of a contemplative house established right at the heart of the city, on the top floors of a high-rise, with the topmost floor, open to the sky, being the sanctuary? Busy men would not have to make long journeys to reach these refuges of silence, of true leisure, of communion and communication with those given to prayer. All these limitations imposed by historical data which are secondary, all these returns to what is primary cannot fail to influence the restoration and devel-

33. See "La vision cosmique de S. Benoît", in *Revue des études augustiniennes*, 13 (1967).

opment of a *ius monasticum* and, more precisely, or over and above it, a *ius contemplativorum*.[34]

Simultaneously, this monastic institution brought back to itself will have to tighten its links with the Church as a whole, and first and foremost grasp more clearly the *raison d'etre,* and the meaning of the separation which it involves. "The place of the monk is not to teach but to weep over himself and over the whole world."[35] By this definition, St Jerome, with some other Fathers of monasticism, affirmed that for monks and nuns the fact of withdrawing from public life and from direct action upon society does not separate them from mankind; it only sets them in material, exterior and superficial isolation in order to encourage a spiritual, interior and profound fellowship. The Christian who chooses God alone, who goes, who runs, who flies towards him, finds in him all those whom he loves and wishes to save.

Was the Saviour not the model and the beginning of this universal love? Eternal Word, he was the principle of every created thing. Perfect man, he had a heart which was without limits because without egoism. For that very reason, was he not the only one without sin in the midst of men? Could he not, must he not have felt lonely? "He came unto his own and his own received him not." It is in the acceptance of this refusal, in the forgiveness of this rejection, that he proved his

---

34. Under the title "Tradition et évolution dans le passé et le présent de la vie religieuse", in *Vivre ensemble l'aujourd'hui de Dieu* (Ramegnies-Chin-les-Tournai, 1968) pp. 79-98, I have pointed out, in another context, "what is lasting" and "what is changeable" in the present phase of the evolution of the religious life in general and monasticism in particular.

35. *Contra Vigilantium*, XV, PL 23, 351: "Monachus autem non doctoris habet, sed plagentis officium, qui vel se, vel mundum lugeat." Allusions to the solidarity of monks with everyone else are more frequent in ancient monasticism than is sometimes thought. I hope one day to assemble a number of them.

love. His solitude was the condition of his universality.[36]

Thus, in his Church, the only legitimate solitude is the solitude of love. We only have the right to isolate ourselves in order to love more; we only have the right to separate ourselves in order to be united.[37] We have these rights, but the bare fact of living cheek by jowl with mankind is not in itself a condition of charity. It is possible to hate one another communally. What unites us and makes us love is the presence of Love. And if we devote our lives to seeking it, within ordinary society or outside it, we realize our Christian vocation. We participate in the total solitude and in the universal solitude of Jesus Christ.

We must still endeavor to empty ourselves of all selfishness, deny ourselves, allow ourselves to be hollowed-out deep down, and sometimes painfully, in order to open ourselves and to allow ourselves to be filled, invaded by the universal love which the Spirit of the risen Jesus sheds in the hearts of Christians. Solitude is not an observance, an enclosure, a grille. It is a presence. And because it is the presence of Jesus

36. If Christ has been described as *solitarius*, it has sometimes been in the sense that he was the only son of the Father (for example Vincent de Lerins, *Commonitorium*, XII, 17; Ed. G. Rauschen (Bonn, 1906) p. 30.: "Cum scilicet Christus homo communis primum et solitarius natus sit . . . "; See St Hilarius, *De synodis*, 81, PL 10, 534; but the context has sometimes given the word another nuance: "Homo solitarius sub Pontio Pilato passus crucifixus et mortuus est," *Expositio fidei*, in Schwartz, *Acta conciliorum oecumenicorum*, 1, 2, p. IX, 1.15. In the Middle Ages, Peter of Celle, in writing of the temptation of Jesus in the wilderness, was to say "Magnus ille eremita Iesus", in the treatise *De afflictione et lectione* which I have published in *La spiritualité de Pierre de Celle* (Paris, 1946) p. 233. On the subject of Christ as *eremita* and the cross as *eremus* from which he makes waters flow for the salvation of the whole of humankind, a text of Odo of Cheriton is quoted in *Chances de la spiritualité*, p. 271. Among our contemporaries, J. Guillet SJ, "Rejeté des hommes et de Dieu", in *Christus*, 13 (1966), pp. 83-100.

37. Cassiodorus, *In Psalm. 132*, I, CCSL 98, p. 1206: "Illi in uno habitant qui eremi solitudines pervagantur; qui, quamvis corpore videantur discreti, fidei tamen concordia non probantur esse divisi". Among the other monastic authors of the Middle Ages, see Baldwin of Ford, *De vita cenobitica*, PL 204, 548: "Amor solitarius ipse sibi cruciatus est et quodammodo seipsum odit, cum omnino nolit esse solitarius, ne non sit mutuus"; Adam of Perseigne *Epist.*, 5, PL 211, 596; ed. J. Bouvet, in SCh 66 (1960) letter 9, 91, p. 158.: "Nihil certe tam facit ad amoris negotium quam solitarium esse, id est monachum. Nam religiosa et quieta monachi conversatio ipsa est quam sanctus amor desiderat solitudo."

Christ, it is, as was his whole being, as his whole existence expressed, mediation, encounter, shouldering the burden, accepting responsibility, offering, reconciliation, union with all and, with them and for them, access to the Father.

Concretely, monasticism will be able to contribute—and is already contributing—to the dialogues of Christianity with other religions, especially, without question, those of the Far East, and to the dialogue between Catholicism and other Christian confessions.[38] But its role will always go beyond what can be seen of it; in the spiritual dimension it is, like God, invisible and universal.

In bringing man nearer to God, if only in a small number of individuals, the contemplative monastic life brings man nearer to himself and to everyone else.

Who would dare assert that prayer, even the prayer of a being isolated from the community, is not valuable on the entire cosmic scale, on the whole evolutionary scale if not on the limited scale of humanity at a given moment? Isn't it in the mystical experience of these solitary beings that nature seeks out and tries out new processes of thought in order to accomplich that 'translation' of the religious archetype into conscious symbols, so as in the end to enable man as a species to understand what evolution demands of him?

And then, without going so far as that, should society not encourage this search of some among us towards the deepening of themselves? As long as man devotes some of his zeal to encouraging the efforts of certain others to find means to set man against himself (by research in armanents, for example), will it not be highly desirable that there should exist simultaneously a handful of living creatures who will consecrate their lives to meditating on the true vocation of man? [39]

38. On the subject of the Far East, see the recent volume of Dom Bede Griffiths, *Christian Ashram, Essays towards a Hindu-Christian Dialogue*, (London, 1966); the last of the "essays" is entitled "The Future of the Church", pp. 243-249.

39. Jean E. Charon, *L'homme à sa découverte* (Paris, 1963) p. 136.

Forecast

We already know that tomorrow will be neither like yesterday nor like today. But what will the monk of tomorrow be? Who can foresee it? The Holy Spirit is free with his gifts, and he has the right to surprise us. Who could have foretold the grace of an Antony, a Pachomius, a Benedict, a Bernard? Nearer home, the mission of a Dom Guéranger, a Père Muard, a Lambert Beauduin? The monks of tomorrow will be diverse, as those of yesterday have been. But we can see that more and more they will be monks, in forms which will vary with continents and cultures, and with the social environment in every type of civilization. It would not be surprising if there were founders or reformers among them. There will be in any case—and there are already—renewers. Will they be exceptional men? There is nothing to rule it out. But, increasingly, responsibilities will be collective, shared by whole areas.

Ideas or plans will not be the guides, but fervent groups, determined, enthusiastic communities. Nothing will be accomplished on the basis of nostalgia for the past, still less of resentment of the past, but by a leap towards the Eternal. The future will belong to the young, to those who, whatever their age, have received the Holy Spirit and have kept, have cultivated, that freshness, that ardor, that sense of going forward, without which institutions can continue, can grow old, can almost outlive themselves, but cannot live, grow, and develop. Bringing legislation up to date, still less defending it, is not enough. Not that institutions are becoming redundant; they remain necessary. But they are body to a spirit without which laws would be no more than dessicated bones.

Much of the work done by monks in other periods of history, in other types of civilization, may well pass into other hands. Already the task of putting the liturgical reform into effect is falling on those responsible for pastoral ministry. The pictures of the learned Benedictine, the librarian, archivist and palaeographer, or of the liqueur manufacturer, run a grave risk of being shoved out among the pictures of

Epinal. Amateurishness in all fields will be ruled out. People will only be taken seriously if they have a skill, if they are specialists in a discipline or function for which nobody else in the Church or in the city is trained. We have already seen that monks specialize in the search for God. Will they, in addition, have some new function? There is nothing to rule it out absolutely, although increasing subject specialization would rather lead one to believe that they will come more and more to grips with the peculiar demands of their vocation, which will require of them a human balance and other aptitudes whose prevalence cannot be guaranteed.

Saints and men of genius will doubtless be, as always, rare among them. But it will be harder for all the others to remain average monks, to keep that *aliquid honestatis* which St Benedict demanded, if the environment becomes more opaque to what is spiritual, more resistant to what is religious. The call may become more exacting, perseverance more costly, numbers consequently more limited. At all events this situation will only encourage a more intimate participation in the mystery of the cross of Christ, and, accordingly, in his redemption and in his resurrection, and a more intense communion in the work of the salvation of the world.

PART TWO:

SKETCHES OF MONKS

THE RELIGIOUS UNIVERSE OF ST COLUMBAN*

HAS THE LAST WORD BEEN SAID about St Columban? His biography and the chronology of his itineraries have been the subject of historical research. His influence in very diverse fields has been illustrated. The authenticity and the textual tradition of the documents about or by him have been examined by philologists. And yet, there remains perhaps material for what is called today a study of mentality. The teaching of St Columban is transmitted to us by his writings.[1] But it is above all thanks to the *Vita Columbani,* which Jonas, a monk of Bobbio who had not known him, wrote ten years or so after his death, that his religious psychology and that of his circle are known to us.[2] This account gives us as much information about the practices of the monastery and of the age when it was composed as it does about the hero who is its subject.[3] The limits of its value and its objectivity were defined by its editor, Bruno Krusch, in an excellent preface from a period when people still knew how to write Latin. We can explore this long hagiographical text here not as a source of information on the actions of Columban, but as a witness to the behavior and inward attitudes that his biographer attributed to him, thoughts which were familiar to Columban and to the monastery in which and for which he worked.

* Published in *Revue d'ascétique et de mystique,* 42 (1966) pp. 15-30.

1. It is in light of these that I attempted to characterize his teaching in *La spiritualité du Moyen Age* (Paris, 1961) pp. 47-55.
2. See B. Krusch, *Ionae Vitae sanctorum Columbani, Vedasti, Iohannis,* in *MGH Scriptores rerum Germanicarum* (Hanover-Leipzig, 1905) p. 240, note 1.
3. Ibid., p. 42

The most general impression which forces itself upon a reader of the *Life* of St Columban is that, contrary to what might be expected from a legend, this text is full of life. It describes actions far more than ideas. He speaks of souls, and of different things and creatures that cause them to react. A whole *universe* is thus evoked, and because it is considered in its relation to God, it is a *religious* universe. We are invited to follow a route which goes from matter to God, from creation to the Creator and Saviour. Nature and animals, men and angels, God and the saints are there present, and the relations St Columban has with them all are marked by both violence and gentleness.[4] Let us consider each of these realms in which the contradictory personality of the founder of Luxeuil and Bobbio moved.

Nature

It is difficult for us, in our age of urban civilization, in our cultivated countryside, where all the soil has been tidied up and put under the control of man, to imagine what life could be like in an untamed world. To have spent some time in tropical Africa, to have measured there the effects of tornadoes and drought, to have seen, in monasteries, monkeys protecting fowls against boas, helps one to grasp the importance of natural setting. When Jonas described the rapid waters of the river Bobbio becoming, in the thaw and rainy season, a torrent which bore away boulders, uprooted trees, and threatened to carry off the monastery mill,[5] you can well believe that he had seen what he was writing about. Throughout the *Life*, water plays an important part. The biography is very largely an account of voyages by sea or waterways, particularly on the Loire and the Rhine. But eighteen other watercourses are mentioned, from the Aubertin and the Aubois to the Trebbia and the Vienne. Six

---

4. Ibid., pp. 53, 55-57, 162, note 3, *et passim*.
5. *Vita Columbani,* II 2, ed. Krusch. p. 233. The *Vita* will henceforward be quoted in this edition (pp. 1-294), without further references other than the book (in Roman numerals), then the chapter, and finally the page.

times it mentions a skiff, *scapha*, and one long chapter recounts the "naval itinerary" of a boat which reached port without having its tiller held, simply by following the current. True the description includes a phrase from St Jerome —*pennigero volatu*—which reminds us that literature brings to these recollections an element of artifice.[6] Six times the Atlantic is named, three times the Gulf of Brittany; the rowers and their art—*remigera arte*—are mentioned on three occasions. Similes from the sea are not lacking. In this 'floating' world harassed by tornadoes, faith is threatened by the violent blasts of tempests.[7]

There is rain,[8] and a mill which the stream sets in motion,[9] water which was miraculously turned into milk,[10] and, for drinking, there is a spoon, that is, the "cockle shell" whose shape it takes.[11] And here, at Luxeuil-les-Bains, are those "hot waters" which had formerly been used for thermal treatment and which had become the subject of superstitious rites.[12] In recording this, Jonas echoes the memory of the *fontanalia*, those feasts in which the amazing combination of water, which is normally cold, with fire emanating from celestial thunderbolts was celebrated.[13] In the eleventh century, a successor of St Columban, the Abbé Dogon, was to restore hot baths in the monastery of Luxeuil. After all, hadn't a Council under Charlemagne authorized monks to take the waters and recommended it during Lent? Later many other monks—Benedictines of Canigou and Saint-Amand-les-Eaux, Vallombrosians and Camaldolese, not to

6. I, 22, pp. 200-203.
7. I, 1, p. 152. B. Krusch, *Praefatio* p. 31, quotes this phrase from a letter of St Columbanus, ed. MGH, Epp., III, p. 170: "Vigilate, quia mare procellosum est et flabris exasperatur feralibus; ideo audeo timidus nauta clamare: Vigilate, quia aqua iam intravit in ecclesiae navem, et navis periclitatur."
8. I, *Hymnus*, p. 277, 4.
9. II, 2, p. 233.
10. II, 21, p. 277.
11. II, 9, p. 249 and note 4.
12. I, 10, p. 169. We know that St Columbanus and his disciples usually established their monasteries on sites that had been occupied previously.
13. See P. Balme, *Essai sur le rattachement abusif de nos sanctuaires et de nos pèlerinages aux anciens cultes des fontaines sacrées* (Clermont-Ferrand, n. d.) pp. 52-56.

mention the Celestins of Vichy—were to provide facilities for thermal baths in their hospitals.[14]

The sun is called Phoebus[15] and mention is made of Titan;[16] mythology here is mingled with the observation of nature. Precious stones are enumerated according to the Apocalypse.[17] The wind which shakes the tall plane trees is described in virgilian terms—another indication of the part played by literary reminiscences in these descriptions.[18] Side by side with these clichés, what a lot had been actually seen and experienced! The landscapes of the Juras and the Vosges, the earth, the fields, the furrows, the harvest, the hard labor of breaking new ground, form a real part of the conditions of life. The same way with the wine-harvest: Jura wine is kept in vats with precise names, *tonna, tiptrum, cupa, gilbo.* Other items of food mentioned are butter, flour, peppers and, especially, those little reddish berries, bilberries or blueberries, which were called *bullugae* and which are still named in the *patois* of the Vosges, *"belues".*[19] And let us not forget the granary nor the smell of cider, nor the *cervisia* or barley beer, a kind of beer mentioned seven times. All this gives the setting in which the life of St Columban unfolded, and which living creatures are now going to animate.

14. Some facts and texts are quoted by H. Guitard, *Le prestigieux passé des eaux thermales* (Paris, 1951) pp. 42-45 and p. 269-270.

15. I, 2, p. 155.

16. I, 2, p. 153.

17. I, *Versus,* pp. 225-226.

18. II, 9, p. 168, note 1; I, 27, p. 216, note 1. Krusch does not suggest any equivalent of the world *bulluga*. Du Cange, *Glossarium,* ed. Favre (Niort, 1883) vol. I, knows the term in our text and gives it the forms *bulgula, bolluca, bulluga*; to this last article, the editor of 1883, p. 778, adds: "Hinc forte vox apud vulgum *Breluque* quasi *Buluque* pro re minori". Jean-Joseph Claude, known as Claude Descharrières, in his *Histoire du Val d'Ajol* [MS preserved at the Mairie of Val d'Ajol] (1925) ch. XLVIII, pp. 162-164, mentions bilberries among the shrubs that grow in the Vosges forest, in the region of Remiremont, Plombieres, Le Val d'Ajol and Luxeuil: "arbustes: génévrier, putiet, sureau, houx, épines de différentes espèces, coudrier, ronce, framboisier, myrtille (vaccinium myrtillus). Ce dernier arbuste êtait appelé en basse latinité Bulgula, que le patois lorrain traduit par brimbelle (cf Jonas, *Vita Columbani,* cap. VIII). Le peuple les appelle Belues." This term is still that of the patois of the Val d'Ajol, which pronounces it B'lues. This reference and this last detail were supplied by a "vosgien" colleague, Dom A. Galli, whom I thank.

Animals

Animals are present everywhere in life in the wild, that is to say, life in the jungle, in forests whose fauna are constantly a danger.

One day as the man of God was walking along the paths of a dense forest, carrying a book and discussing holy Scripture in himself, suddenly his thought burst in upon him: Would he choose rather to be a prey to the insults and injustices of men or to suffer the cruelty of the wild beasts? . . . . And he said to himself that it is better to bear the ferocity of the beasts and not to give to others occasion for sin, than the fury of men accompanied by danger of their souls.[20]

These animals haunted his imagination. How many similes he borrowed from them! Pardoned sinners are like ewes snatched from the jaws of wolves.[21] He who detracts from the observance is like a rodent whose teeth try to devour the good reputation of the monks, or like a grunting hog.[22] Errors are words infected by the poison of the serpent.[23] To leave the religious life and return to the world is to behave like the dog who goes back to his vomit. This strong image may come from the Book of Proverbs.[24] But the description of the hog whose snout searches out food seems to come from observation.[25]

For the man of God, the beasts are not merely elements of his everyday surroundings. No more are they enemies to be feared, for they become friends. It was told that Columban had often been seen commanding wild creatures, beasts and birds, to come to him. They all obeyed immediately and he caressed them. The birds played around him as kittens play around their master. A baby squirrel got into the habit of coming down from the trees and settling in his hand. He

20. I, 8, p. 166.
21. II, 1, p. 232.
22. II, 9, p. 248.
23. II, 10, p. 253.
24. II, 19, pp. 271-272; see *Prov.* 26, 11.
25. II, 22, p. 278.

would put it on his neck and let it clamber over him, and from time to time its head would be seen peeping through the folds of his habit.[26] As might be foreseen, fish were no less eager to respond to the orders of St Columban, as a miraculously plentiful catch witnessed.[27] In his journeys, he was careful to allow the mounts the rest they needed,[28] and they repaid him when they guided towards him a visitor who had lost his way.[29]

On the day when he had generously agreed to be eaten by wild beasts rather than succumb to the sin of men, he was rewarded, by seeing twelve wolves coming up all around him. He did not move, repeating a verse of Psalm 38, "O my God, be not far from me, make haste to help me, O Lord of my salvation". The wolves came up and sniffed his garments. He remained motionless and fearless, and watched them go peacefully away again. A little farther on, he found a bear in his cave. He told him to leave those parts and not come back again, and gentleness was communicated to the animal, who obeyed.[30] Specialists in pre-history and ethnology have shown the importance of the bear in the life of primitive peoples. One of them went so far as to write: "Where man is compelled to adapt himself to cold, the bear has had a role of first importance in his metaphysics".[31] The same author has collected the rudiments of a vast "eulogy of the bear", that animal that seems to know everything,[32] who is most like man and who has an astonishing memory.

Where man leaves him in peace, as in the reserves in the U.S.A., he becomes bold and even friendly. Whoever lives on an understanding with the bear has nothing to fear from

26. I, 17, pp. 185-186. Cf I *Hymnus*, p. 228.8.
27. I, 11, p. 172; see Krusch, *Praef.*, p. 26.
28. II, 5, p. 237.
29. I, 7, p. 165.
30. I, 8, pp. 166-167.
31. I. Lissner, *Dieu était là. Les croyances et les pratiques religieuses de l'homme pré-historique éclairées par celles des peuples primitifs d'aujourd'hui* (Paris, 1965) p. 67. On the fact that "human palaeontology" can help us to know certain aspects of man and his life in the Middle Ages, see M. R. Sauter, "Quelques contributions de l'anthropologie à la connaissance du haut Moyen Age", in *Mélanges offerts à M. Paul-E. Martin* (Geneva, 1961) pp. 1-18.
32. Lissner, *Dieu était là,* pp. 165-169.

him, and in Siberia innumerable tales are current whose heroes are 'grateful bears' who have become the 'friends' of those who have saved their lives.[33]

These facts help us to understand, perhaps even to believe probable, certain tales in the *Life* of St Columban. He too, in the snowy forests, met bears. One day, he saw one preparing to devour the body of a stag killed by some wolves. Anxious not to lose a hide needed for leather with which to make shoes for the monks, the saint ordered the bear to go away, an order he carried out straightway without the slightest murmur. Even the vultures refrained from coming near.[34] Another day, when the time had come to pick the plums the brothers liked so much, they noticed that a bear had got there first who seemed to be leaving them nothing. They went and told the man of God, who decided to share: they were to leave one section of the trees for the bear and pick from the other section for themselves. And from then on the animal never went to feed in the places which were forbidden him.[35]

Finally, there were birds. One day Columban had laid the gloves which he wore for manual work on a stone of the refectory door. A crow came and took away one of them. After the meal, the theft was noticed. All the brethren began asking one another who the culprit might be, but the abbot thought it could only be that creature who left the ark of Noah and did not return. He threatened to stop feeding its young unless the thief flew swiftly to make restitution. Everyone waited. The crow arrived and, not content to put down the glove, instead of flying off, he stayed, waiting for his penance.[36] In another situation, during a famine, the miracle of the quails of Egypt appeared to be repeated: the birds came and allowed themselves to be caught, and never had the monks eaten such good game.[37] Should we be surprised at this friendship between the inhabitants of the sky

33. Ibid., p. 168.
34. I, 17, p. 181.
35. II, 27, p. 216.
36. I, 15, pp. 178-179.
37. I, 27, p. 215.

and a man whose name meant the dove? *Columbanus etenim, qui et Columba.*[38]

Men

In this wild and domestic natural world, in the midst of this violent and friendly animal life, what were the human beings like? By temperament, they were in harmony with the harshness of everything. Their hearts were capable of atrocities, but they could respond to kindness. Jonas' tale of the adventure which befell the monk Meroveus says a great deal about their feelings. When he had set fire to the divinity who was the object of a woodland cult, he was bound, beaten, and wounded with arrows. They wanted to drown him, but the river refused to receive him. So they had the idea of putting such a heavy weight on his body that it would make him sink to the bottom of the waters.[39] And yet, the same generation was able to show affection. The parents of a monk, suffering at being separated from their son, insisted on his coming to see them, and he was granted leave for this from the Abbot Attala.[40] Abbot Attala, before dying, consoled those around him.[41] Another, Theodald, full of gentleness all his life, died joyfully, radiating loving kindness, to the sound of a melody.[42]

Jonas contrasts with these men of God the obstinate sinners. The cruelties of Brunehild are compared with those of Jezebel.[43] The king Theoderic is called a dog.[44] Columban

---

38. I, 1, p. 152; see also I, 17, p. 183. A study of the same kind as that which has been attempted here has been sketched out, for a later period of the Middle Ages (tenth-twelfth centuries), by P. Rousset, "L'homme en face de la nature à l'époque romane", in *Mélanges offertes à M. Paul-E. Martin* pp. 39-48; it treats a man "at once rooted and immersed in a Nature that is still wild" (p. 39), Nature "at once threatening and benevolent, terrible and gentle" (p. 48). On "the place of animals in nature and the links of solidarity which bound them to man", especially in hagiographic literature, see pp. 45-48.

39. II, 25, pp. 289-290.

40. II, 5, p. 237.

41. II, 6, p. 240.

42. II, 25, p. 292.

43. I, 18, p. 187.

44. I, 22, p. 202.

did not spare him accusations, even insults. One would think from his violent expressions that he wanted to provoke him. But he condemned the stupidity and irreligion of Theodebert in wanting to harm his enemy, the same Theoderic.[45] In order to get Attala to come and cure a sick child, the parents upbraided the holy man with "terrible oaths".[46] The Abbot Euthasius, for his part, was able to give "terrible" reprimands.[47] The expressions which speak of pestilence,[48] ridicule,[49] madness,[50] and ravings,[51] convey the same violence of emotion. Krusch is probably right when he says that Columban sometimes behaved towards the king with more importunity than was strictly necessary,[52] and he calls him a "vehement and ferocious man by nature". (*Homo vehemens feroxque natura*). At least he was able to oppose fearlessly (*imperterritus*) those who did not agree with him and he maintained frankness towards everyone.[53] One day he heard of a prison full of men condemned to death. He went there. He preached. The prisoners promised to amend their ways if they were released. Columban freed them, took them to the church and defended them against their warders. And from then on, nobody dared mistreat them.[54] This way of protecting captives had always been the symbol in monasticism of that interior liberty which the man of God possesses and communicates to others.[55] It was also a sign of charity on his part.

The same combination of gentleness and vigor appears in the women of whom Jonas speaks. A stream of invective

45. I, 28, pp. 218-219.
46. II, 5, p. 236.
47. II, 7, p. 243.
48. I, 25, p. 208: I, 25, p. 213; II, 24, p. 288.
49. II, 9, p. 247.
50. II, 10, p. 253.
51. Ibid.
52. *Praef.*, p. 13.
53. Ibid., p. 33.
54. I, 19, pp. 191-193.
55. On this subject, pending a fuller study, I have given a few indications under the title "L'obéissance, éducatrice de la liberté, dans la tradition monastique", in *La liberté évangelique, principes et pratique* (Paris, 1965), pp. 67-69.

which would be denounced as anti-feminist today was put in the mouth of a recluse, who addressed the young Columban (who had come to consult her) in these terms: "Dost thou not remember Adam, who fell because of Eve, Samson whom Delilah seduced, David who fell from his virtue because of the beauty of Bathsheba, Solomon who was led into error by love of women? "[56] One consecrated virgin, it is said, spoke with virility.[57] Several nuns were kept within the enclosure only by the three locked doors. One night they tried to escape by means of a ladder.[58] And yet, what a serene picture is painted of Ercantrude, mirror of purity, patience and gentleness! [59] How beautiful were the deaths of Deurechilde, Domma and two young Sisters! [60]

Such is the society which allows us to grasp the figure of St Columban. It belongs to him and it resembles him. He shared its roughness and harsh virtues, and like it he was sometimes capable of a delicacy most apparent in his relations with the Hereafter.

Saints and Angels

St Columban and Jonas of Bobbio lived with the invisible. The biographer was familiar with the saints; he claimed as his authority the great Latin Doctors who were the "pillars of the Churches in times of trouble."[61] He appealed to accounts of the exploits of St Antony, St Paul, St Hilarion and other ancient models of the monastic life.[62] He was inspired by Sulpicius Severus' memoirs of St Martin,[63] and his narrative

---

56. I, 3, pp. 156-157.
57. I, 10, p. 253.
58. II, 19, pp. 271-273; see *Praef.*, p. 43.
59. II, 13, pp. 262-263.
60. II, 15-16, pp. 264-268. [The French edition says *morts amères* where *morts amenes* was intended - ed.]
61. I, 1, p. 152.
62. Ibid., p. 151.
63. Ibid.

contains reminiscences of the *Life* of the Bishop of Tours. [64] St Columban, travelling on the Loire, made his boatmen stop in that town where he spent the night praying at the tomb of St Martin. [65] When he had left his family, he is said to have walked over the body of his mother who barred the way by which he was to leave. Was it he or was it his biographer who was inspired in this by the advice given Heliodorus by St Jerome? [66] Either way, Jonas was certainly familiar with the monastic texts of the hermit of Bethlehem. [67] He also set out to imitate characters mentioned in the Bible: Moses, [68] Jeremiah, [69] and Job. [70] Conversely, the example of Cain allowed him to castigate a fratricide. [71]

Among angels, not all remained faithful to God. It cannot be said that *diableries* hold a very important place in the life of St Columban. But the devil is present. He insulted the saint—who gave as good as he got—in the course of a confrontation in Paris. [72] Nearly twenty times, the obsessed and the possessed, diabolical ardor, rage, deceit and plague occur, the terrible features of the devil, [73] or the cunning of "the old serpent". [74] These are allusions rather than descriptions. They are enough to show that in the eyes of St Columban and his sons, the powers of evil really existed and were active in the world, but that we should not exaggerate their influence.

Good also existed in the persons of the angels. They were by no means models of disembodied virtues, but of virtues thoroughly human, serenity of character and kindness in speech. [75] Their voices were heard at the death of monks. [76]

64. I, 3, p. 155, 1.6; I, 29, p. 219, 1.20. See Sulpicius Severus, *Vita S. Martini*, IV, 5, CSEL, p. 114.
65. I, 22, p. 201.
66. I, 3, p. 157, and note 1.
67. I, 22, p. 201, note 2; I, 27, p. 217, note 1.
68. II, 9, p. 246.
69. Ibid.
70. II, 10, p. 253; II, 13, p. 262.
71. II, 9, p. 246.
72. I, 25, p. 208.
73. Cf pp. 357-358: *Daemon.*
74. II, I, p. 231; II, 19, p. 272; II, 22, p. 278.
75. I, 5, p. 162.
76. II, 17, p. 270.

They intervened as witnesses of God, whose glory they sing.[77] Thus every creature is seen in relation to the Creator. They help man or hinder him in his progress towards the Lord. But in the end, everything depends on the personal encounter of the Christian with his Saviour.

God

How can we go to God, unite ourselves with him, receive him within us? Columban and Jonas give to this question the traditional answer: they teach faith in the words of God, the efficacy of sacramental grace, the necessity of prayer and finally the cultivation of the virtues, especially those of charity and mortification.

As has already been seen, Scripture provides the biographer with his chief examples of virtues or vices. More than seventy Biblical quotations have been pointed out by the editor of the *Vita Columbani*, to which may be added unidentified reminiscences.[78] One account of a *miracle* is so directly inspired by a passage of St Matthew that it has more value as a hagiographic theme than as historical fact.[79] The "pages", the "treasures", the "order", the "learning" of the Scriptures are praised more than once.[80] Columban was steeped in its study,[81] he loved to "satiate himself with the word of life".[82] He discussed it with himself.[83] He made it a remedy for heresy.[84] Willesuide, the nun, acquired an astonishing knowledge of the books of Moses and the mysteries of the Gospel.[85] The Psalms were especially beloved, a staple diet for reading,[86] or for the Office.[87]

77. II, 20, p. 275.
78. For example I, 20, p. 170, 1.5 (cf Acts 4, 32); II, 15, p. 265, 1.12 (cf Acts 7, 55).
79. I, 17, p. 183; cf Mt 14, 21.
80. See p. 364: *Scripturarum pagina*, etc . . .
81. I, 3, p. 157.
82. I, 6, p. 163.
83. I, 8, p. 168.
84. I, 30, p. 221.
85. II, 17, pp. 268-269.
86. I, 3, p. 158.
87. II, 16, p. 267; II, 19, p. 274; II, 23, p. 284; II, 25, p. 291; I, 3, p. 158.

If God reveals his truth in Scripture, he imparts his life in the sacraments, and primarily in the grace of baptism, which is several times described as a sacred bath which purifies man from sin.[88] The celebration of the Eucharist, of *missarum solemnia*,[89] involves the participation in the body and blood of the Lord.[90] Jonas puts into the mouth of a nun singing after communion an antiphon of thanksgiving which is found in the Bangor antiphoner: "take into yourself the sacred Body and Blood of the Lord and Saviour unto eternal life".[91] In accordance with the tradition expressed, for example, in the Rule of St Benedict, St Columban limited the exercise of the priesthood of monks to the needs of community worship: "to the priests, except in the case of a particular need, he gave no special authority over either the people or the things in the monastery."[92]

It is known that St Columban, like the Celtic Christians of his time, attached great importance to penance, which normally fell to bishops and priests to impose upon sinners in order to reconcile them to the Church.[93] Monks had always been asked to admit even slight faults and sinful thoughts to their spiritual father. In Ireland this secret confession had been associated with the sacrament of penance, and under the influence of Columban and his kind, this custom gradually penetrated the continent. This confession even became frequent, and was followed by punishments which were at times harsh.[94] Among themselves, the nuns practised it up to three times a day.[95] It was the "mother", that is the abbess, who heard the avowals[96] which formed a preparation for the reception of the Body of Christ.[97] But the temptation could come from the devil to hide serious faults, that is, those of

88. See p. 355: *Baptismus*; p. 360: *Lavacrum*.
89. See p. 361.
90. II, 16, p. 266.
91. II, 16, p. 267, and note 1.
92. Krusch, *Praef.*, p. 40.
93. See Krusch, *Praef.*, p. 27.
94. Ibid., pp. 22-24; cf. p. 357: *Confessio*.
95. II, 19, p. 272, and note 2.
96. II, 17, p. 269; II, 22, p. 279.
97. II, 13, p. 263; II, 19, p. 274.

one's past life, or those committed in everyday frailty.[98]

If there are frequent references to the sign of the cross,[99] and if we are told that it was often made,[100] and that it was used as one would use a weapon,[101] this is because the Crucified was the vanquisher of the fault of the first Adam.[102] The devotion paid to this standard of his glory is full of hope, a source of joy. But the Cross was also the symbol of the renunciation which they came to practise in the society of monks.[103] To take up the Cross and to follow Christ carrying it stripped of everything—there we have the whole of Columban's program,[104] and that of his successor Bertulf.[105] In all this there is nothing which is not in a real sense religious.

The conception of the monastic life was equally traditional. It was that of a life of prayer and asceticism, lived in community but far from the world, and at times involving complete solitude. The vocabulary used in speaking of it is that of earlier monasticism: there is mention of "devoting oneself to" prayer,[106] of staying and remaining (*resedere*),[107] of singing psalms.[108] Jonas readily applied to the activity of prayer the word *desudare*, to sweat,[109] because there was nothing more worthy of effort.[110] They sat down to read.[111] Attala did not think of setting out on a journey without taking books. Columban prepared himself for Sundays and feast days by withdrawing to a hermitage in order to be free from

98. II, 19, pp. 272-273.
99. Cf. p. 364: *Signum crucis.*
100. II, 9, p. 249.
101. II, 19, p. 274.
102. II, 6, p. 239.
103. I, 4, pp. 158-159.
104. I, 6, p. 163.
105. II, 23, p. 281.
106. I, 4, p. 259; I, 7, p. 164; I, 17, p. 185.
107. I, 6, p. 163; I, 9, p. 168; I, 10, p. 169. It is curious that these terms, so characteristic of the vocabulary of the contemplative life in monasticism, should not have deserved a place in the copious *Index rerum et verborum* compiled by Krusch at the end of his edition.
108. "Psallendi officio", II, 23, p. 284; see above, note 87.
109. II, 5, p. 237 - though the term had acquired an attenuated meaning.
110. II, 9, p. 251.
111. I, 20, p. 194. (twice); I, 28, p. 218; see *Praef.*, p. 28.

everyday cares and dealings with men.[112]

The ascetism was strict. It naturally included fasting,[113] which did not exclude on certain days of rejoicing "singing at table".[114] "Contempt for this life" was referred to without emphasis.[115] The virtues admired were simplicity,[116] and the humility which liberates from vainglory.[117] An exercise in mortification known to the whole of ancient and medieval monasticism was peregrination, voluntary exile, which gave occasion to travel in discomfort and poverty. This form of ascetism is found from the beginning to the end of St Columban's life:[118] leaving one's native soil,[119] imitating Abraham who went out from his country, his people, and the house of his father,[120] not turning back,[121] behaving like a stranger,[122] persevering in the condition of an exile.[123] All these phrases betray a conviction dear to St Columban and his circle.

Peregrination for them as for the whole of the tradition was a means of isolating themselves from the society of men. Jonas readily used the vocabulary of the desert. The *eremus* was characterized by a term inherited from antiquity: it is "vast".[124] You live there in a "cell".[125] As we have seen, Columban withdrew in this way fairly often,[126] and the spiritual benefit which he derived from it was expressed in two words from Cassian: *heremi libertas.*[127] The fidelity of Jonas

112. I, 9, p. 167.

113. On the food of the Columbanian monks, see Krusch, *Praef.,* p. 30.

114. Witness the *Versus in festivitate eius (Columbani) ad mensam canendi*, K. I, p. 224.

115. II, 1, p. 231.

116. II, 25, p. 292.

117. Krusch, p. 26.

118. I, 3, p. 156.

119. Ibid., p. 157.

120. I, 4, p. 159.

121. I, 20, p. 195.

122. I, 21, p. 199.

123. I, 24, p. 207; I, 27, p. 212.

124. I, 6, p. 163 (twice); I, 7, p. 165; I, 8, p. 167.

125. I, 3, p. 156; II, 6, pp. 238-239.

126. I, 28, p. 218; see above, note 112; see Krusch, *Praef.,* p. 17.

127. II, 1, p. 231; cf Cassian, *Conl.,* XIX, 5, 6, CSEL 13, p. 540.

of Bobbio to the hermitage of ancient monasticism can be seen even in the details of his language.

The body of monks lived in community and formed a *coenobii collegium*,[128] with a single will.[129] The power of the abbot was described as a "monarchy",[130] or as a "ministry", a service.[131] When the number of monks rose, Columban divided them into groups. At the head of each he placed leaders, *praepositi,* reserving the right to visit them in turn.[132] At the beginning of his vocation to exile, after having spent many years in the monastery, he felt the desire to occupy himself not only for his own benefit, but for the good of others.[133] And, in fact, every time he arrived in a new place, he proclaimed the Gospel.[134] But his life was not organized for preaching, not even at the time when, having had to leave Luxeuil, he became a temporary missionary,[135] "in spite of himself", as has been said.[136] B. Krusch has written with some objectivity that he "had by no means left his native land in order to convert the heathen, but that he had come to this later". And indeed he could be accused, Krusch adds, of not persevering in what he had undertaken.[137] In the steps of St Columban, moreover, St Attala did all he could to discourage the monk Agrestius from going out to preach. Having no success, he let him to go. The apostle first tried in Bavaria but achieved no success. Then he went to Aquilea, where he fell into schism and heresy.[138] This example, quoted with satisfaction by Jonas, insures that the bulk of St Columban's sons will not be shown as missionary monks.

128. I, 10, p. 169.
129. I, 5, p. 161.
130. II, 10, p. 252 (*monarchiae institutis*: the variant *monachiae* is also given—translator)
131. I, 9, p. 168.
132. I, 10, p. 170.
133. I, 4, p. 159.
134. I, 5, p. 161.
135. I, 27, p. 213; I, 27, pp. 216-217.
136. The expression is that of P. Riché, *Education et culture dans l'Occident médiéval. VIᵉ - VIIᵉ siècles* (Paris, 1962) p. 375.
137. *Praef.,* p. 33.
138. II, 9, pp. 246-247.

Conclusion

The part played by St Columban and his sons was not only that of converting to the faith, when the occasion arose, those who did not yet believe, but also of christianizing the baptized who lived like pagans.

> Those who had been washed by the bath of regeneration, but who were kept in bondage by profane error, he, by his warnings, like a good shepherd, brought back into the lap of the church.[139]

This society, Christian in part, was also partly unbelieving. As always, there had to be a struggle for the good and the truth. St Columban had the temperament and the grace of a fighter: he was a soldier,[140] a conscript, a volunteer enlisted for the duration of the war.[141] The very name of his disciple Congal meant "fighter".[142] The monks and nuns were described ten times as making up a troop, a "cohort".[143] A vocabulary passed on in these expressions from the literary tradition must be taken into account, but the fact remains that the dominant feature in the character of the abbot of Luxeuil, the one which Jonas of Bobbio emphasizes in ending the *Life*, because it sums up all the others, in his vigor, his strength, his *strenuitas*.[144]

We have seen how this vigor could reach the point of violence, and could be accompanied by harshness. This was due, in part, to the character of St Columban. An admirer of Irish monasticism, who often had the kindness to speak to me of it, the late Fr. Paul Grosjean, a Bollandist, used to like to draw a contrast between the culture of many Celtic monks—their love of study pursued by the means at their disposal—and the tendency peculiar to St Columban—to sacri-

---

139. I, 27, p. 214.

140. I, 3, p. 155: in the phrase: "sed cum se egregius milis tantis *pilis* undique urgueri conspiceret . . .", the editor gives, for *pilis,* the variant *pliis*: one wonders whether not to read *praeliis.* (Indeed one variant given is *pliss*—translator).

141. I, 4, p. 159.

142. Krusch, p. 158, note 3.

143. See p. 356: *Cohors.*

144. I, 29, p. 224.

fice erudition to efficiency. A man of action first and foremost, he was without any doubt the saint needed by his time. He made himself all things to all men: one might even add, a barbarian among barbarians. Surely it is one of the signs of the church's vitality that, in her saints as in her legislation, she has been able to adapt herself to every historical situation, endeavoring always to raise the human condition out of its own heaviness, and in some small measure succeeding?

Don't we find a reflection of this partial success in the *Life* of St Columban? To the same degree in which struggles and invective occupy the first book, in which the life of the saint himself is recorded, serenity dominates the second, which is devoted to his disciples. [145] One has the impression that after this saint-for-violent-times, everything calmed down. The women in particular, by the gentleness of their character, make up for the impression of aggressiveness left by St Columban. Certainly he had been the man of God needed by his time. This man of violence had prepared peace.

Jonas of Bobbio praised his gentleness and kindness: *Tu lenitate polles benignate clares.* [146] And he recorded that many men built and peopled monasteries "for love of Columban and his rule". [147] If St Columban, with less richness of character and less refinement of intellect than St Bernard, like him exercised great appeal, isn't it because, like Bernard, he was attractive to his contemporaries? He was able to touch in them a fibre which perhaps no longer vibrates in us, or which no longer has the same resonance. He knew how to give them a delicate conscience, [148] to prepare them to live with loving-kindness, [149] and to die to the sound of music. [150] Finally, interior balance surely remained the ideal to which everyone aspired? The portrait painted by Jonas of Attala, the first successor of St Columban at Bobbio, says a good

---

145. II, 10, p. 252: "Eusthasius mitis animi...”; II, 23, p. 283: "Honorius ... dulcedine et humilitate pollens ... dulcia promeret effamina...”
146. I, *Versus,* p. 225.
147. II, 10, p. 255.
148. See II, 1, p. 234.
149. II, 25, p. 292.
150. Ibid.

deal about the human qualities for which everyone still yearned and which they endeavoured to approach:

He was pleasant to all, remarkable for his fervor, and had an exceptional liveliness, and showed perfect charity to the poor and strangers. He was able to resist the proud, obey the humble, speak to the wise in their language and instruct the simple; he resolved difficult questions with sagacity, he was strong and vigorous against the attack of the heretics, he was brave in adversity, moderate in success, measured in all things and endowed with discretion. He overflowed with affection and with respect for his subordinates, with sound teaching for his disciples: around him nobody was sad or bored, or allowed himself to be puffed up with excessive elation.[151]

151. II, 4, p. 236. Since these pages were written, Don Michele Tosi has published at Piacenza in 1965 a new edition, with Italian translation, of the *Vita Columbani*, using the MS of the Metz Seminary (ninth century), to which I had drawn attention in *Analecta Bollandiana*, 73 (1955), p. 193-196.

SAINT MAJOLUS AND CLUNY*

DIVERSE SOURCES are at our disposal for becoming acquainted with the personality of St Majolus.[1] There are the non-Cluniac texts, originating from Peter Damian, Orderic Vitalis, or various chroniclers. The others are Cluniac. These are in the first instance charters and other diplomatic documents, and then the hagiographic texts. It is this last file, so instructive of the history, the legend and the portrait of St Majolus, which we will examine here. Of what papers does it consist? They are thirteen in number, and it will be sufficient here to indicate their chronological sequence.

We have first of all a fairly short letter on the death of Majolus, which occurred on 11 April, 994. This was written shortly after the event, perhaps by one of the abbots of the

---

* Paper read to the Congress held at Pavia in September 1967.

1. The most recent bibliography is that given by Dom J. Hourlier, art. "Mayeul (Saint)", in *Bibliotheca sanctorum*, vol. 10 (Rome, 1967) cc. 1261-1263. I wish to thank the author of this article, to whose advice the paper that follows owe much. A bibliography on Cluny and St Majolus has likewise been given by P. Zerbi, "I monasteri cittadini di Lombardia," in *Monasteri in Alta Italia dopo le invasioni saracene et magiari (sec. X-XII)*, (Turin, 1966) pp. 298-300. The most recent contribution to the biography of St Majolus deals with what may have been his birthplace (J. Barruol, "L'inscription médiévale du prieuré Saint-Symphorien près d'Apt", in *La Provence historique,* 15 (Aix, 1965) pp. 147-157; on pp. 152-153, there is a plate representing "the birthplace of St Majolus".

diocese of Rheims, and addressed to St Odilo.[2] Soon afterwards, Syrus, a monk of Cluny, told the life of the departed in a *Life,* the first version of which was edited, in the form of a second version, by the monk Aldebald, who then added various pieces of verse and borrowed from other sources, all of which resulted in yet a third edition.[3] These were used in the composition of an abridged *Life.*[4] In 1033 or later, St Odilo published a *Eulogy* of St Majolus.[5] After 1142, Cluny saw yet another *Life* appear, the work of the monk Nagoldus,[6] and still another, anonymous, one.[7] At a date after 994 a series of marvellous deeds or *Miracula* was collected.[8] In the eleventh century, hymns were composed with a view to the celebration of his feast.[9] Finally, on two successive occasions, notes on this abbot were introduced into the Chronicle of Cluny.[10] There is here an exceptionally abundant succession of hagiographic texts proceeding from the same milieu and reflecting a tradition which lived on there.

What value have they? Everything depend on Syrus. How much faith can we have in him? Discussions which have arisen over his objectivity have resulted in a fairly favorable

2. The general bibliography, as far as sources are concerned, is given in the *Bibliotheca hagiographica latina* (= BHL) (Brussels, 1900-1901) pp. 768-770, n. 5177-5187. The references to the different texts are given in the notes belonging to each. The first, the *Epistola de morte maioli,* has been edited by E. Sackur, "Ein Schreiben über den Tod des Maiolus von Cluny," in *Neues Archiv,* 16 (1890-1891) pp. 180-181.

3. Syrus, *Vita Maioli, libri* III, ed. G. Waitz, in MGH, 55, IV, pp. 650-655 (also PL 137, col. 745 sqq. Waitz' edition is incomplete—translator). On the successive versions, see L. Traube, "Abermals die Biographien des Majolus", in *Neues Archiv,* 17 (1891), pp. 402-407. This *Vita* will be designed by the name of its author, Syrus. K. Hallinger, *Gorze-Cluny,* Studia Anselmiana, 22 (Rome, 1950) p. 47, n. 10 has pointed out an example of "stylistic exaggeration" in Syrus.

4. *Vita brevior,* ed. in M. Marrier, *Bibliotheca Cluniacensis* (Paris, 1915) 1763-1782. This text will be designed by the abbreviation VB.

5. *Elogium ab Odilone,* ed. PL 142, 943.

6. Nagoldus, *Vita Maioli,* ed., AA SS, Maii II, 3rd. ed. pp. 657-667.

7. *Vita anonyma,* ed. *Bibl. Clun.* pp. 1783-1786.

8. *Miracula libri* II, ed. AA SS, Maii, II, 3rd ed., p. 690-698.

9. PL 142, 961-964. To the four hymns published there should be added that edited by G. Morin, "Le Passionaire d' Albert de Pontida et une hymne inédite de S. Odilon", in *Revue Bénédictine,* 38 (1926) pp. 56-57.

10. *Chronicon Cluniacense, Bibl. Clun.,* 1619-1620 (designated by *Chronicon* I) and 1635 (*Chronicon* II).

verdict, at least as far as chronology is concerned.[11] But did the author mean to write history, or draw a portrait, or merely illustrate the Cluniac way of life? Did he shuffle his own views in with the facts? Certainly he used themes and sources. He drew on Scripture, on *Lives* of St Benedict[12] and St Martin,[13] and on the Rule of St Benedict.[14] And yet he recorded facts which seem to have been drawn from life—for example, the confession of the Bishop of Coire is certainly what one would expect of a zealous prelate of the period.[15]

Let us examine the document left by Syrus and its successive accretions. This will not be the last word, but at least we shall know those things which the Cluniac tradition wanted to reserve. We shall discover some unexpected aspects which the ordinary historiographer scarcely mentions. These themes will be set out in an order corresponding to their apparent importance, according to the place they hold in the first texts and to the frequency with which they are mentioned. In each case, the chronological order of the sources will be followed.

From the outset of Syrus' Life, the place given to academic study is noteworthy: it is considered the answer to Majoulus' destiny, a preparation for his future function, and a privileged gift of God.[16] This is said of the first education he received at his native Valensole, where he was born about 906-915, but it is said again in connection with his stay at Mâcon where, after the death of his parents, he took refuge with a cousin who recognized his capabilities and wanted to

11. See L. Bourdon, "Les voyages de S. Mayeul en Italie", in *Mélanges d' archéologie et d'historire publiées par l'Ecole française de Rome,* 43 (1926) p. 62.

12. For example, Syrus I, 3; III, 5.

13. For example, Syrus I, 9; III, 11.

14. For example, Syrus I, 5-6.

15. See below, Conclusion, on the subject of the account of Majolus' old age. On the subject of the confession of the bishop of Coire, Syrus II, 16.: "Et studuit confiteri delicta, in multis se confitens offendisse, maxime in elatione, et quod boni egerat, per inanem gloriam se perdidisse timebat".

16. Syrus I, 3.

make a monk of him.[17] There is fresh emphasis on the question of when Majolous spent time at Lyons. There is mention of "philosophy", of the "philosophers", of "zeal (*studium*) for the liberal arts", of "competence (*peritia*) in the liberal disciplines", of the "schools", of the "gymnasium", of "eloquence", of the "arts" which the young man "professes", of the zeal, the desire, the ardor with which he was "touched" (*artium profitendarum afficeretur studio*), and even of a final examination (*examinatus*).[18] Farther on, there was a question of the "literary profession".[19] In the Eulogy, St Odilo was to say that "human knowledge" was subordinate to "spiritual understanding", to the "research" pursued in Holy Scripture.[20] He came back to "ecclesiastical studies", "spiritual learning", "humanities", "philosophy", and "liberal studies".[21] And Nagoldus expressed himself in the same terms.[22] There is a revealing insistence on their interest in the intellectual life.

This interest was maintained thanks to books and it is understandable that they are mentioned several timse. Majolus looked after them as librarian and above all as a reader. In 948 he was appointed steward and in this capacity had charge of the monastery's books. "He was both an edification and a terror to all", declared Syrus, and he illustrated this opinion by the following incident, which is indeed both edifying and terrifying.

> This man of God had formerly read the books of the ancient philosophers and the lies of Virgil. He would not have them either spoken of or read by others. He would say, 'let the divine poets satisfy you: you have no need to defile yourselves by contact with the licentious eloquence of Virgil.'[23]

17. Syrus I, 4.
18. Syrus I, 5. I have collected various testimony on the meaning of *studium* under the title "Les études dans les monasteres du Xe au XIIe siècle", in *Los monjes y los estudios,* (Poblet, 1963) pp. 106-110.
19. "Litteratoria professio", Syrus III, 8.
20. *Elogium,* PL 142, 944.
21. Ibid., 948.
22. Nagoldus, 2; 658.
23. Syrus, I, 14. On *apocrisiarius* meaning "librarian" in this kind of text, see K. Hallinger, *Gorze-Cluny,* p. 92.

A severe attitude indeed. Why should Syrus, in the *Life* of this man of God, have introduced a quotation from the Aeneid,[24] in violation of the precept left by the hero whose virtues he was recounting? This is enough to hint at the extent of rhetoric and exaggeration in all this. In spite of Majolus, Syrus not only read Virgil but set a passage before all his readers. Together with his reviser, Aldebald, he shows that study was held in honor at Cluny.[25]

He corrected his own first assertion when he spoke of "moments when Majolus read secular philosophers and books". In what spirit did he do it? In conformity with the interior dispositions suggested by the traditional theme of the "fair captive": avoiding everything that could be harmful to the faith and virtue, and drawing profit from everything else. The result was a culture which can be said without pejorative undertones to be general—acquired through this "assiduity in reading". It was drawn from sources which the biographer enumerates in precise hierarchical order: Holy Scripture, monastic texts, canonical texts, then the laws and decrees, and finally "philosophical arguments".[26]

An example is in order. Majolus used to read the *Hierarchies* of St Denis. Odilo added that he did it at St Denis. What was his method? During the day he read; then at night he meditated: "he deposited the book in the library of his heart". But one evening he abandoned himself to reflection while he still had the book before his eyes. He fell asleep, his candle fell on to the volume and burned out without damaging the page it had touched. What was the reason for Majolus' consternation on waking? "He was horrified at the thought that the fire could have consumed this work which was found almost nowhere else."[27]

"He gave himself up so continually to reading that on a

---

24. Ibid., III, 7; cf. MGH, 55, IV, 653.
25. See L. Traube, "Abermals die Biographien", pp. 302-307.
26. Syrus, II, 4. On the theme of "la belle captive"—a foreign woman taken prisoner in time of war whom an Israelite might marry under certain conditions according to Deut. 21, 10-14—see H. de Lubac, *Exégèse médiévale*, I (Paris, 1959) pp. 289-304.
27. Syrus, III, 17.

journey he frequently had a book in his hands. Thus, as he rode, he rested his mind by reading". And Syrus tells us what happened to him over the treatise of Pseudo-Jerome on the Assumption, the day he was taken prisoner by the Saracens: "He was in the habit of handling the book which Blessed Jerome published on the Assumption; he lost on that occasion all the books that he had brought, but that one, he noticed, he had on him"—we would say, in his pocket (*sub tegmine*).[28]

Lady Poverty

"Majolous has always concerned for the poor", and Syrus indicated the reason for this preoccupation: that charity of which the Lord had given both the example and the precept. Two texts which are traditionally fundamental on this point are quoted, the beatitudes and the eschatological discourse in which the Lord proclaims the reward given to those who have served him in the humble and weak of every kind. The way in which Majolus fulfilled this duty consisted in giving to each according to his need, in accordance with an "ordered charity" (*ordinata caritas*).[29] Nearly all the miracles attributed to him consist in coming to the help of the poor.[30] He "succored the oppressed",[31] and so he was frequently "surrounded with beggars".[32] Above all, he prayed for them.

His kindness was the fruit of an interior poverty, which was nothing other than humility. "For the love of eternal life, he had embraced voluntary poverty. All that he found in the treasure of his heart he gave to Christ; he attributed nothing to his own merits".[33] If he refused to be Pope, it was, so Syrus tells us, in order that he himself and his community might remain detached. He did not want to abandon the little

28. Ibid., III, 3.
29. Ibid., I, 9.
30. Ibid., I, 10, II, 17; II, 18.
31. Ibid., II, 6.
32. Ibid., II, 12.
33. Ibid., I, 14.

flock which it had pleased Christ to entrust to him. He
wanted to live in poverty with him who had come down from
the celestial heights into our poverty.[34] Here the Cluniac tradition rightly saw in the very Incarnation the essential poverty of Christ.[35] "In his spirit", the biographer declared once
again, "evangelical poverty reigned".[36]

The theme was developed in later hagiographic texts. "Little given to secular affairs and at times poor in worldly goods,
he nonetheless always lived rich in the goods of heaven." So
speaks the author of the short *Life*, which further on once
again praised "the poverty of Father Majolus",[37] and added
that, seized with pity for the poor, he bore them up in his
prayer.[38] When Odilo, in the course of a stay at Romain-
môtier in a time of general need, wrote a eulogy of St
Majolus, it was with the intention of obtaining resources
which would allow him to "succor the poor", concern for
whom was causing him sleepless nights. One night as he was
praying to St Majolus, he seemed to receive his promise of
help and it was this which persuaded him to compose the
text. Fundamental to the vocation of the man whose praises
he was about to celebrate (as was true previously with St
Anthony and would happen later with St Francis of Assisi)
—is this saying of the Lord: "If thou wouldst be perfect, go,
sell all that thou hast, and give to the poor".[39] According to
Nagoldus, the compassion that he felt for the poor made him
suffer as if fire had burned him. The selflessness which he
exhibited lent lustre to his program of reform: "He had no
use for dishonest gain but he distributed for the use of the
poor the revenue attached to his position". Beneath the
wretchedness of one of them, he recognized Jesus.[40] So it

34. Ibid., III, 8. As for the fact of an abbot refusing the episcopacy, we meet it
in other Lives: see K. Hallinger, *Gorze-Kluny,* pp. 513-514.

35. See above, pp. 55 "He was rich, yet he made himself poor".

36. Syrus III, 8.

37. *Vita brevior,* 1766 B-D.

38. Ibid., 1767 E.

39. *Elogium,* PL 142, 945 C.

40. Nagoldus, 6, 659.

was that the Chronicle of Cluny could say, "for a wife, he had chosen humble poverty".[41] These hagiographic testimonies agree with what is known from other sources about the cult of poverty at Cluny. They reflect the thoughts of this monastic *milieu* in a time of need and of reform.

Solitude

Solitude was dear to Majolus for two purposes: recollection and humility.

He had had a "little oratory" rebuilt and dedicated to St Michael, where he might "in secrecy and tranquillity, devote himself more attentively to the divine service by prolonged prayer".[42] Let us note that this refers only to private prayer, as at Cluny the service of God was not identified with the Divine Office. "Alone or travelling, wherever he was, he contrived for himself every day some hidden corner where, separated from men, he used to unite himself more closely to God. . . .[43] When travelling, he often journeyed apart from those who accompanied him. Far from the world in order to be always close to God, wishing to remain hidden, he sought the shade in order to remain there with Jesus, his spouse."[44] He went apart not through a need for peace and quiet but through a desire to pray more. "One day, journeying through a forest, he sent all the others ahead of him, and was going on alone; he was separating himself from them because he was offering to God a sacrifice with tears".[45]

41. *Chronicon* II, 1636. On the cult of poverty at Cluny, I have collected testimony in *Temoins de la spiritualité occidentale* (Paris, 1965) pp. 135-154. On Majolus and the Poor see P. Lamma, *Momenti di storiographia Cluniacense* (Rome, 1961) pp. 168-169, 181.

42. Syrus, I, 10.

43. Ibid., II, 9. The expression used here by Syrus: "secretum sibi adhibebat locum moeroris amicum" recalls that of John of Fecamp: "Locum dilectae solitudinia, amicum moeroris", in the *Lamentation* which I edited in *Un maitre de la vie spirituelle au XIe siecle, Jean de Fecamp*, (Paris, 1946) pp. 194, 225. On the possible connection between John of Fécamp and Majolus over the aspiration to solitude, see this work, pp. 198-199..

44. Syrus III, 8.

45. Ibid., III, 15.

Solitude is necessary for the famous who are exposed to the illusions of success and glory. Their purity of heart depends on it. In order to defend themselves against honors, they need sometimes to pass unnoticed, to live *incognito*. With this motive of humility is associated the only allusion made in our texts to the celebration of the Office. Syrus says that during a stay in Pavia, "in order to avoid being the object of the stares of the crowd and in that way to purify the eye of his heart from all pride, Majolus, in the silence of the night, anticipated the canonical hours".[46] At Avignon, he lived on an island in the middle of the Rhône, "to keep himself from the multitude".[47]

The short *Life* reproduces the reference to the oratory of St Michael. Nagoldus said that Majoldus' reason for coming to Cluny had been "the desire for solitude and peace",[48] the will "to imitate in some way the heavenly solitude".[49] And he emphasised his behavior in travelling: "Having sent ahead those who were with him, he used to ride behind all the others: solitary, living with himself, speaking with himself, he always contrived this solitude for himself. The others used to go on ahead of him; for his part, he followed, alone."[50] In this way they liked, at Cluny, to stress the importance of recollection.

Monastic Peace

The conception of the monastic life attributed to Majolus by Syrus is what the themes already pointed out would lead one to expect. If the Abbot of Cluny wished to see vocations appear among the people he met, especially among the great, he did so that they might find it possible to detach them-

---

46. Ibid., III, 16.
47. Ibid., III, 18.
48. *Vita brevior*, 1766 B.
49. Nagoldus, 10, 660. Taken up in *Chronicon* II, 1635.
50. Nagoldus, 39, 667. On the sources and meaning of the expression *secum habitare*, see P. Courcelle; " 'Habitare secum' selon Perse et selon S. Grégoire le Grand", in *Revue des études anciennes*, 69 (1967), pp. 266-279.

selves from the world and attach themselves to God, and to devote themselves in contemplative solitude to the true cares, those of the spiritual life. "During his intimate conversations with them, he found the means to bring help to the oppressed. What is more, it was his intention to win for God a few men from the world or from the clergy so that, according to the teaching of the Lord, they might give up everything, break away from the cares of this age and apply themselves to serving God in tranquillity".[51]

Towards this union with God in renunciation the main observances and occupation of the life of the cloister were directed. The importance of reading has already been noted.[52] Yet another text gives proof of it. "It was not only by day that he devoted himself to reading as far as he could; but during the night he prolonged the office of reading".[53] Here again, "the office" referred to is not the liturgical celebration but private reading. Another pious practice is worth noting. When the triple tiara was offered to Majolus, he set himself to ponder and pray. Then, "when he got up from prayer [for which no doubt he had prostrated himself], he saw by chance the book of the Acts of the Apostles. He opened it, and at the top of the page he saw this text through which he believed God wanted to teach him. 'Be on your guard; do not let your minds be captured by hollow and delusive speculations' . . .[54]

This attitude of prayer demands and engenders peace: "he orders everything patiently, in tranquillity of soul".[55] "This *semper et idem*".[56] He longed for heaven and made others long for it. "He taught men to go towards the eternal city, the heavenly Jerusalem".[57] "Because he was directed unswervingly in the desire for heaven, he earned the grace of

---

51. Syrus, II, 6. On the idea of peace and gentleness in Cluniac hagiography, see Lumma, *Momenti,* p. 149.
52. See above, p.
53. *Vita brevior,* 1777 A.
54. Syrus, III, 8. And the end, quotation from Col. 2, 8.
55. *Elogium,* PL 142, 950 C.
56. Ibid., 954 A.
57. Syrus, II, 10.

divine contemplation".[58] In his case, the (very monastic) theme of the foretaste of heaven is filled out by a metaphor which appeals to the sense of smell. The image may not be to our liking but it shows that the analogy of the five spiritual senses served to evoke realities that translate into concepts only with difficulty. "He tasted in advance how good is the God of Israel to upright hearts, and he savored with the nostrils of piety the sweetness of life. . . . He had attained the purity of the monk. Having come from Jericho to Jerusalem, from that obscure and wretched land to the country of light and peace, he had scaled heights filled with joy".[59] It is understandable that he should have delighted in St Gregory the Great. We are told that he frequently read his work, listened to it being read, and liked to speak of it.[60] He quoted him.[61] St Gregory is after all the doctor of delight and repose in God, of detachment and contemplation. All these themes, which the renewed monasticism of the twelfth century was to develop at Citeaux and elsewhere, were present at Cluny in the eleventh century.

With the exception of an allusion to the fact that Majolus attended Matins on the Feast of Candlemas,[62] nothing is said in these Cluniac sources about the Divine Office. A surprising silence, indeed, after all that has been written of the predominance of the liturgy at Cluny. Is it not mentioned because it went without saying that they devoted themselves to it? No doubt. Or must we conclude that it played no part in their spirituality? There is no evidence for this. At least it must be recognized that it held no place in the theory, the doctrine, and that it certainly did not have in practice the preponderance attributed to it. Another genuinely monastic trait is that nothing is about priesthood. The only allusion made to it is the statement that at Besançon, when they wanted to make a bishop of him, Majolus refused. "Never did

58. *Elogium,* PL 142, 952 B.
59. Nagoldus, 10, 660.
60. *Elogium, Praefatio,* 943.
61. Ibid., 953 A.
62. *Vita brevior,* 1774 B.

they succeed in swaying his free will to make him consent to
this promotion and exercise the priesthood [the word may
have here the sense of bishopric], he who avowed himself
totally unworthy even of the diaconate". What was his
motive in refusing? To remain a contemplative. This idea is
expressed by Biblical images. "This man worthy of God did
not want to rise before the day [we should take this to mean:
to give himself up to action], but rather to sit and be humiliated with Christ, in order that if he took the lowest place at
the meal, the voice of Heaven might resound for him, 'Go up
higher' ".[63]

When, with reference to Majolus' monastic youth before he
became Abbot, there is mention of the *sacramenta ordinis,*
this means only "humility and obedience". He wanted to be
truly and entirely a monk. "When he had become a monk
through and through, the monk shone forth in everything
about him; and living by the law of the monk, he attained to
the summit of monastic conduct".[64] In short, he was a "real
monk".[65]

As such, he frequently accused himself in all sincerity of
weaknesses in himself which he considered serious.[66] He felt
the need to ask forgiveness by reciting the *Dimitte nobis* of
the *Paternoster,* in order that, "the sovereign Master having
washed his feet, the word might be fulfilled: He who is holy
shall be sanctified".[67] The intention of virginity was to give
him a way of giving himself to God, "he who had nothing

---

63. Nagoldus, 8, 660. On the meaning of *sedere,* see *Chances de la spiritualité
occidentale* (Paris, 1966) pp. 313-328. On the attitude of Cluniac monasticism
towards clerical life—an attitude at once of respect and independence—and on the
meaning of the refusal of the tiara attributed to Majolus, see P. Lamma, *Momenti,*
pp. 56-57. On the historicity of this refusal, see E. Sackur, *Die Cluniacenser in
ihrer kirchlichen und allgemeingeschichtlichen Wirksamkeit,* I (Halle, 1892) p.
293.

64. Nagoldus, 10, 660.

65. Nagoldus, II, 659.

66. Syrus, II, 9: "Se quae levia contingeret, quae pro humana fragilitate solent
evenire in cogitatione, tali haec eadem plorabat moerore, ut gravissimorum
criminum eum crederet rerum. Porro quia iustus in principio accusator est sui,
ipse saepius se accusabat, se reum esse clamabat".

67. Syrus III, 5.

better than himself to give".[68] He demanded the same attitude in his subjects,[69] and this emphasis on chastity may partly be explained as a reaction against the incontinence of many. Not that he was excessively severe. His discretion and moderation in all things are praised, particularly in the matter of fasting.[70]

Finally, his charity went out to all. First in his monastery, where he strove to maintain that unanimity of which the apostolic community gave the example. Indeed, like all who worked for reform, he used always to look towards the model given by the early Church.[71] "Although the monks were of different nationalities, they were united in spirit, so that in them what we read of the newborn Church in the Acts of the Apostles was fulfilled: 'they were of one heart and one mind'."[72] What Syrus says here of the mother house, the short *Life* applies to all the dependent monasteries. "In the different regions of the earth, he invited the numerous monks of the same order to unanimity in the monastic life".[73] The charity of Majolus was universal; he felt a solidarity with all men, fulfilling each one of the beatitudes by making himself poor with the poor, and meek with the meek. "With those who are declared blessed because they mourn, he wanted to mourn for the negligences and the afflictions of his sons and of the whole world, in order to attain eternal consolation together with all his own".[74] Nobody ever does anything on his own in the realm of salvation. Majolus had as vivid a sense of catholicity as he had of solitude; he went apart in the interests of all.

68. Nagoldus, 3, 659.

69. Syrus II, 5.

70. Ibid., II, 7-8. On the discretio of Majolus as a Cluniac theme, see Lamma, *Momenti* p. 51.

71. See G. Miccoli, "Ecclesiae primitivae forma", in *Chiesa Gregoriana* (Florence, 1966) pp. 225-99.

72. Syrus, II, 6.

73. *Vita brevior,* 1769 A.

74. *Elogium,* PL 142, 952 B.

He was animated by "the love of the monastic order".[75]
Sometimes "he would sit among his brethren for a general
colloquy".[76] When he came to Pavia at the request of the
Empress in 980, he pleaded on her behalf with her son and
reconciled them.[77] Very much the monk, very much the
solitary, he was at the same time very human.

Spiritual Fatherhood

Having been coadjutor to Aymard, Abbot of Cluny, when
the latter became blind in 954, Majolus was elected Abbot in
965. Nearly thirty years later, in 993, he designated his own
coadjutor in the person of St Odilo. How did he see his
office, or how was it seen at Cluny relative to the way he
exercised it? The archaic title *abba,* in the not-yet-latinized
form of the word, was often applied to him.[78] Already as an
archdeacon at Besançon he had taught clerics.[79] But as abbot
he became a "spiritual father". Those of his sons who were
weary, tempted perhaps to discouragement (*lassabundos*), he
exhorted with sermons. "Others he led imperceptibly to taste
and see, by the zeal for assiduous reading, that the Lord is
good."[80] We have seen that this was his own particular consolation. He knew how to remain a monk among monks.
"This good father filled these good sons with joy: with them
he remained one of them, he gave in everything the example
of an invincible humility".[81] And he made the whole Church
participate in the overflow of his contemplation. Once again,
the short *Life* emphasizes this universal character of Cluniac

75. Elogium, 946 D. Other monasteries also felt they had a solidarity with
Cluny: St Majolus was included in the martyrology of Saint-Maximin of Trier, see
G. Tellenbach in *Neue Forschungen über Cluny und die Cluniazenser* (Freiburg-
im-Breisgau, 1959) p. 7; on the relations of Cluny with Marmoutier under St
Majolus, see H. Diener, "Das Verhältnis Clunys zu den Bischofen vor allem in der
Zeit seines Abtes Hugo (1049-1109)," in *Neue Forschungen,* p. 267.
76. *Vita anonyma, Bibl. Clun.,* 1784.
77. Syrus III, 9, see Lamma, *Momenti* 68-69, 94-98, 108-109.
78. Syrus II, 2 C; *Elogium,* PL 142, 951 A.
79. Syrus I, 11.
80. *Vita brevior,* 1769 B.
81. Ibid., 1772 C.

piety. He prayed "for his salvation and that of the whole world. . . . Sacrificing himself entirely on the altar of his contemplation, and by the practice of everyday mortification, he became a victim pleasing to God. . . . And by faith, like all Saints, he acquired for the Lord the people of many nations".[82] The contemplative life involves a sacrifice but one which is efficacious for the whole world.

How was this spiritual fatherhood transmitted? If there was heredity in the designation of a coadjutor, was there freedom of election on the part of the monks? The working of the abbatial election at Cluny is worth considering. This institution differs from the conception which we have in our day of an election, and yet it was described as such in the written testimony of a long tradition.

There was first of all the election of Majolus according to the account of Syrus. Aymard, being blind, said to his monks: "Elect someone from among you". And "he urged them to elect the one among them who was suitable" for the abbacy. A consensus was taken of the monks and the clerics, the people of the country and of the town. "All" pronounced themselves in favor of Majolus. He resisted. For three days they prayed. He accepted. At this point, Aymard in his turn elected him: he decided that Majolus should be elected. In other words, he confirmed the election that had already been made and submitted Cluny and all its dependencies to him. A deed was drawn up whose signatories proved their consent. This document has been preserved and it coincides exactly with the account of Syrus.[83] The same text exactly was drawn up when Majolus had Odilo elected.[84]

---

82. Ibid., 1779 C.

83. Syrus II, 1-2. Here are the expressions that mark the phrases of the election: 1. The words of Aymardus: "Ex vobis ipsis eligite . . . ut eligerent adhortans". 2. Consensus on the part of monks, clerks, laymen, *plebs rustica, plebs urbana, cuncti, omnes* . . . 3. The words of Aymardus: "Fratrem ac filium Maiolum reeligimus et abbatem esse decernimus, . . . vinculis oboedientiae astringimus . . ., et abbatem unanimiter omnes proclamamus." 4. Record of the minutes of the election that is "universitatis consensu roborata".

84. PL 137, 777-780.

The same procedure would have been followed.

Let us now examine the account transmitted by Odilo of the same event.[85] Aymard "began by talking of preserving order in the monastery and of the election of his successor, to brethren known for their religious sense and their spirituality. He discussed the matter with them on the spiritual level".[86] Then an enquiry was made from which it transpired that all of them wanted Majolus. He was thus "chosen by the community".[87] He resisted, accepted, and, finally was "elected by the brethren": he was honored as lord and abbot.[88] So there was at once designation by the predecessor and election by the monks. The one proposed the candidate for the choice of the monks, and the monks ratified the choice.

According to the short *Life*, Majolus, before declaring Odilo his successor, was to make this declaration: "It is not for us, dear son, to choose you as abbot".[89] But in the account which Nagoldus has left of the election of Majolus, the juridical, psychological and spiritual aspects of the operation are clearly formulated: "It is upon you", said Aymard to the monks, "that the election falls. But since you have submitted your liberty to our decision, I urge and instruct you to put Brother Majolus in my place". The predecessor here appeals to their obedience at the same time as to their liberty.[90] Indeed, "they immediately elected Majolus", who refused, spent three days in prayer with them, and finally accepted in

---

85. PL 137, 707.

86. *Elogium*, PL 142, 950-951: "De ordinatione coepit monasterii suique successoris electione cum spiritalibus et religiosis fratribus spiritaliter tractare".

87. Ibid., "Facta est autem ab omnibus inquisitio et ad quem omnium fratrum tendebat, ad domnum scilicet Maiolum, pervenit electio. De cuius electionis negotio . . . Electus advocatur. . . ."

88. Ibid., "Postremo a fratribus eligitur . . . et ab omnibus domnus et abba honoratur.'

89. *Vita anonyma,* 1785 C: "Non est nostrum, filii charissimi, vobis abbatem eligere".

90. Nagoldus, 13, 661, "Vobis quidem abbatis incumbit electio . . . Sed quoniam in nostrae discretionis iudicio vestri quoque posuistis arbitrii liberatem . . ., hortor atque commoneo ut Fratrem Maiolum . . . substituatis".

an act of obedience.[91] This virtue came into it freely on both sides.

What then is the purpose of this procedure? Sackur, then Dom Hourlier, have explained it clearly.[92] The resistance of the abbot-elect has a double significance: it was probably intended to show that there was no question of simony in his designation but it also shows that the choice of the community was a free one. That was an essential point for Cluny. This monastery had been founded with a view to restoring and affirming the abbots' and communities' independence of lay proprietors. Thus in the case of St Majolus, as of his successors, there was on the one hand designation of the candidate by his predecessor—which secured continuity of tradition—and on the other the acceptance of this designation by the community. The whole process, made up of these two operations, constituted an election.

But if Cluny was independent, not only from the laity, but also from the bishop of the diocese in which it was situated, it was attached to the See of Rome, and had a special devotion to it which marked the whole history of the abbey. This devotion to the Apostles was devotion in both senses of the expression: reverence for St Peter and St Paul, and devoted loyalty to them and St Peter's successor as head of the Church of Rome. Syrus tells us of the emotion which Majolus experienced at the tombs of the Apostles, his joy when he arrived there and his sorrow when he left.[93] He prayed to St Paul.[94] When he was taken prisoner by the Saracens, he saw in a dream the bishop of Rome clad in apostolic vestments.[95] The short *Life* adds that when, following his capture and liberation, the Saracens were driven out

---

91. Ibid, "Domnum Maiolum protinus in abbatem elegerunt".
92. See J. Hourlier, *S. Odilon* (Louvain, 1964) p. 37, quoting Sackur. This procedure was imitated in other monasteries; see K. Hallinger, *Gorze-Cluny*, pp. 567-568.
93. Syrus II, 15.
94. Syrus, II, 17. On devotion to St Peter, in Syrus, as a Cluniac theme, see Lamma, *Momenti* p. 52.
95. Syrus, III, 3.

of the Alps, the road to Rome, which leads to St Peter's, was once more open to all.[96] According to Nagoldus, Majolus attributed to St Peter several of the miracles that he performed.[97]

A Vigorous Monasticism

Having attempted to portray the spiritual features of St Majolus, we must note the limitations of this portrait. It was drawn according to hagiographic texts or family chronicles. These documents certainly do not tell the whole story, the whole truth. Like all Christians, all monks, and even all the saints, Majolus remained a man. But at least we know the image of him which was preserved and maintained, and which after him continued to act with the force of an idea or, more precisely, of an ideal.

The sources examined here bear witness to a consistent tradition. The original narrative of Syrus contains precise formulations borrowed in part from earlier great examples but stated with an emphasis which is peculiarly Cluniac on certain points: education, poverty, solitude, the peace of the cloister, spiritual fatherhood. It has a vocabulary which does not mislead, and mentions commonplaces whose repetition betrays their environment. In this sense, Syrus was a valid hagiographic source. What he set forth was later developed, but little was added.

96. *Vita brevior,* 1771 E - 1772 A. On relations with Islam, as a Cluniac theme (over the captivity of Majolus), see Lamma, pp. 134-135. The importance of the consequences attendant upon the capture and liberation of Majolus has been underlined by P.-A. Amargier, "La capture de Saint Mayeul de Cluny et l'expulsion des sarrasins de Provence", in *Revue bénédictine,* 73 (1963) pp. 316-323.

97. Nagoldus, 15, 662. On the reform of Saint-Pierre-au-Ciel d'or and, on that occasion, the restoration of a pre-Cluniac exemption, see Diener, "Das Verhältnis Clunys", p. 334, no. 96. On the relations of Majolus with the bishops who, under his abbacy, made more donations to Cluny than they had under his predecessors, see ibid., 232-299; 278 and 325 (relations with the bishop of Châlons-sur-Saône), 279 (with the bishop of Autun), 287-288 (with the bishop of Vienne); for a list of donations made by the bishops of Majolus, see pp. 339-360. See also Miccoli, "Ecclesiae primitivae forma", p. 51.

What was then the secret of Majolus, and of Cluny? Nagoldus affirms that his whole program was to live by Christ and to bring others to do the same.[98] All the rest— detachment, prayer, reading, study—followed from it. Majolus was an abbot who taught himself and taught others, who had something to say about Christ. He was not merely a superior who administered and governed, he was a master. He had a doctrine, he formed and guided his monks. This could no doubt be claimed of many abbots and it should be possible to proclaim it about all. How did he himself realize this ideal?

There exists a record concerning Majolus' old age which seems revealing. At an age when others live less intensely, he devoted himself to "concentrated hard work": "as though he were still a new creature, as though all the vigor of youth were still fervent in his whole body, he persevered in the service of the Lord with an incredible fervor of spirit".[99] In this phrase, the idea of fervor occurs twice, to underline all the interior energy which continued to animate Majolus. What did he do in this state? What he had always done, but with an even greater emphasis on solitude. For two years, "whether in the monastery or in one of the cells round about, he saw the brothers, he gave them counsel; [we should say today that he gave spiritual direction]. But more often still, far from everyone, alone, he united himself to God alone".[100] This alternation of prayer, reading, and the spiritual overflowing had occupied all his life as a monk. Now, freed from the cares of administration, he could devote himself still more exclusively to them.

His solitude increased in that he could see all his con-

---

98. Nagoldus, 14, 661: "Christum sapere, Christum loqui, terrena postponere, ad aeterna suspirare".

99. Syrus, III, 19: "Senectutis tempore, quo solent ceteri remissius vivere, acri se labore ... et quasi tunc novus accederet ac iuvenilis vigor in toto corpore ferveret, ita incredibili mentis fervore divino famulamini insistebat."

100. Ibid., "Aut in monasterio, aut in quadam suarum cellula pro fratrum utilitate immorari cupiebat ... aut saepius remotis omnibus solus soli deo inhaereret."

temporaries disappearing. Then "his sole consolation was the *lectio divina*".[101] Once again, note that nothing is said about the liturgical office. It is even suggested, or supposed, that Majolus did not attend choir. He prayed alone, far from everyone, and sometimes in a cell. He lived in the desire for that peace which, in his native land, would follow this exile, this *peregrinatio*.[102]

And so in the last years of Majolus, there was no trace of softness, of mediocrity, of letting things slide or of letting himself slip, of passive and resigned acceptance, but there was a continued impetus. This is what enabled Cluny to last two centuries without growing old, and to spread its influence to Pavia and elsewhere. There is only one remedy for the force of habit and the weight of institutions: renewal and rejuvenation.

This record of an abbatial old age must be based on the memories of first-hand experience, and it confirms the mark of a whole life: that vitality, that *alacritas* of which Odilo speaks in connection with Majolus,[103] that vigor which the anonymous *Life* emphasises: *Vigebat . . . vigebat.* The courage of a monk striving to the end.[104] He announced his end with joy and alacrity.[105] The strength of Majolus, and of the great abbots of his line, and the strength of Cluny in its first two centuries came from this continued tranquil fervor, this blending of vigor and peace.

---

101. Ibid., "Solamen sibi sola divina praebabat lectio."

102. Ibid., "Omnia quieta et tranquill perspicere."

103. *Elogium*, PL 142, 950.

104. *Vita anonyma,* 1784 B: "Vigebat animus omnino irreverberatus, vigebat armis sanctitatis munitus, miles invictissimus . . . Fortis agonista. . . ."

105. *Vita anonyma,* 1785 B: "Finemque suum laetus et alacer imminere praedixit."

ST JOHN OF GORZE AND THE RELIGIOUS LIFE

IN THE TENTH CENTURY*

IS ST JOHN OF GORZE OF ANY INTEREST to us? Even during the "golden age" towards the end of the last century, when Joris-Karl Huysmans, the president of the Goncourt Academy, wanted to become a Benedictine oblate and had to choose the name of a patron saint, he wrote: "I have found a John of Gorze, a Benedictine Abbot, a perfect man, who loved plainsong, art and so forth. I shall therefore be Brother John. . . ."[1] The unfortunate thing is that although we are exceptionally well-informed about this character, we know nothing, or next to nothing, of his abbacy, and to go by what we do know makes him seem a spiritual person, certainly, but less an artist than an administrator. Let us try, going beyond the clichés of Neo-Romanticism, to discern what his character was. It will not be our concern to study his acts, their chronology, or their influence on institutions, but the mentality they presuppose in his environment and express in him.

Our principal source of information is the hagiographic record composed by John of Saint-Arnoul. Probably born shortly after the beginning of the tenth century, the Abbot of Gorze died about 976. About 12 years later, his biographer set to work. He admitted having done so without having conferred with his subject, and so without much knowledge of the different periods of his life which he had not himself

* Published in S. *Chrodegang* (Metz, 1967) pp. 133-152.

1. Letter to the Abbé Mugnier, quoted by R. Baldrick, *La vie de J.-K. Huysmans* (Paris, 1958) p. 343.

witnessed. This should be enough to set us on our guard. From the very beginning of his text, he piles up hagiographic themes: the rarity of saints in his time, the contrast between *otium* and *negotium*. Then, faithful to the law of an *ordo artificialis* which, ever since the *Ars Poetica* of Horace demanded that the natural order of events should not be followed, he began by recounting the death of his hero, introducing into it a familiar type of lament. All this is enough to confirm us in our apprehensions. Are we going to meet here more rhetoric than history? Yet towards the end of his preface the author devoted a good page to making excuses for the saint of whom he is to speak because, like John the Baptist, he performed no miracles either in his lifetime or after his death. Here is something which begins to make him sympathetic to us. We are about to read of a man like any other. John of Saint-Arnoul adds that he will say nothing of his hero's childhood because he knows nothing about it. A further sign of good faith which inspires our confidence. Indeed, this *Vita's* qualities of style and composition, which have earned praise,[2] in no way detract from the veracity of details, the flavour of the narrative, nor the charm of the characters. The abbot of Saint-Arnoul has recorded a great number of things from firsthand experience. His text, composed during the years preceding the year one thousand, reveals to us in the Christians of the so-called iron century an astonishing delicacy.

The life of John of Gorze consisted of four periods: he was for a long time a layman, then as a monk the bursar of his monastery, then in charge of a mission in Andalusia, and finally abbot. John of Saint-Arnoul died before being able to record the details of this last phase. Let us however examine his record of the three preceding periods.[3]

---

2. E. Auerbach, *Litteratursprache und Publikum in der lateinischen Spätantike und im Mittelalter* (Bern, 1958) pp. 122-123.

3. The most recent bibliography of Jean of Gorze is in the *Bibliotheca sanctorum*, VI, (Rome, 1965) col. 814. The text of the *Vita* will be used in the Pertz edition, in MGH SS, IV, pp. 333-377, reproduced in PL 137, 239-310.

Adventure in Lorraine

John of Gorze was neither a saint from the cradle nor miraculously converted. He became a monk as the result of a long and slow development, which was not completed until late in life and in the course of which was a whole series of episodes. Faithful to his promise, the biographer says nothing of his childhood, but he gives a discreet picture of family life at the beginning of the tenth century. John's father was a farmer at Vandières, near Pont-à-Mousson. He did not belong to the nobility. Kind, generous, lovable and beloved, he suffered when he had to part from his son, who was sent to be educated at Metz. When he died, John became the support of the family—*totius familiae domesticae curator.* And so he returned to oversee the fields, the livestock and the workshops of his father's farm. He made it prosper and succeeded in making friends for himself among the great men of Church and state. The little he had retained from his years of study he forgot in his business activity. It was only as an adult that he put himself under the tutelage of Bernac, a deacon of Toul. Then he learned grammar, a necessary "introduction" to Holy Scripture. He led the life of a layman, sanctifying himself in his state and doing good. He sent to a convent a young girl seeking her path, and he took in an old foreign priest who thought aloud, prayed aloud and struggled at the top of his voice against temptations. These details illuminate both the psychology of the time and the place of the psalms in its spirituality.

John felt himself moved to a more complete conversion by the example of a pious woman called Fredeburge and her friend Geisa. He realized he had lost time, almost lost his soul—*perdite vivendo*—and he began to feel within himself the monastic vocation. Where was he to fulfil it? In his district he saw no abbey where life was regular. He searched, he made retreats which sometimes lasted a month or more with several men of God, in particular with two holy priests of Metz. One day, having made up his mind to take the final step, he decided to become a recluse in a cell close to the church of

Saint-Saviour. He went, tried, hesitated, and finally opted for rural solitude rather than urban. He heard of a recluse at Verdun, a certain Humbert. He went to him, opened his soul to him in general confession and remained with him, sharing his austerity and his prayer. Then he heard of the existence of another solitary in the valley of the Argonne. This simple man, Lambert, was a sort of fool for Christ. John went and spent some time with him.

What was to become of him? He was advised to make a pilgrimage to Rome. He prepared for it with Bernac of Toul and a group of companions (*comitatus*) for it was safer in those days not to travel alone. The expense of the collective journey required money, which John found and took with him, and which made it possible for him to be generous when occasion arose. From Rome, John and Bernac decided to go as far as Mount Gargano, where Saint Michael is said to have appeared, and they set off with only a few other pilgrims. Stopping at Monte Cassino on the way, John collected information. Soon he was to marvel at the sight of the smoke rising perpetually from Mount Vesuvius (*perpetuo vapore fumantem miratus*). If he was no tourist, he certainly did not refuse to wonder at the beautiful things in the world. On his return, he renewed contact once again with Humbert, the recluse of Verdun. Since neither had yet found the right place to which to retire, John decided for the present, to stay home doing good. So there he was, a monk in the world, bearing the cross of Christ.

It was at this point that another solitary came in, Ainold, former archdeacon of Toul, who had withdrawn into a cell adjoining the clerics' cloister and who entered the church but rarely. Humbert went to see him and suggested that he should go with him and live in nature rather than in town. Off they both went beyond the Moselle to a cave where they intended to become "perpetual hermits". Some clerics came to dissuade them, and each returned to his beloved cell (*amica cellula*)—one at Toul and the other at Verdun. But they met again for long conversations. There really is something marvellous in the role of spiritual friendship in all this.

Among other subjects (*inter cetera quae familiaritas illa
parere solet colloquia*), they mentioned John of Vandières.
Humbert suggested to Ainold that they meet. They fixed a
rendezvous at Toul. In the joy of this new threefold friendship (*familiaritur, adgaudentes*), they looked for a means of
withdrawing from the world together.

John sought the advice of his Messinian friends who approved the idea. Back at Metz, Humbert, having tasted the
"sweetness" of mutual companionship, "found a prolonged
absence difficult to bear." He and John met again, sometimes
in company with Geisa and a group of devout women surrounding her, with Salecho, a cleric of St Martin beyond the
Moselle, with Randicus, a priest of St Symphorien-en-l'Ile,
near whose church they sometimes withdrew in order to be
quieter, and finally with Bernac, their travelling companion
in Italy. John and Humbert, at least, met every day to read,
pray and talk of God. They had a kind of secular institute at
Metz in the tenth century. Then Ainold joined from Toul,
urging them to cut themselves off completely from the
world. So they set out to find a place where they could lead
"the common life". Since they saw no possibility of this in
their own country, where all the monasteries were decadent,
they considered living abroad. John recalled his happy
memories of Italy and spoke of the deserts of the Benevenuto
region. "He saw, [he said,] solitary places where they could
live by the labor of their hands, after the example of the
saints of old." There was also Monte Cassino, and Saint
Saviour near Vesuvius. Filled with enthusiasm, they decided
to set off as soon as possible.

Since no secret can be kept, however, the whole project
came to the ears of the bishop, Adalbero of Metz. Bernac,
who knew him well, undertook to tell him everything in the
hope that he would try to hold back the would-be exiles. He
appealed to the prelate's vanity, showing the dishonor this
lost opportunity would be to his episcopate. The bishop was
won over, decided to help, and suggested offering Gorze to
them, but he too asked for secrecy. Indeed, the affair was no

simple one. Gorze belonged to a violent count, Adalbert, who rented the monastery property from the bishop but whose brother-in-law, Lambert, not on good terms with him, could interfere with it. Lambert, when he heard of it, advised the group (who did not know why) to bide their time. Two different plots were being hatched in secret until in the course of a meeting of everyone with the bishop the situation was cleared up. He made his suggestion, and mentioned Gorze. Disappointment assailed the group. They had become accustomed to the idea of exile—*peregrinatio* was exactly synonymous with *exsilium*. John, who wanted more ardently than anyone to go abroad, said he agreed, knowing it would be impossible to get Gorze from Adalbert. But unforeseen things happened. Adalbero recovered the abbey and gave it to the group. He loved Gorze and had long cherished the idea of raising it out of its wretched condition.[4] After this swift, unexpected but not unhoped-for, *denouement*—the bishop had trusted in Providence—we find our community (*conventus*) taking possession of the monastery. The community consisted of several priests and a deacon, whose names are already familiar to us. They were joined by others, as well as by an adult layman, John of Vandières, and two young men, Ainold's servant and Randicus' nephew. This restoration of Gorze took place in the year 933.[5]

What impressions of the whole emerge from these facts and in these surroundings, as John of Saint-Arnoul knew them, or at least imagined and reconstructed them? First of all, we cannot fail to notice the part played in this spiritual movement by women. The mother of John of Vandières intended one day to go and live with him at Gorze. We have already seen him guiding a young girl towards the monastic life. It was under the direction of Fredeburge and Geisa that he

4. While he was still young, Adalbero had witnessed the great neglect into which Gorze had fallen: "qui altaria cuncta perlustrans sagaci industria invenit fimum tam asinorum quam reliquorum animalium in circuiti altarium"; *Miracula S. Gorgonii*, ed. MGH, SS, IV, p. 241 Information on the state of Gorze and its possessions at its restoration has been assembled from various sources by Dr Lager, "Die Abtei Gorze in Lothringen", in *Studien und Mittheilungen aus dem Benediktiner - und Cistercienser-Orden*, 8 (1887) pp. 45-53.

5. See K. Hallinger, *Gorze-Kluny*, pp. 51-52.

plunged into *lectio divina.* The program of studies ascribed to them, which included all the disciplines, was no doubt idealized. Nevertheless it shows their idea of what all they should know, and shows that pious ladies of Metz were regarded as having more learning than a former pupil of the schools. Similarly, it was through the example of these religious in the world, as it were, that he advanced in the interior life.

Another character who frequently intervened is the hermit. Nothing was done without him. First of all there was Humbert, the recluse of Verdun. Then, in the forests of Argonne came Lambert, an ignorant man, but one who attracted Humbert and other learned men, in particular the islanders, those cultivated "Bretons" whom the northern invaders, the Normans, had driven from their own country. Then there was Ainold at Toul and finally, just as they were deciding to take over Gorze, Benno of Einsiedeln was named. John of Vandières had long been drawn to the solitary life himself. At that period as in all times of reform, the hermit appears as the instigator of renewal, the example of total renunciation and utter commitment. And this sort of society had two kinds of leader: on the one hand the prelate or temporal lord, on the other the recluse. The final decision fell to the bishop but the spiritual counsel came from a man of God of another sort.

Finally, one preoccupation which emerges from one end of the record to the other is poverty. No doubt this *Life* forms part of a literature of reform and reaction against the excessive wealth of the nobility and some clerics. From the start, the principle is affirmed that the true condition of the free man is freedom from slavery to vice. True nobility is not nobility of blood: it is possible to possess it while poor (*egenus et pauper*). The vocabulary is biblical. So are the examples: David and St Peter pursued humble trades. Again, it is asserted that through the Word and the Spirit of God a man is free and not a serf. A long discourse emphasises the difference between the nobility and sanctity. Is it not possible to read in all these declarations a concern for freeing the churches and monasteries from the domination of the ruling families? At Metz, Bernac was a cleric with a knowledge of letters and even of arithmetic, who lived as a poor man and had given everything to God. At Toul, Ainold, an important member of the clergy, had given away all his wealth before becoming a hermit. The dominant idea of John of Vandières as he was getting his friends to accept the projected trek to Italy, was living by the labor of their hands, following the example left in ancient times by the apostle St Paul and by the first monks. The Church of the poor can only be conceived in the image of the apostolic church, and monasticism, in its authentic periods, has as its mission to set this example.

Sketches of Monks

So here is the established community.[6] From the outset it was taken for granted that it would be "monastic", not orientated towards the priesthood or conditioned by it and the activities which govern it. John of Saint-Arnoul said without any possibility of misunderstanding that those who came wearing the clerics' habit took it off and put on the habit of monks. They elected Ainold abbot, and John of Vandières was put in charge of administering the property. The few survivors of the community existing before the reform consented willy-nilly, in fact by force (*coacte*), to the new state of affairs. As for John, he saw to his property, made out his inheritance in favor of the monastery, and assured an income for his mother, who came to live close to the abbey with some other women who gave their services (*serviens*) especially in the wardrobe. Let us note here again that women play a part. Other members joined the community in the service of God (*divina servitus*), some of them wealthy. The narrator mentions once again the conversion of Humbert and his life as a recluse at Verdun, and recalls that he had established two "religious women" in cells where they received spiritual exhortations through a window. Two others were living in the same way at the time in the same town, and one of them was to become Abbess of Bouxières-aux-Dames.[7]

6. This part of the story begins at n. 44 of the *Vita*.
7. N. 44-55.

What were the occupations of all these people? John of Saint-Arnoul enumerated the different forms of what he called the *opus fratribus consuetum.* They were cooking, laundry, gardening, shoe-cleaning, the duty of hebdomadary in choir, in short, the whole organization of the life of prayer and of the cloister (*ordo omnis claustri et orationis*).[8] All took part in this life of worship and manual labor on an equal footing. There is no mention of cultural activity. Prayer consisted in three activities: orison, psalms and reading (*pensum orationum, psalmorum vel lectionum sanctarum*).[9] The Divine Office is mentioned here only in second place, and is described as psalmody, the custom at Cluny and elsewhere in conformity with monastic tradition. These exercises in prayer lasted a long time (*multo prolixiores*). This last word, designating the "prolixity" of the liturgy, was also found at Cluny.[10] John of Saint-Arnoul quotes a series of examples of prayers which were added at the end of Offices, and which could number thirty psalms or fifteen canticles. He adds that later on this quantity, which answered the fervor of the early days but did not suit the "pusillanimity of the weak", had to be reduced. Was this an indication that, wherever it was possible to maintain this lengthy psalmody, as at Cluny, that first fervor was always retained? The fact remains that at Gorze it had to be somewhat reduced (*in nonnullis*) but no doubt it was still long, and the only reason given for this relative diminution in vocal prayer is the *pusillanimitas imbecillium.*[11]

Many other details about the observance are given in passing. Thus the brief phrase *licita colloquendi invicem tempora fugiens* leaves us to understand that there were times of free conversation from which it was possible to absent oneself—for nothing is said of asking or receiving permission not to take part. You could compel someone to come to it (*si forte compelleretur*) but not to remain for long. Occasionally, baths were allowed as *recreationes,* as a means of "refresh-

8. N. 62.
9. N. 68.
10. See *Aux sources de la spiritualité occidentale* (Paris, 1964) p. 143.
11. N. 81.

ment".[12] The wardrobe comes up again, the store-room, the bakery, various cleaning jobs, and even washing up—which a devoted monk sometimes did alone (*vasa refectorum solus elavit*)[13]—in short, every form of work (*opus*).

In his life of John of Vandières, John of Saint-Arnoul inserted a brief biography and portrait of some of the members of the community. These secondary records are worth pausing over. They help a great deal in grasping the atmosphere in which the principal hero spent his life. First of all there was Anstée. An archdeacon, he really turned himself into one of Christ's poor (*ex archidiacono in pauperem Christi vere mutatus*).[14] For some clerics then, conversion consisted in becoming poor. This one was very well educated, blessed with a fine voice and richly endowed with various gifts: a commanding presence, fluent speech and a knowledge of architecture. In the new community he became dean (*decanus*), that is, the abbot's assistant. Later he became abbot of Saint-Arnoul and was able to exercise his taste for building. We have been introduced to several types of holy monks distinguished by eremitical tendencies here, in Anstée, is an extrovert destined to become a superior.[15]

Yet another, Blidulf, had been archdeacon of Metz. Prudent to the point of seeming crafty, he fell ill, but not so seriously that he could not be taken to the monastery. There he received the habit, after which he recovered and was able to remain in the community. A few years later, endowed with a grace which filled him with a greater courage (*maiori calore virtutis tactus*), he went off with a companion, Gundelach, to a hermitage in the Vosges where he was to spend ten years in prayer and poverty.[16] Gundelach had proved himself capable of action: he had been sent successfully to several communities before going to be a hermit with Blidulf.[17] As for Isaac, he was another introvert (*totus*

12. N. 63.
13. N. 77.
14. See "Documents sur les fugitifs", in *Analecta monastica*, 7. Studia Anselmiana, 54 (Rome, 1965) pp. 90-92 and 117-118.
15. N. 57-65.
16. N. 69.
17. N. 70.

interioribus animae bonis deditus).[18] The abbot Ainold was himself a man of prayer who, at the beginning of his abbacy, was afraid of being taken from the contemplation of God, the *divina speculatio,* by his administrative duties. It was then that John of Vandières offered to free him from this anxiety: "Let your concern be purely with interior realities (*Interioribus tantum, ut cupitis, animum intendite . . .*)." And so he was able to be entirely free for spiritual matters, (*cum in solo Deo vacationem assumpserit*).[19]

Beside these men of high virtue, there were others—and no doubt they were in the majority—for whom the violence of their temperament made the common life difficult. Hence the scenes of anger and repentance, of severe sanctions and public humiliations, which John of Saint-Arnoul did not fail to record for us. They convey a good deal about primitive psychology, which we know is the monopoly of the age of iron.[20] A child whose parents had given him to the monastery decided to follow the example of the grown-ups (*quemadmodum maiorum ducebatur exemplis*). He returned to the world and lived there indifferently (*indifferenter*). He too had to repent and return.[21]

This was the environment in which John of Vandières lived at Gorze. What was said of him is marked with the same realism.[22] He was critized in the community by small minds. What base motives were not attributed to him! What calumnies were not spread about him! If he was economical, he was charged with avarice. He was accused first of hypocrisy and then of rigidity. He was accused of fraud. At least all these accusations had the virtue of being in no way secret: they were made publicly, they were hurled at his head (*in faciem dum iacularentur*). The angry scenes he had to endure are not passed over in silence. He himself, in his austerity,

18. N. 71.
19. N. 72.
20. N. 74. Think, for example, of the humiliations that Saint Jean-Marie Vianney suffered at the hands of the Abbé Raymond; see R. Fourrey, *Le Curé d'Ars authentique* (Paris, 1964) p. 324.
21. N. 55.
22. N. 76.

seemed to be lacking in moderation (*ipse sibi austerus et pene indiscretus*). He was incapable of remaining idle. After he had paid a visit to the altars, in the interval separating Vigils from Lauds, he would go out to check the sky to see what the weather was doing, then he would mend nets or start on some work, or attend singing practice. As though it were his job, he was quick to put out the dormitory lamps, or lower their wicks, when he judged that daylight made them unnecessary. This is easy to imagine, for this is a "firsthand experience" of things which happen in community everywhere and in every age.

Comments on reading no doubt bear the marks of literary themes.[23] But it is easy to believe that he preferred above all the *Morals on Job* and the *Homilies* on Ezekiel by St Gregory. This is another characteristic which he had in common with Cluny and all contemporary monastic life. He was attracted by "Scholasticism" and its problems once after reading the *De Trinitate* of St Augustine, and his abbott had to suggest that he content himself with Holy Scripture, (*sacra lectio*), since he would find in it more "learning" and, more important, more "edification" than anywhere else. As at Cluny, and later at Cîteaux, as in the monastic renewals of every age including our own, ancient monasticism was a cult at Gorze. Antony, Paul, Hilarion, Macharius and Pachomius are mentioned—and the last is one of those who loved solitude (*heremi sectatores*)—Martin of Tours, and finally Germanus of Auxerre. John of Vandières knew by heart the life of an Eastern saint, John the Almoner, once patriarch of Alexandria.

One of his most admired traits was that, cellarer though he was, he hardly ever went out, and when he was obliged to, he came back as soon as he could. He saw to it that as many outside jobs as possible were done by lay people, so that monks could be kept "in the cloister".[24] Once again, John

23. N. 83-84.

24. N. 85. Similarly, Lambert, the cellarer of Hautmont, was praised later for going only as seldom as possible to the market in the neighbouring town of Avesnes; the text is in Martène, *Thesaurus Veterum scriptorum . . . amplissima collectio* (Paris, 1729) vol. VI, col. 1214.

implies that he was the object of envy and criticism, as are all who are in the public eye and achieve something.[25] In fact, he embellished the church and, in connection with the circles of lights which were hung from the ceiling, it is interesting to see the biographer use the same rhetorical device of *praeteritio* which St Bernard used against the art works at Cluny *taceo coronas. . .) .* [26] His activities as Bursar did not prevent John of Vandières from working in the garden like all the brethren.[27] He always arranged to have himself bled long enough before the liturgical feasts to be recovered for their celebration. It is curious that he was praised as cellarer,— unless praise came at the beginning of the eulogy of his virtues as abbot—because he was content with the food served to the community. "He was never heard to say 'I do not take this, bring me or prepare me such and such' " (*Hoc non utor, illud affer vel para; nunquam ex eo auditum*).[28]Having a delicate stomach, he accepted herbal teas but not drugs. If he was invited out, or on feast days when the fare was better, he was ready to appreciate good food. A whole series of tales show him skilful in recovering the revenues of territory which had been usurped, or for which the rents were refused. One day, in the course of one of these disputes caused by the alienation of monastery property, a count set out to have a scandalous operation performed on him, but the usurper's wife rescued him from the violence and had him escorted home. Almost everything said of the actions and deeds of John of Vandières concerns his activity in the economic field. It is as though it were difficult to remain a saint while dealing with business matters. He was admired for having succeeded.

The Mission at Cordova

The last part of the record of John of Saint-Arnoul concerns John of Gorze's journey to and stay in Andalusia from

25. N. 87.
26. N. 90.
27. N. 94.
28. N. 100-114.

953 to 956.[29] These are among the most interesting pages.
They abound in details instructive from many points of view.
In order fully to appreciate them, it is necessary first of all to
place the events of these three years in their context in the
history of the relations between Islam and the West, and
between Eastern and Western Christendom. The gulf was not
as wide as it was to become at the beginning of the Crusades.
To quote only one example from Lothringia, we know that
merchants of Verdun continued economic relations with
Moslem Spain.[30] Indeed, the sufferings of the Christians
living under Muslim rule stimulated interest in their churches.
In the Holy Roman Empire, the nun Hrotswitha put into verse
and set as a drama the passion of St Pelagius,[31] martyred at
Cordova in 925, soon after the beginning of the long reign of
Abd-el-Rahman III of the Omayyad dynasty, who was caliph
from 912 to 961.

The visit of John of Gorze towards the end of his caliphate
likewise gains significance in the whole context. Monastic
journeys were more numerous, longer and more important in
their consequences than has sometimes been thought, especially when their objective was the East or Spain.[32] In
both places, monks had been given welcome or protection by
the Muslim authorities, at least by some of them.[33] It seems
that, from the Carolingian period on, problems in doctrine
raised in Islamic centres of Spain were known in the Holy
Roman Empire and became the subject of research.[34] Later,
exactly a hundred years before the excursion of John of

29. This part of the story begins at paragraph 115 of the *Vita*. W. von Giese-
brecht, *Geschichte der deutschen Kaiserzeit*, I (Leipzig, 1881) pp. 506-513, has
related the events following this text.

30. Pertz pointed this out, following the *Antopodosis* of Liudprand, a
contemporary chronicler, in PL 137, 299, note 411.

31. *Hrotsvithae opera*, ed. K. Streckler (Leipzig, 1930) pp. 54-66.

32. See "Les relations entre le monachisme oriental et le monachisme occidental
au Moyen Age", in *Le millenaire du Mont Athos,963-1963*, II (Chevetogne, 1965)
pp. 61-70 ("Psychologie des Voyages monastiques").

33. This appears, for example, in the Life of St Willibald; summary, ibid., p. 64.

34. Witness the work of M. Bernards, of which I gave a brief account in
L'Occidente e l'Islam nell' alto medievo (Spoleto, 1965).

Vandières, Usuard, a monk of Saint Germain-des-Prés, had gone to Cordova to look for the relics of St Vincent, and he had brought back with him relics of the Christians martyred c.825 under the Caliph Abd-el-Rahman II. Usuard had set out with Odilard, another monk, in the winter of 857-858. At Barcelona, the bishop got them an introduction to the Moslem chief Abdilumar, who entrusted them to a caravan making its way towards Cordova. On the return journey, they were given permission to accompany the army of the Emir Muhammed, who was marching on Toledo. Although "the Saracens do not allow veneration of the martyrs they themselves have made", they came back with the relics and pleasant memories of the way in which they had been protected by the Moslem chiefs in Spain.[35]

In the vicissitudes of alternating persecution and toleration, the period of John of Gorze's visit was peaceful, at least as regards the religious life. In the military and economic sphere, the Moors of Spain were abandoning themselves to piratical expeditions which reached the southernmost regions of the Empire, especially Italy, and led Otto I to protest against the damage. The Caliph of Cordova sent to him a Spanish bishop to offer his excuses. But the letters brought from Abd-el-Rahman seemed to the Emperor "to contain blasphemies against Christ". Accordingly, he got his brother Bruno, Archbishop of Cologne, to compose a missive correcting them. The problem was to find a bearer and, as the expedition involved some risk, they thought of the monks of Gorze. Being "dead to the world", they would have sufficient courage to speak freely and fearlessly in front of the potentates. Abbot Ainold designated two of his monks, Angilram and Guy. But now there occurred once again one of those violent scenes familiar to medieval life, even monastic. Only a few days before he was due to set out, Guy, reprimanded in front of the community for some negligence or other, allowed himself to be carried away by such a fit of anger towards the

---

35. According to Dom J. Dubois, *Le Martyrologie d'Usuard* (Brussels, 1965) pp. 130-132.

abbot and whole convent that he had to be dismissed. Now nobody had enough daring—the text seems to say aggressiveness (*id aggredi*)—to replace him. It was then that John of Gorze volunteered to go, fired by a "perfect charity" which made him long for martyrdom. Accompanied by only one other monk, Garamann, he set out from Gorze and entered the Saracen kingdom via the Rhône valley and Barcelona. There the authorities had him escorted with great honor as far as Cordova.

On the state of the Mozarabic Christians when they arrived the historians' judgments differ. Father Garcia Villada, relying mainly on the *Life* of John of Gorze, is inclined to be pessimistic.[36] But Edward P. Colbert takes a more favorable view of what he calls—in a phrase adopted thenceforward by the Holy See in its agreements with certain Peoples' Republics or various Muslim states—the *modus vivendi* by which the Christians coexisted peacefully with the Muslims.[37] And he emphasises the fact that at that time the Mozarabic Church retained its own culture, liturgy and theology.[38] One treaty in particular, which seems to date from the tenth century and is still preserved in the archives of the former mosque, now the cathedral, at Cordova,[39] attests to this.

But let us continue the story. The monks from Lorraine were subjected to a system of supervision and cunning investigations—*dum callide cuncta explorant* is said of the Caliph's men—in an atmosphere of secrecy. *Clam* is used repeatedly. Kept informed by his secret police, Abd-el-Rahman suspected that these envoys and their message could cause an unnecessary incident in his then peaceful kingdom. The text speaks for itself. It seems full of lifewise details, even if the name of

36. Z. Garcia Villada, *Historia ecclesiastica de España,* III (Madrid, 1936) pp. 162-4.

37. Edward P. Colbert, *The Martyrs of Cordoba (850-859): A Study of the Sources* (Washington D.C., 1962) p. 383.

38. Ibid., p. 387.

39. I have published this text under the title "Un tratado sobre los nombres divinos en un manuscrito de Cordoba", in *Hispania sacra,* 2 (1949) pp. 327-338.

the first emissary it mentions, Hasdeu the Jew, seems to have the symbolic meaning of "prudent" or "wise man". In point of fact, it was John of Gorze who was to show a fine Lorraine tenacity, whereas the caliph's representative was more moderate (*temperatior*).

The Caliph, apprehensive and undecided, scenting danger to himself, tried by every means to avert it. He sent them first of all a Jew by the name of Hasdeu, with the commission to probe them with utmost skill. (Our people were to affirm later that they had never heard or seen a shrewder man). This character had learned by hearsay that John was the bearer of an Imperial commission. He set out first of all to conciliate him, assuring him that no harm would come to them, and that they would be sent back to their own country with honor. Then he impressed upon them the laws of the land, and how they ought to behave in public. The young men in particular should be on their guard against too much freedom in word and gesture. Nothing was so trivial that it did not come to the ears of the caliph. If they were allowed to go out freely, they must take care not to make unseemly gestures to the women out of sheer high spirits, lest they should have to pay the penalty for their rough behavior. Whatever they did would be closely observed, and if the smallest transgression were found out they could be hanged.
John replied courteously, thanking the Jew for his good advice. . . . After an exchange of various topics of conversation, he [the Jew] came gradually to the heart of the matter and asked what the travellers had brought with them. Seeing John hesitate to speak (for until then everything had remained secret between him and his companions) Hasdeu promised to keep silence and even, if necessary, give him sound advice. Then John told him in detail what had brought him to Cordova: the presents from the Emperor and the letter to be read to the Caliph. Without this last, he had the right neither to produce the presents nor to present himself at the Caliph's audience. And he went on to disclose the contents. 'That is very dangerous', exclaimed the Jew. 'To see the Caliph with such a message! . . . Be very

prudent when it comes to giving a reply to his envoys. You
know the severity of the law. Take every precaution to
protext yourself against it.'

After this several more months elapsed. Then it was the
bishop who was sent to them a certain John. The conversation turned on a variety of subjects, as happens between
believers. Questions and answers followed one another in
swift succession, after which the bishop hinted that they
would do better to come before the Caliph with only the
gift. 'What! ' exclaimed John, 'what about the letter from
the Emperor? Haven't I been sent mainly to deliver it?
The Caliph has blasphemed; his absurd errors must be refuted by devastating arguments.' 'Be so good', said the
bishop mildly, 'as to take into consideration the conditions
under which we are living. Through our sins we have been
brought into subjection to the heathen. But we are forbidden by the Apostle to resist authority.[40] This much consolation is left us in such adversity, that our masters do not
forbid us to govern ourselves according to our own laws.
They even enjoy the company of those whom they have
seen to be faithful. Christians, respecting them and welcoming them. On the other hand, they detest the Jews. Therefore, it seems wise to us for the present, since our religion
suffers no detriment at their hands, to submit to them over
the rest, and to obey their orders in so far as they do not
hinder our faith. So I repeat, it is much better to hold
your peace, and suppress that letter, rather than provoke,
when their is no pressing need, a scandal to you and yours
which could be extremely dangerous.

While he spoke John felt rather annoyed. 'It ill befits a
bishop such as you to say things', he said. 'As such you are an
upholder of the faith and your noble rank makes you its
defender; you ought not yourself to be corrupted and to
restrain others through human respect from proclaiming
the truth! Would it not be much better for a Christian to
suffer the most serious injury to his reputation than take
part in the meals of the heathen to the downfall of others?
What is more, I have heard said of you something that the
whole catholic church detests and condemns: that you have
been circumcised. Have you forgotten the admonition of

40. Rom. 13, 1-5.

the Apostle that, 'If you receive circumcision Christ will do
you no good at all'.[41] And what about the foods that you
eschew so as to keep on good terms with them? 'To the
pure all things are pure'.[42] And elsewhere: 'There will be
doctors, great talkers and seducers, who will teach this and
that'[43] among others, 'abstinence from certain foods,
though God created them to be enjoyed with thanksgiving
by believers',[44] for they are 'hallowed by God's own word
and by prayer'.'[45]
The bishop answered: 'Necessity compels us to act in this
way, for otherwise there would be no possibility of coexisting
with them. Moreover, these customs come to us from our
ancestors who had them from a long and well-established
tradition.' 'Never,' replied John, 'shall I approve a way of
behaving that makes you, under the dominion of fear, good
fellowship and human respect, transgress the statutes of
God. As you are restricted in this way you argue the necessity of accommodating yourselves to the infidel. The
grace of Christ has freed me from such necessities. Through
the mercy of the Lord my heart is fixed, so that nothing,
not fear nor solicitations nor favors, will deflect me from
the course which I have undertaken at the Emperor's order.
It is with his letter, and without removing or altering one
jot or one tittle of it, that I shall present myself before the
Caliph. If someone should take it into his head to rail
against those things in it which we hold as the sound
Catholic faith and to oppose them with contradictory affirmations, I shall resist him to his face, and I shall not
shrink from bearing witness to the truth even for the love
of life itself'.

This lively quotation is very instructive, first of all on the
personality of John of Gorze; his strong, even rigid, personality and his habit of interpreting Scripture literally; then on
the difference between the two states of the Church, Christianity under Otto the Great and Christianity in the Mozarabic world, where religion did not mingle with politics. For

41. Gal. 5, 2.
42. Tit. 1, 15.
43. See Tit. 1, 10.
44. 1 Tim. 4, 3.
45. 1 Tim. 4, 5.

more than two years, the episodes in the drama continued, and it would be interesting, but drawn out, to record them all: secret diplomatic conversations between the bishop and the Caliph's men, disquiet on the part of the Caliph, vigorous assertions from John of Gorze, who the Caliph realised "would not be afraid to die"—which would solve nothing. Finally, the Caliph decided to send a fresh embassy to Otto to obtain the withdrawal of the letter entrusted to the monk for him. A Christian employed in the service of the caliphate, who spoke Arabic well, a certain Recemundus, was sounded out, and accepted only on condition that he was made a bishop before setting out. Abd-el-Rahman, "to whom it mattered little that it was an infringement of the canons", in the words of Fr Garcia Villada,[46] granted his request. Here again, Edward P. Colbert recalls the services to be rendered to Mozarabic culture by this new prelate, particularly in drawing up an important liturgical calendar.[47] However this may be, the new emissary went off to find the Emperor, got him to give in, and came back with a moderate letter. This duel between Lorrainian firmness and southern diplomacy was to end in a triumphant *dénouement.* Even in this record, in which everything is done to underline the merits of John of Gorze, Abd-el-Rahman emerges as a great prince. The refinements of the high degree of civilization which he maintained at his court were to appear on the day when, at last, he agreed to converse with our monk. Let us listen once more to the account of this princely reception and the brilliant fantasia of which it was the occasion:

> John was at last released from the imprisonment in which he had been held for nearly three years, and he was commanded to prepare to appear before the Caliph. When the Caliph's messengers told him that he must present himself to the royal gaze with his hair trimmed, and his person washed and decked in magnificent clothes, he refused. Concluding that he had no change of clothes, they informed

46. *Vita*, p. 103.
47. *Vita*, pp. 386-388 and 402.
48. Saturday, 21 June 952.

the Caliph of this. He immediately sent John ten pounds in cash to enable him to buy what was needful to be presentable to the Caliph's eyes. For it was not permissible among his people to present oneself before the gaze of the sovereign meanly clad. Undecided at first whether or not to accept the gift, John reflected at last that it would be better used for the poor. He thanked the Caliph for considering him worthy of his solicitude in showing this munificence and so refused. Then he added this, the reply of a true monk: 'I do not spurn this princely gift; however I will wear no clothes or other than those permissible for a monk, neither burnose nor anything of any other color than black.'

When this was reported to the caliph, he said, 'I can see by this reply the strength of his character. Let him come dressed in a sack, I shall see him willingly and he will please me all the more.'

On the day fixed for the audience, every kind of parade was contrived to display the magnificence of the Caliph. From their lodging all the way to the city and on to the royal palace, colorful troops thronged the route. Here infantrymen stood with fixed spears while at a distance others, brandishing javelins and darts, made a show of attacking one another. There followed others mounted on mules and lightly armed [and] after them, cavalrymen spurring their horses on till they neighed and reared. In addition to these, there were Moors whose unfamiliar appearance struck fear into the hearts of our people.... Thus by an excessively dusty route, which in itself the drought was enough to cause (for it was the summer solstice), they were led to the palace. Various nobles came forward to meet them, for the whole of the pavement immediately outside the palace was spread with the most costly tapestries and coverings.

When they came to the room where the Caliph dwelt alone, like some divinity, rarely if ever accessible, they found everything hung with curious draperies. The floors vied with the walls. The Caliph himself was reclining on a divan of utmost magnificence (for it is not the custom of these people to use thrones or seats; for conversation or for meals they recline on couches or divans, their legs placed one over the other). As John approached, the Caliph held out his hand for him to kiss the palm—a favour granted to no one, either of his own people or foreigners . . . but to those of the highest rank who were to be entertained with the greatest pomp. . . . A seat was brought forward, and he made a sign for John to sit down. A long silence followed. Then the caliph began. . . . And the two tried to outdo one another in compliments.

The situation was very nearly wrecked once again in the course of the ensuing conversation which revealed that the Caliph was well informed on Otto I's policy, which he condemned severely.

Some time later, John was once again summoned to the Caliph, who engaged him in friendly conversation about the power and wisdom of our Emperor, the quality and number of the soldiers, of his glory, his wealth, his campaigns and victories, and so forth. Moreover he bragged that in the strength of his army he excelled all the kings of the world.

To this John spoke a few words calculated to soothe the Caliph a little, but he added: 'I must say that there is no sovereign in this world known to me to equal our Emperor in either infantry or cavalry'.

The Caliph, his wrath appeased or suppressed, replied; 'It is a mistake to praise your king! ' 'See for yourself', said the other, 'whether I am right or wrong.' The caliph answered, 'I could accept everything else you have told me about him: but in one thing he has certainly not been very prudent.' 'What is that? ' John asked. 'He has not kept all power in his own hands but has allowed certain of his followers wealth and power which should be his own. Thus he has shared parts of his empire among them, as if that would make them more loyal and obedient to himself. Far from it! For in this way pride and rebellion are fostered, and now this very thing has happened in the case of his own relative, who has kidnapped his son by treachery and is openly tyrannizing the Emperor, compelling him to allow a foreign tribe, the Hungarians, to pass through and ravage his territory.'

It is at this stage in what may well be called diplomatic conversations between Abd-el-Rahman and John of Gorze that the account of John of Saint Arnoul ends unfinished. What happened next? We only know that our monk returned to Gorze, was its abbot from 967, and died there in 976.

Conclusion

The more we read of the *Lives* of saintly monks of the Middle Ages, the more we shall catch glimpses of their customs which make it possible to fill in and elaborate the finer points of those matters which historical syntheses are bound to simplify. The account which John of Saint-Arnoul wrote of John of Gorze is valuable on several scores. There is less evidence of culture at Gorze than at other monasteries, particularly Cluny, but this text, whose Latin is of a high standard, bears witness to it. Moreover, it is a reminder that reforms were not made possible solely through the agency of institutions or political influences. Of course, the juridical aspect must not be neglected. It continues to give distinctive character to various great monasteries which exercised an influence in the tenth century. On the very borders of the diocese of Metz, in the diocese of Trier, Saint-Maximin had a quite different emphasis.[49] But for the structures to be recognised as beneficial anywhere, they had to have energetic personalities behind them.

The record of John of Saint Arnoul does not tell us what John of Gorze's abbacy was like. We can assume that he retained the qualities which he had shown in his previous life. Because of his extreme reserve and his taciturnity, one historian has concluded that he was withdrawn.[50] Indeed, his biographer, who had known him well, doubted whether he

49. This fact has been studied by E. Wisplinghoff, "Die Lothringische Kloster-reform in der Erzdiozese Trier," in *Landeskundliche Vierteljahrsblätter,* 10 (1964) pp. 145-159.

50. L. Zoepf, "Die Verschlossenheit seines Charakters", *Das Heiligenleben im 10. Jahrhundert,* (Leipzig-Basa) 1908) p. 102.

had any close friends capable of wringing from him the least confidence.[51] He was always a solitary in the midst of men.[52] In this he was only putting into practice the aims of the greatest monks of all times. His outstanding virtue seems to have been his courage (*fortitudo*).[53] He showed it in his action in the economic field and in his Spanish mission. He also gave proof of it in his asceticism, which the prologue to his *Life* asserts was more important than miracles. It has even been said that the whole record was "a piece of propaganda in favour of asceticism".[54] Similarly in his death, his strength was apparent: For five days, he suffered violently (*acerrime, dolor nimius*). This agony, this "combat in him between life and death", was a last ordeal, an *examinatio*, right up to the moment when death came with difficulty (*dure moritur*). But he had used his tenacity in defending the weak, and a throng of lowly folk (*minorum quorumcumque turba non modica*) came to witness the joy in his face even in the midst of pain. The day after the onset of his illness, all the monasteries in the neighbourhood were informed. He himself was talking of nothing but the happiness of the next life. Now he is in the presence of the light of the glory of Christ (*in praesentia claritatis Christi assistit*).

---

51. *Prol.* "Si tamen quisquam ille intimas ei existeret, qui aliqua ex eo extorquere se posse confideret."

52. N. 49: "Cum ita vitam egerit, ut solitarius inter multitudines vixerit."

53. This fact was pointed out by E. Auerbach, *Litteratursprache*, pp. 122-123.

54. Zoepf, *Das Heiligenleben*, p. 98.

ST BERNARD AND THE CHRISTIAN EXPERIENCE*

IT IS HARD TO OVERESTIMATE the influence of
that great reformer of the church and monasticism, Bernard of Clairvaux (1090-1153). Moreover, the doctrinal
message he left behind him has enormously enriched theology. But it is above all by his spirituality that he has acted
upon his and every following age, including our own. Catholic tradition, and an entire stream of Lutheran tradition as
well, has always been sensitive to the profoundly religious
element in anything he says about God, about man, and
about the manner in which God and man are united in Christ
and Christians. The truth is that he lived his entire life under
the sign of an intense experience of his own wretchedness
and of the consolation afforded him by the redemption.

Gifted as he was with an extremely rich nature, he felt
more acutely than others, and in a way sometimes approach-
ing violence, every stirring which nature and grace are capable
of arousing in man. It is for this reason that this twelfth-
century monk is still so real even in our times. He might have
aspired to a fine ecclesiastical career, but he deliberately retired to the cloister. Even there he found himself caught up
in many fields of action, partly because his services were in
such demand and partly because he felt a certain need for
activity. Though ill and overworked, he was an agreeable and
even attractive personality. He was often successful in his
undertakings; sometimes, however, he met with misunder-

* Published in *La Vie Spirituelle,* 116 (1967) pp. 182-198; English translation in
Worship, 41 (1967) pp. 222-233.

standing, resistance, and failure. But this divided man analyzed himself with an inexorable lucidity, and he found in his
faith the power necessary to bring about unity between the
diverse and sometimes contradictory tendencies which he saw
within himself.

This is the synthesis which he taught in a style as varied as
it is splendid. Bernard was a poet, but he was also a writer
who has been shaped by the laws of a rhetoric inherited from
both patristic and classical literature. Thus, despite an apparently casual style, he practised a writing technique which
was very exact in composition and in editing. His vocabulary,
in particular, was consistent and was perfectly adapted to
what he wished to say. Bernard's thought was strongly
marked by reading Origen, St Augusting, and St Gregory. But
it was shaped even more by his experience of monastic life
lived according to the Rule of St Benedict and handed down
by a long tradition which had been simultaneously recorded
and experienced.

To all this that Bernard gave expression in texts which,
whether *Sermons on the Canticle,* other sermons, treatises, or
letters, do scarcely more than comment on holy scripture.[1] All
of these writings give us a glimpse of his personality and in all
we can recognize a style that has been fashioned by Bible and
liturgy. We may say that the core of his spiritual teaching
consists in revealing through analysis the double experience
that he had continually undergone: the experience of himself
and his own destitution, and the experience of God, whose
mercy gives him salvation in Christ.

His doctrine lacks neither amplitude nor speculative vigor.
To make a synthesis of it would require lengthy development, and this has already been done many times.[2] Here we
shall do nothing more than mark the genesis of his teaching
as it issued from life itself. And since we cannot say everything, we shall only consider the texts which speak explicitly

1. Bernard's works are in Migne's *Patrologia Latina,* 182-183, and in the new
edition, *Sancti Bernardi opera,* 4 volumes (Rome 1957-66).

2. In a book entitled *S. Bernard,* in the collection *Maîtres spirituels* (Paris,
1966), I have given the findings of the most recent research on St Bernard and his
works, with bibliography.

of the Christian experience, usually by the use of terms like *experiri, experientia,* and *experimentum* or words like *sensus* and *sentire.* We shall see in these texts that sentiment played a lesser part than did reflection upon the fundamental themes of all Christian experience.

The Experience of Self

Bernard's self-knowledge and the self-knowledge which he wanted to help his reader acquire in no way belonged to the realm of theory. It did not flow from abstract philosophy but from concrete, everyday experience: the experience in every man of the existence of sin, shown by the attraction to evil. Bernard insisted on acknowledging his personal wretchedness. He said that his flesh was "tainted by an evil habit," and he mentioned his temptations to murmuring, impatience, and illicit suggestions.[3] In realistic terms he described how his memory had been turned into a dirty "sewer" by the remembrance of past sins and how it needed constant purification. "Our own experience together with the testimony of the sacred text enlightens us about the heaviness of our flesh which weighs down and oppresses the spirit. The inward gaze which we turn upon ourselves is hazy and blinded, such is the frequent experience of one who would walk according to the spirit."[4]

And what a lengthy treatise on concupiscence we read in the sixth sermon for Lent. It is almost entirely concerned with the "obstacles" and "hindrances" which delay our union with God: ignorance of our true good, the pleasure we find in hurting others, the delight we take in doing wrong, bitterness, envy, detraction, discords and enmities, every kind of injustice and weakness, satisfaction of the natural desire for eating and sleeping, finding pleasure everywhere, and

---

3. *In Quadragesima* 5:1-4. The following abbreviations for Bernard's works will be used: IQ (*In Quadragesima*), DC (*De Conversione*), DD (*De Diversis*), QH (*In Ps. Qui Habitat*), SC (*Super Cantica*), DE (*In Dedicatione Ecclesiae*), IA (*In Adventu*), DDD (*De Diligendo Dei*). The titles of works referred to only once will be given in full in the text of the article.

4. DC 30.

finally the difficulty we have in knowing what God wants us to do. Elsewhere Bernard wrote about concupiscence as a stain which taints man's nature through and through, a "pest in many forms," a "pestilential virus" which leaves nothing undefiled. The inward and outward senses are attacked, the soul is inclined to ambition, avarice, envy, contumacy, voluptuousness, in a word, to every known vice. "Everything that the world and the flesh can offer by way of attractions, the just man experiences as so many temptations and tribulations. . . . From the soles of my feet to my head, there is no sign of health within me; the law of sin lies within all my members, and concupiscence has infected me throughout. On every side death seeks to enter through the windows, and filth seeks to lay hold on everything."[5]

This wretched state is brought home to us whenever we suffer temptations, which no one ever escapes. God's enemy assails us, employing our very own nature against us. Bernard depicts him tying us up in knots with our own belts and then beating us with our own stick.[6] Each of us has only to "consult his own experience" in order to measure his beggary. And even more than the body, the spirit is wounded within us. The soul's possessions are no less an object of struggle for us than are those of the body; there is war on every side. What shall we say of the "aridity that dries us up," and—Bernard never hesitated to use the words—the "stupidity" of our "imbecile mind" (*hebetudo stolidae mentis*), which we must so often own.[7] "Each day and each night the words of the prophets, the gospels, and the apostles are read to us. . . . Whence comes it then that so many vain, harmful, lewd thoughts torture us first through impurity, then through pride, ambition, and so many other passions, to such an extent that we can hardly exist in the calm of holy thoughts? Woe to us because of the slothfulness and the drowsiness of our hearts!"[8]

5. DD 25:4.
6. IQ 5:2.
7. SC 9:3.
8. DD 16:1; cf 28:6.

We become aware of this state by means of what Bernard often called *consideratio*—the inward gaze which we turn upon ourselves and which must be pitilessly discerning. It is not easy to do this: "How often thine eye is closed in slumber, blurred by smoke, wounded by a speck of dust, clouded by bad temper, sore with searing suffering; and in the end death will blind thee."[9] But even as this consideration reveals our lowliness to us, it also brings to our notice the need we have of raising ourselves up to God. There is within us a disconcerting incoherence, an astonishing alloy of contrary aspirations, "a wedding of reason and death."[10] Deep within we possess a capacity for God, a reflection of his grandeur. The very proof that he is present to us and that he wishes to set us free is the "conscience" which he has placed in us and which Bernard saw as testimony to the Spirit of God dwelling in our hearts. He is there. He it is who maintains in us the awareness of good and the desire to do it. It is he who is continually judging us.

Conscience is that inner voice by which God accuses us and by which he also calls us back to himself. Through conscience he defines our duty and urges us to do it. He is constantly questioning us, pressing us for an answer. In a word, we may say that conscience in us is the inward witness to our divine adoption and our moral obligation.[11] Thus, though he sometimes felt himself on the brink of "despair",[12] Bernard did not lose confidence in himself[13] because God was at work within him. He turned over in his mind the misery he had come to know so well. He saw clearly that his wretchedness had not tainted his "flesh," his body, but his "heart." And this is the very core of man. It is here that he comes up against the depth of his weakness. But here, too, he comes face to face with the image of God. The soul is bowed down, it must be straightened up. It has moved into the "region of

9. QH 8:6.
10. DE 5:7.
11. Cf. P. Delhaye, *Le problème de la conscience morale chez S. Bernard* (Namur, 1957) pp. 13-41.
12. DD 28:5.

dissimilitude" and must be brought back to its model, that is,
to God who created it and to Christ who recreated it.[14]

There is a remedy for this wretchedness, but it is not an
easy one to apply. Here again experience shows that it is
effective. They who join fasting to prayer are well aware of
this[15]. Since it entails lighting up our inner gaze, which "by
frequent experience" we know to be so often darkened, it
does not suffice to "swill the sewer" once and for all. There
must be an ever-renewed purification. Water is not enough.
Fire, symbol of suffering, must do its work as well. It can be
done. It begins here below in faith and will be completed
when, face to face with him, we shall be for God stainless, "a
glorious bride."[16] Meanwhile, we must confess our sins and
those inclinations to evil which are revealed in our wicked
tendencies. This is an act of voluntary humiliation, the first
step along the road to humility.

Then we shall have to watch carefully over our intentions,
our thoughts, to keep peace with all, in a word, to "strive to
tend towards eternal good things".[17] Commenting upon the
sentence of the prophet Habacuc, "I will stand on my watch-
tower" (2:1), Bernard recalled the voice of God speaking to
the heart of man, ceaselessly recalling him to this center
within himself, where he hears reproaches and warnings, but
also counsels and consolations. This is a bittersweet word. It
chastises for our correcting. Let us then be vigilant. Let our
habitual preoccupation turn "not to the dunghill of his
wretched body, but to the heart where Christ indwells".[18]

As we see, it is always an intimate experience which serves
as a touchstone, and it is the discovery of our "misery" that
urges us to cry out for "misericord," to use a play on words
which Bernard fancied. "What shall we do? Despair forthwith? Not at all! On the contrary, hope, and that as much as

14. Cf. B. Stoeckle, "Amor carnalis—abusus amoris. Das Verständis von der
Konkupiszenze bei Bernhard von Clairvaux und Aelred von Rievaulx," in
Analecta monastica, VII. Studia Anselmiana, 54 (Rome, 1965) pp. 147-74.
15. IQ 4:4.
16. DC 30.
17. DD 16:5.
18. DD 5:14.

we can." For Christ has mortified sin in us. He has sent us the Spirit of wisdom and goodness. There lies our "consolation," another of Bernard's favorite words.[19] The dignity of man, healed, liberated, redeemed by the Son of God, is greater than his wretchedness. His strength, that of the resurrection, is mightier than his enemies'. It is up to us to ask for help, and this is no easy thing, for the experience of temptation filters even into our pleading: "We return from prayer in the same state in which we went: no one answers us a single word. . . ." We must then believe in prayer as in a mystery of faith, and persevere.[20]

We must search. The need to search comes up again and again in more than one of Bernard's pages; it is like a theme which haunted him. He played freely, for example, on variations of the word *quaerere* by using biblical texts in which this word occurs. He cited the word fourteen times in some ten lines.[21] "We can hardly state briefly all the needs that we actually experience," he declared in another place. But it is those very needs which make us long for counsel, help and succor, and all this has been given to us by Jesus Christ. He came "to us, into us, and because of us," he has remained "with us" and fights "for us," because we cannot escape from our misery by our own power alone.

The incarnation and the redemption were, and they remain, our necessary salvation, but we only fully appreciate the profound worth of salvation when we have experienced our radical need for it.[22] Then we begin to "respire," a word which Bernard readily borrowed from the liturgy. Resurrection follows upon death; the spiritual man who has acknowledged his sins and who has thus tasted bitterness, now has "experience of the wine which cheers his heart." They know it well who, "aware of the wiles of the devil and all his thoughts, are enlightened by the Spirit of wisdom, and taught by their own experience."[23] For them there remains only

19. DD 28:2, 5,.
20. IQ 5:2-5.
21. DD 37:9.
22. IA 7.
23. SC 44:1.

unfailing desire and perpetual light. Thence comes "this
burning desire which they experience of seeing at long last
what they do now hear and believe." The concupiscence of
the eyes has given way to another, concupiscence of vision
(*concupiscentia videndi*).[24]

The Experience of God

Bernard, and in him the Christian whose states of soul he
described, fathomed his wretchedness. Out of the depths of
the abyss he cried out to God. He believed and he hoped; he
even knew by experience that his cry was heard. He was
saved, and little by little he would be delivered from his sin,
at last to enter into the full brightness of divine glory. But by
what forms did this answer come to him from God? In Jesus
Christ, of course. And how could he, a sinful man, bring
about this encounter? By a combination of all the means
through which God communicates himself: the sacraments,
faith nourished by scripture, and mystical experience.

The only spotless one is the slain lamb, Jesus, who, born of
a virgin, offered himself to his Father.[25] Salvation is only in
his sacrifice and his victory. Since the Word was made flesh,
not only can we imitate God as a model, a being who is apart
from ourselves, but we may actually participate in his
mystery, that is to say, enter into it and make it our own.
Here we have Bernard's whole doctrine concerning what we
may call the "sacramental imitation" of Christ. In Jesus God
has imitated us: he has come down to us, into us, so that we
may return up to him, into him, and with him. We must
therefore pass through his "mysteries," his *sacramenta*. How
shall that be?

By living them over again, as it were. By rendering them
present within ourselves through our voluntary imitation of
his actions, by the remembrance (*memoria*) which we always
have of them, and above all, by communion with them in the
holy sacraments. Without this *communicatio*, the *recordatio*,
the *representatio*, and the *imitatio* would be in vain. Now this

24. IQ 8:3.
25. DD 28:1.

"commemoration" of salvation is accomplished in the church's liturgy, above all in the eucharist. Here the benefits, the graces (*charismata*) of the authentic Pasch are unceasingly renewed, given to those who eat Christ's body and drink his blood; those whose sins are forgiven them after they have already been initiated by baptism into his death and resurrection.

What we are actually doing here is speaking about "active participation" in Christ's mysteries, not only because this participation involves the complete effort of faith and ascesis, but also because it makes possible in us the indwelling of the Father, who is glorifying the Son, and of the Holy Spirit whom the Son sends to his church. It identifies us, so to speak, with their desiring; it instills into us strength for the struggle against the wicked tendencies which remain (as daily experience shows us) but no longer dominate. It is at the origin of every inner light we receive and is already a seed of our resurrection.[26]

Nurtured by the very life of God, in this way, man can, and must, feed on his word, which has been consigned to a book whose secrets are revealed to us by the church in her liturgy. Bernard's Bible was the one he heard read and interpreted in the divine office. He assimilated its words, scrutinized its meaning, and was satisfied only when he had experienced their teaching and content. "Rejoice in your hope, be patient in tribulation, be constant in prayer", he said, commenting on Romans 12, 12. "Whosoever amongst you feels that come about within him, knows what the Spirit wishes to say, he whose voice and whose action are never separated. He it is who understands what is said, because what he hears without, he feels within."[27]

Elsewhere he wrote, "Lend your inner ear, gaze with the eyes of your heart; and you will grasp, by your own experience, what is meant here."[28] It is essential that God's word

26. Under the title "Christusnachfolge und Sakrament in der Theologie des Hl. Bernard," in *Archiv für Liturgiewissenschaft* 8 (1963) 58-72, I have brought these texts together.

27. SC 37:3.

28. DC 4.

"pass over" into life, that it be assimilated by the whole being, and penetrate the whole area of man's conduct.[29] A spiritual "relishing," a gift of the Spirit, has to make us "savor" the word; this is one aspect of that "wisdom" Bernard talked about so often.[30] The reader must transcend the text in order to rejoin him by whom it has been inspired. He must discern what this universal message has to say to him. After that he will be able to give back to God with enthusiasm and thanksgiving the words which the Lord first uttered. They become the nourishment of his praise and his spiritual son, *carmen spiritus*.[31] Thus holy scripture is always an occasion for God's personal intervention in the life of the reader. It is for him to discern the "spiritual sense" which it bears for him within the wider meaning which it has for the church as a whole. Bernard even saw in the "inspiration" which the sacred writers have received a grace similar to that enjoyed by mystics, and on this point he continued the patristic tradition. Now we see more clearly the distinction between these two kinds of charisms. At least their assimilation by Bernard shows that, for him, both writer and reader find in scripture an occasion for experiencing God.[32]

Finally, entertained and already satisfied in faith by the sacraments and the Bible, the desire for God is the stimulus for that prayer in which the entire spiritual experience finds expression and full flowering. For, despite frequent periods of aridity which cannot pass unnoticed, the soul is sometimes irrigated by a river of peace, by the joy of a good conscience, and by a relish for virtue, but also by the "delectation" born of affection for God, the *affectus*.[33] More than once Bernard revealed confidences concerning the joy he felt in prayer; and

---

29. IA 5:2.

30. Cf. R. Keretzy, *Die Weisheit in der mystichen Erfahrung bei hl. Bernard von Clairvaux* (Westmalle, 1963).

31. I have given several texts in the article "Ecriture sainte et vie spirituelle" in *Dictionnaire de spiritualité*, IV, I (1960).

32. Cf. D. Farkasfalvy, *L'inspiration de l'Ecriture sainte dans la théologie de S. Bernard*. Studia Anselmiana, 54 (Rome, 1964).

33. IQ 5:6-7.

the aspect of rhetoric, of literature, which he injected into these texts seems to be aimed at showing that he intended proposing a doctrine applicable to others as well.

Sometimes he made veiled allusions to that "unction" which helps one accept crosses,[34] to that appetite for God with which "experience" reveals he had been filled,[35] to the "kiss" that had been received, to the "inebriation" felt in prayer.[36] Sometimes in explicit if not clear terms he described these visits of the Bridegroom:

> Although oftentimes he has come within me, never have I known his coming in. I knew him to be there, I remember him to have been; sometimes I felt him coming. But how he entered and how he left, I know not. . . . I lifted me up above me: the Word was higher still. I probed my inner depths: and yet the Word was deeper. . . . How then, you will ask, since his ways are so unsearchable, did I know that he was present in me? He is living and effectual. No sooner had he entered me than he awakened my drowsy soul, he touched my stony heart. He removed whatever was unwholesome, he began to plant; he watered what was withered; he enlightened the dark recesses, opened what was locked; he set the ice ablaze, made the crooked straight and the rough ways plain. And so did my soul bless the Lord, and all that was within me did bless his holy name. . . . My heart's moving told me he was there. I knew the power of his glory from the fleeing of my vices and the repression of my fleshly passions. From the rebuking and admonishing of my hidden sins I was astonished at the depth of his wisdom. And from the gentle progress of my life I knew the kindness of his meekness. And seeing my spirit—that is, my inner being—all renewed, and as it were reformed, I perceived something of the loveliness of his beauty. And at the vision of all these things together, I was awed by the multitude of his greatness.[37]

We may wonder whether this page—which in Latin has a musicality lost in translation—describes extraordinary mystical states. Is it not rather a poetic, but nonetheless true,

34. DE 1:5.
35. DC 26-27.
36. SC 9:7.
37. SC 74:5-6.

evocation by means of biblical symbols of that purification
which the experiencing of our wretchedness has made necessary, and which the grace of the sacraments and the frequenting of the word of God have made possible to all who live by
faith and who practice asceticism? There is here a wonderful
continuity between self-knowledge, as it has been analyzed in
Bernard's texts already quoted, and this sudden awareness of
God's presence. This, too, is part of the condition of redeemed man.

There is no doubt that in its highest forms there may be
some going out from self, which Bernard calls, according to
the cases, *excessus* or *extasis*: it is then a "brief moment, a
rare experience"[38] But this sublime ravishment is an upper-
limit, and in no way necessary, case which illustrates the
"experience" of the union of man's will with God's, an
experience to which all may aspire.[39] There are degrees and
varieties in the experiencing of God.[40] Bernard did not even
hesitate to say that it can be an everyday affair. Commenting
on St Paul's words "The Spirit himself asketh for us with
unspeakable groanings" (Rom 8:26), Bernard wrote: "And so
it is. He who makes us to groan is himself represented as
groaning. And though there may be many who are thus heard
to groan, it is but a single voice which resounds from every
lip. And whose, if not the voice of him who gives to each
what he shall say in every need? And the manifestation of
the Spirit is given to every man for profit. A man's voice
makes him known and indicates his presence. And I hear
from the gospel that the Holy Spirit has a voice: 'The Spirit,'
saith he, 'breatheth where he will, and thou hearest his voice,
but thou knowest not whence he cometh and whither he
goeth.' Indeed he knew it not, this dead master who taught
the dead letter which killeth. We who have passed from death
to life by the Spirit who quickeneth, know by a certain and
daily experience—he himself by his enlightening does give us
proof—that our vows and our groanings do come from him,
and do go to God, and there do find mercy in his sight. When
indeed would God disdain his Spirit? He knoweth what the

38. SC 85:3; DDD 27.
39. SC 1:11.
40. SC 4:1; 31:4-5; DDD 39.

Spirit desireth, because he asketh for the saints according to God."[41]

And again, this experience supposes faith, and those to whom it is not given, or who, on account of their misery, do not presume to receive it, must be able to trust themselves to those to whom it has been given and who have borne witness concerning it.[42] This experience must always remain spiritual, it is not sensible. Given otherwise than in faith, such an experience is "fallacious".[43] Nor can it come from book-learning,[44] nor from mere intelligence.[45] It is itself the best of books.[46] The "comprehension" it bestows is the fruit of holiness, not discussion.[47] Just as it is in "the flesh" we feel the concupiscence of sin, in "the heart" we experience this new birth which comes from the Holy Spirit, and thanks to which we can say with St Paul: "But we have the mind of Christ".[48] Such is the blessed "experience which we have of the fullness of intimate sweetness." It flowers in solitude and silence, in recollection and expectation.[49]

Mysticism and Asceticism

Mystical experience after the manner of St Bernard has often been spoken of. The first thing to remember is that it cannot exist without an experience in ascetical living. The one and the other are, as it were, two slopes of the same mountain, both leading to the same peak, or, if you prefer, they are like two panels of a diptych. If only one is seen, the tableau is incomplete. There is a certain amount of rhetoric, but also of realism, in the way in which he described these two aspects of every Christian life: the depths of human misery and the heights of union with God. It is only after we have groped about in the abyss that we can stretch up to-

41. SC 59:6.
42. SC 38:2; 84:7.
43. SC 28:8-9.
44. DC 25.
45. SC 22:2.
46. SC 3:1.
47. *De consideratione* 5:30.
48. *De laude novae militiae* 24; cf I cor 2: 16.
49. *Epistola* 128:2.

wards the peak. Both are described for us in breath-taking, even exaggerated, terms so that the image may be all the clearer. Let each one recognize himself. It is for the saint devoured by love, for the writer of genius wholly possessed by God, to express, in the name of all who have not received these exceptional gifts, what goes on in them—in their own way and according to their own measure.

In this sense Bernard's message is useful to all, and we could apply to him this same character of "practicality" which Jacques Maritain once attributed to the vocabulary of St John of the Cross.[50] Over and above a poetic style and an analysis of spiritual states which remain exceptional, his writings manifest a kind of teaching which many can put into action and realize in their daily life. These texts, which seem so sublime that they become discouraging or pass for rhetoric, describe nothing more than the difficult ascent of every Christian to God, beginning with his experience of his own weakness. The mystical writings will only be understood if we bear in mind the ascetical pages which must never be separated from them and which are preparatory to them.

Mortification of the flesh leads to radiance of the spirit. We do not even have two successive phases here. They co-exist, they alternate or mingle, to the point that the absence of one can prevent the grasping of the other. It is for the theologian to help us to see each of them clearly, distinct yet inseparable. He helps us not to lose courage at the sight of our destitution, not to lose courage in the face of marvels of which his grace is both capable and (often under very lowly appearances) accomplishes in every one of the faithful. He reminds us, too, that the religious experience does not depend on psychology or on speculation, but that it is rooted in faith, in frequenting the word of God, in the participation of the mysteries of salvation, especially by the sacraments and above all by the eucharist. So it is that Bernard's testimony is stamped with a vigorous realism which explains his sparkle. Here every Christian may discover his own advance

---

50. J. Maritain, "La 'practicité' du vocabulaire de S. Jean de la Croix" in *Distinguer pour unir ou les degrés du savoir* (Paris, 1932) pp. 647-67.

along the way which is life in Christ and which leads from sin to glory.

Here, too, the message is consoling. In a first redaction of the fifth of his Sermons on Diverse Things, Bernard had quoted this verse of St Augustine: "O God, may I know thee, may I know myself (*Deus, noverim te, noverim me*)."[51] Bernard had added: "Such is the true philosophy: this twin knowledge is required for salvation: the first gives birth to fear and humility, the second to hope and charity."[52]

Then, in the definitive text, Bernard developed this thought in terms which might well serve to conclude an exposé of all his teaching: "These two realities are the résumé, the summa of the spiritual life. By the consideration of ourselves we are first troubled and saddened, so that we may forthwith respire in God-sent salvation; then it is that we are gladdened by the Holy Spirit. And this is consolation."[53]

51. Augustine, *Soliloquia* II, 1. PL 32, 885.

52. Text edited by J. Leclercq, *Recueil d'études sur S. Bernard,* II (Rome, 1966) p.199.

53. DD 5:5.

THE LESSONS OF THE MILLENARY OF

MONT SAINT-MICHEL*

O N GLANCING THROUGH THE VOLUME of
Mélanges published on the occasion of this millenary,
one has the impression of knowing a good deal, but
no all.[1] What kind of things do we know? What kind of
interest do they enkindle? Although the first part of the
volume (286 pages) has been given the title *Historical Survey,*
it can at most hazard a few suggestions on the subject of the
even whose thousandth anniversary is being celebrated, and
of the long procession of facts, happy and unhappy, which
escort it up to our day.

What the Chronicles Say

As to the facts recorded for the centuries following this
event, we can abandon ourselves to apparently disillusioned,
but ultimately encouraging, reflections on the misleading
character of monastic history as it can usually be written, and
also, in a general way, on the limitations of historiography
when it is applied to spiritual undertakings. If, knowing
nothing of Mont Saint-Michel, you read the volume of
Mélanges with an open mind, you cannot fail, in turning over
the pages, to make two kinds of observation: it treats the

* Published in *Nouvelle revue luxembourgeoise,* 3 (1966) pp. 243-252; in Italian
in *Vita monastica,* 19 (1965) pp. 122-120.
1. On the history of this dictum, see H. Silvestre, "A propos du dicton
'Claustrum sine armario quasi castrum sine armentario'," in *Medieval Studies,* 26
(1964) pp. 351-353.

material rather than the spiritual, and troubles rather than holiness.

To begin with, one marvels at the mass of material which the scholars have drawn and illustrated from their sources. But the most frequent vocabulary applied to them and to the problems which they raise, concerns goods, possessions, domains, treasure, revenues of every kind, donations, oblations, allowances, rents, grants, disputes, usurpations, robberies, restitutions, deals, settlements, claims, agreements, contracts, concordats, covenants, chirographs, charters, diplomas, bulls genuine or false, the acquisition, theft and receiving of relics, purchases, expenses, exchanges, allowances, quit-rents, honoraria for Masses, emoluments, benefices, rents, tithes, annates, prospective favors, overlord's lodging rights, patronage rights, burial rights, and the *regale,* monopoly of the purchase of fish, alienated tithes, and goodness knows how many other expressions relating to the temporal!

There are also references to the buildings: constructions and enlargements, subsidence, repairs and reconstructions; and to the ceremonies which buildings witnessed or caused: dedications, processions and so on. Names of dependencies are found—fiefs, churches, parishes, villages, houses, cells, obediences, lands, estates, islands, holdings, mills, vineyards, fishing grounds—deeds of partnership and lists of abbeys. Of the last, we know chiefly administrative documents. In contrast to the many names of princes, lords and bishops, of great men in the world and in the Church, very few monks are mentioned. On the rare occasions when there is mention of them, their functions and not themselves as people are referred to. Only one list of monks for the Middle Ages has come down to us, and that does not appear in the book. It belongs to the end of the tenth and the beginning of the eleventh centuries—to be exact, it goes from 996 to 1009, covering about fifteen years. The brethren are divided into two categories, as if ready for the last judgment: the living and the dead (*haec sunt nomina vivorum fratrum . . .* and *haec nomina defunctorum*). There are about fifty on the first list and about forty on the second. But this document tells us nothing of a single one of those it mentions, except that, like everyone else, they lived and they died. Moving in its terseness, this is the only testimony that we possess of a generation of inhabitants of Mont Saint-Michel.

So, as soon as an interest in men is aroused, the question cannot fail to arise, where are they? Who are they? How did they live, pray, suffer? From time to time, it is true, there are some vivid glimpses of the life, more vivid as they are rare: the care taken of the feverish (*febricitantes*) and the chilly (*frigoritici*) at the time the monks venerated St Sigismund and his relic; the "comical figures" with which they insisted on enlivening the austere cartulary; the romance of Guillaume de Saint-Pair, a mediocre pilgrim's handbook, which costs its author many a vigil:

> *Un moine l'a ainsi escreite*
> *Et mise en français du latin*
> *Mout i pensa soir et matin.*

(A monk hath thus written it, and set in French from the Latin; mightily did he think thereon by day and by night).

There are instructions about menus and even about kitchen utensils. Copious details are given in several places of the way in which, through Chapter, the Council and the customary, the abbot's authority, and sometimes authoritarianism, or simply his opinions on observance were held in check. In this way we learn that "the cantor and sub-cantor are excused from attending the *Alleluia* and the responsories at Mass". True, the cantor was not necessarily someone who had a good voice and used it, but someone "who, as is known, directied the liturgical and intellectual life in the ancient monasteries". It is understandable, if regrettable, that he should not have had time to be there for the sung parts of the Office.

The side of the monks' existence for which we have most information is the life led in priories from the end of the tenth to the beginning of the fourteenth centuries. In about twenty places, often near but sometimes very far away from the abbey, there lived forty religious or so—slightly more than the number of monks resident at Mont Saint-Michel. In each of these priories were generally two, occasionally three, but usually a single monk on the spot while the other was visiting the property, "whose administration, even reduced to the daily routine, was a heavy burden". At Tombelaine, a relay priory, the time was divided between solitary prayer and the care of pilgrims. Monks came there too from the monastery for periods of "spiritual exercises" or retreat, and "the alternation of the cenobitic and the eremitical life" was thus made available to many. In those of the priories which were pious foundations, monks prayed with a special intention for the donors. In the hermitage priories, which were generally situated in beautiful surroundings so as to "bear the spirit towards God", separation from the world, and the absence of pastoral work were more marked.

Everywhere the life was "eremitical rather than cenobitic"; "liturgical prayer was simplified to such an extent that it must have differed very little from private prayer, nourished by biblical texts". In short, in those places where the original monastic tradition of Mont Saint-Michel was maintained, the dangers and opportunities of the idiorhythmic way were revealed. On the one hand, as Dom J. Dubois writes, "the proliferation of these small houses, where the monks had to remain alone with little to do and with insufficient means, could be disastrous"; on the other, "precise and punctilious regulations were inapplicable there. A rigid discipline which crushed all initiative, all thought and even all hope of personal prayer would have been inconceivable. If by their modest proportions the priories did not allow spectacular achievements, they brought each one a peace and tranquillity which alternated pleasantly with the heavy demands of the life at the abbey. Life in the priories corresponded basically with the Rule learnt in the novitiate. The priories of Mont Saint-Michel were not mission centres because the monastic life there was seen as directed towards contemplation. Those most popular with the monks were among the most isolated. Thus at the time when the new monastic orders, Carthusians and Cistercians, stood out in their simple and hidden life, the priories made it possible for the monks of the ancient tradition to follow this ideal too. In spite of the slender organization, or perhaps because of it, the priories made it possible for chosen souls to attain to genuine sanctity". Once again the sources are concerned primarily with the outward life of the priories—their number, their origin, their geographical situation, their organization and the workings of their economy. With them as with everything, human details are rare indeed in comparison with all that is recorded in the realm of the material. Even when it comes to one of the documents most explicit on the subject of the life of the monastery, the customary of 1258, we are warned that "most of the arrangements it contains are not of a spiritual or ascetic nature, nor even definitely disciplinary, but administrative". Such indeed, generally and this case in particular, is the information we are given by the texts in whose light history may be written.

Does this mean that the scholars have made a poor job of it? On the contrary, they have worked very conscientiously. They have added nothing to the sources' evidence, they have interpreted as little as possible, they have not invented, they have not embroidered, they have not indulged in facile apologetics. We should be grateful to them for their professional honesty. But this becomes the question then: have the documents spoken of everything and everyone? We are compelled to answer "no", and to establish here, once again, that it is almost impossible to penetrate the mystery of human history, that is, the history of men, beyond the public records they leave behind. Through the silence of the sources, we must guess at the silence of those who spoke only to God, who made themselves known only to him, and who left no trace in the charters and chronicles: self-effacing, forgotten beings, whose memory is lost to the learned.

And yet, who prayed and lived in these edifices whose dates we establish? Who copied, read and meditated upon the manuscripts whose illuminations we describe? Who obeyed under the jurisdiction whose administration we study? These ordinary people—there is no proof that they were mediocre, and we may be sure that some were heroic—were content simply to live. The annalists, on the contrary, spoke. Their job was telling stories and deeds which are worth telling, which are, as possible, sensational, and, when nothing unusual had happened, even invented. The real life of the majority of men and of monks is utterly ordinary, everyday, without incident but not without thoughts and feelings, temptations, faults and victories, and interior movements in the presence of God.

This part of the history of Mont Saint-Michel, richer in genuinely religious deeds and spiritual experience than studies based on the written record, should not be underestimated. Here is a whole realm of silence for God and of the anonymity which covers forever the innumerable monks who lived for him, with all the spiritual desolation and spiritual resources, the struggles and the opportunities for fervour common to men of all time. Without them, none of the rest would have any value. After reading through so many learned works which refer to the others, justice would demand that we go and, if it still exists in some corner of the church and cloister, meditate on the tomb of the unknown monk.

The Deterioration of Monastic Institutions

Let us admit freely that we do not know the most important part. But, going by what we do know, at least what picture can we form of life at Mont Saint-Michel?

Once again on this point, the normal vocabulary of the *Mélanges* is revealing. So often it tells trials, difficulties, abuses, rivalry, quarrels, conflicts, accusations, tensions. Need we quote a few phrases?

"They had already departed from the monastic ideal. . . ."

"The unfortunate antagonism between Fécamp and Mont Saint-Michel which embittered the years 1020 - 1120" (that is, a hundred years). . . .

"After the true balance painfully achieved towards the end of the eleventh century and maintained at great cost during the greater part of the twelfth, the deterioration of monastic institutions becomes apparent from the beginning of the thirteenth. . . ."

"The abbatial succession became uncertain, resignations or depositions and interregna increased. . . . This anarchy could not fail to have results unfortunate for the temporal and spiritual alike. . . . Thus Mont Saint-Michel had a series of difficult years in the twelfth century from 1085 to 1154", which represents seventy-five years. From 1131 to 1149, in other words, for eighteen years, Bernard of Bec was an abbot after the heart of St Benedict and the great models he had had at his original monastery, Herluin, Lanfranc, Saint Anselm. And yet, "even in the best years, there was not an abbacy which was not marked by difficulties. . . ."

After such chapter headings as "The great distress of the abbey (1149-1154)" and "Anarchy at Mont Saint-Michel (1151-1154)", it is a relief to read about "The renewal of the monastic life . . . under the abbacy of Robert of Torigni (1154-1186)", a period of only thirty-two years. A bit later however, "the monastery . . . neglected by its abbot, at least in all but material things, declined rapidly. . . . The decadence which had set in in the thirteenth century, . . . became more pronounced in the course of the fourteenth. . . ."

During this century, Benedict XII undertook a general reform, but his prescriptions "probably came to nothing in the end. . . ." Finally, "in 1524, the abbey of Mont Saint-Michel fell once and for all into secular ownership and from then on decadence prevailed in spite of the efforts of the Maurists in the seventeenth century".

And for this, everyone was responsible, from the Roman Curia on down.

And so when we consider the march of the centuries, we have the impression of a series of crises, of decadence followed sometimes by efforts at reform, some of which succeeded up to a point. What do we see where we try to assess the institutions? Embezzlement over long periods, living by twos in the priories—these cases "call for the greatest caution"—, lack of freedom in abbatial elections, the almost constant,

sometimes "brutal", intervention of princes. In short, the
continual pressure of the temporal on the spiritual gives the
impression of a period when monasticism—here at least—
could not be its true self, that is the simple venture of searching for God. A period not to be repeated.

What about the men? The only ones who are known are
the abbots. The best appear as great lords, great builders,
great administrators. Where are the great spiritual masters?
Not one saint in a thousand years. One man of God, John of
Fécamp, is mentioned several times, but he did not come
from Mont Saint-Michel. The greatest figure is Robert of
Torigni, "diplomat, architect, historian, a good administrator
and an excellent abbot", in all ways comparable to Suger
except for his literary talent, for "he was always a trite,
muddled and boring annalist". "He had his own private apart-
ments built, ready by the king's first visit in 1158, and he was
able from time to time to go hunting with his prior". He also
possessed a summer residence. One of the fourteenth century
abbots, Jean de la Porte, had "the reputation of being a holy
man even in his lifetime." In the fifteenth century, Pierre Le
Roy was above all else a *doctor famosissimus* in canon law. In
general "at Mont Saint-Michel as elsewhere, the abbot was
absorbed principally by material duties"—quite the opposite
of the program set out for abbots by the Rule of St Benedict.

Be that as it may. If Mont Saint-Michel did not experience
the abbatial sanctity that was to mark, for example, Cluniac
life, neither was it the scene of tremendous scandals. It rarely
happened that an abbot, like Jourdain at the beginning of the
thirteenth century, had to be sent away from the community
to prevent his bad example from infecting others, or that
another, like Jean de la Faë at the end of the same century,
was "accused of nearly every crime". Generally speaking,
Mont Saint-Michel was an ordinary monastery with an
average community "living honestly on the revenues of the
property". The abuses were those which occured everywhere
in an age which constantly mixed the temporal with the
spiritual. From that point of view they are not particularly
serious. There were ups and downs, but the monks often

behaved pretty well, reminding us of minimal level of honesty, *aliquid honestatis,* which St Benedict required. Be that as it may, if the Michelins were not holy monks, they were sometimes good monks. In what proportion? The statistics are God's secret. "Leaving aside a dissolute life", writes the thirteenth century historian," we can be sure that the monks thought it enough to live the life of an honest Christian. . . . They do not constitute a model of fervour, but the spiritual life is not entirely neglected. . . . The Michelin monks were still conscious of their spiritual role, of the example they ought to give and of the prayers and good works they had to accomplish for their own eternal salvation and that of all those, religious, clerics and lay folk, above all, pilgrims who counted on their merits to compensate for what they themselves have not achieved. Their bad habits and the mitigations in their rule do not make them Saint-Bernardin monks."

But what other past religious institution could not elicit the same comment, once the golden age of their foundation was over? If Mont Saint-Michel was not an intellectual centre adorned by a Lanfranc or an Anselm, if it was not granted an Odo or an Odilo, even a Peter the Venerable, it did promote the form of hidden sanctity made possible by such historical circumstances as God allowed. The documents teach us primarily what is sometimes best not to know: the scandals, of which we have spoken. Side by side with them, however, in spite of them, often even because of them, there was the anonymous virtue of those who sanctified themselves, who did not become saints, recognized and canonized, but who were nonetheless holy in God's sight, who, without saying or writing anything, suffered from all the situations whose outward verifiable manifestations scholars study, and which redeemed them. They were able to express their humiliation and their desire only to God in prayer. But their love, which had its beginning within these walls, lives on for ever.

Thus the sincere and objective recollection of all the ups-and-downs of Mont Saint-Michel can still serve as a source of encouragement. Some people say that the world, like the monastic life, is in a state of crisis. The history of a monastery, as it was, as God accepted it, is the story of a series of crises. We must not think that ours is the last, or that we are going, once and for all, to resolve everything. The world will be in a state of crisis and in the process of sanctification until the last judgment.

Early History and Reform

And now, after we have opened this prospective window to eternity, let us go back to the beginning, or more precisely the beginnings. Before the year 966 the area of Mont Saint-Michel had had a great period of monasticism. Renewal should not make us forget origins, the time of its first youth. The whole story about the "monks living in the country about Mont Tombe in the second half of the 6th century" is not known, and the shrewdness of historians like Dom Jacques Hourlier, gives us "a glimpse . . . of a strict religious life within an extremely free and flexible framework. It is a type of monasticism with a primitive, 'unstructured' outward appearance. Of course the necessities of the life would have demanded a basic minimum organization, but this left room for individual tendencies and seemingly independent ventures to appear. Monastic society did not restrict monks. Another trait is the apostolic zeal of these monks, who lived in the midst of territory still strongly pagan. A third characteristic, connected with the first, should be noted: the solitary life, eremitism, practiced to a greater or lesser degree, held an important place with them, either within the monastery itself or, more commonly, in the temporary or permanent retreat of one or several monks in a forest or on an island. Avranches and Cotentin seem in this respect to have been a favorite and attractive region. Taking the different proportions into account, it might be compared to the Coast of Provence with its islands".

Many monks delighted in withdrawing to islands or mountains. Here the two forms or states of solitary life were united. As I have seen happen in a fraternity on an island in one of the Great Lakes of Africa, an hour and a half by canoe from the nearest coast, "the monks made smoke signals". "A priest supplied them with food", while they devoted themselves "in individual cells" to the "secrets of the contemplative life". This priest fulfilled "a function of a different order". The "brethren", who were also called "clerics" and "canons", were still to retain in the time of Saint Aubert, and probably long after, this "ascetic and even more, mystical ideal, utterly devoted to contemplation", with particular emphasis on the recitation of the divine office, a bias which the community of Mont Saint-Michel maintained throughout the Middle Ages, and which was renewed on the arrival of "the twelve Maurists (of whom three were priests and one a lay brother)". Writes Dom J. Hourlier:

> The first monks of Mont Saint-Michel lived their life of contemplation within a very flexible institutional framework. If an organization developed later with Aubert, who accentuated the liturgical service and who may have established an abbey on the Mount itself . . ., the system remained that of the *lavra* as it was known in the East, and as St Benedict had practised it near Subiaco. The details of the organization and the observance escape us, but it is certain that Mont Saint-Michel deliberately practised a type of monasticism distinct from the Benedictine stream. Its example draws attention to those genuine monasteries where the rule of St Benedict did not triumph until very late over the ancient monasticism which, although less structured than the Benedictines born of the reform of Gerard of Brogne and others, nevertheless proved its worth, enabling communities to span several centuries.

Thus it remained until, in 965 - 966, duke Richard I of Normandy introduced monks from Saint Wandrille. Two groups survived: the canons, reduced to two clerks, serving the parish Church, while the monks in another Church maintained the Divine Office. The reform had done its work, and on this subject we might allow ourselves, in conclusion, a few reflections on monastic millenaries.

Indeed, if the monastic institution in the East as in the

West has had at least fifteen centuries existence, reformed or renewed monasticism in the West is about a thousand years old. And so throughout Europe people have been celebrating millenaries for some years, such as those, in 1966, of Mont Saint-Michel and of Saint Pierre de Perouse. Up to a point, they throw light on one another, in the sense that they are all part of a vast reformation whose expression in Italy and beyond the Alps have common features. The general reflections which may be made on this subject consist in recalling that these reforms were not part of a universal and organized enterprise in the Church, but regional. All, however, answered the same deep need which gave unity to this collection of events.

First and foremost, the somewhat anarchic character of the monastic reformation which extended from about 950 to about 1050 should be noted: the century in whose course occured the foundations or renewals whose millenaries we are celebrating at this time. An anarchic or, if you like, acephalous character distinguishes this reformation from that which began later in the so-called Gregorian period towards the middle of the eleventh century, beginning with Leo IX and pursued by Hildebrand — Gregory VII. This first reformation was in no way official. It was not determined by any central authority. No person took the overall initiative in these "monastic reforms", which must be mentioned in the plural. There does not exist a single man—founder or reformer, saint or some kind of leader—who can take credit for having organized it. In particular, the initiative and the vitality did not come from the papacy, which at the time needed reforming itself and would only assist these reforms later on, when it had itself been reformed partly under the influence of monasticism. But it did not reform monasticism.

Nor was it Cluny, any more than any great centre, whose influence extended through the whole of monasticism. In other respects, Cluny was to have contact with other reformed monasteries. No more was the central driving power at the abbey of Gorze, which likewise celebrates its millenary this year. It was not Monte Cassino, for it too was in need of reform. Furthermore the reformation was not the work of an emperor or some prince, as had been the case in the days of Charlemagne and Louis the Pious. It cannot therefore be said that there was, before the Gregorian, *one monastic reform.* There were several of them, and moreover there was a reformation, by which I mean a vast movement of reform which was a spontaneous manifestation of the vitality of monasticism, which itself constitutes one aspect of the vitality of the Church. Every time people have been aware of a renewal of life in the Church, a renewal in monasticism has been observed. And this kind of law is being proved true today as it has at other times.

Thus, before the institutional reform, organized and to a greater or lesser degree centralized, there must be—and there was then—a spontaneous reform to enable it to happen. The vital reaction of the monastic organism precedes organization: the latter can assist the former, but it can also, to varying degrees, stifle it. This anarchic character of the pre-Gregorian reforms may be explained by two fundamental elements in monasticism. The first consists in the fact that monasticism is in itself an institution for reform, but for personal reform, that is, the continual "conversion" of people. If it exists, monasticism cannot *not* reform itself, even if no authority takes the initiative. Authority can help and encourage but in itself it is not enough and it is not always necessary. It was this leaven of personal, ascetic, spiritual reform which in the pre-Gregorian period revealed its activity in monasticism. That in its turn helped to maintain in the whole Church the idea and the ideal of reform. Thus monasticism could, had to, reform itself without the help of a central organization, and it did.

The acephalous character of the monastic reforms of the time is equally linked to the fact that the monastic institution is decentralized, or rather uncentralized. It had no founder in the sense of one particular founder, the only one, but it has had founders, known or anonymous. Saint Benedict did not start monasticism, even in the West, and no saint before him or after him—such as St Benedict of Aniane—had that role. We can only say that slowly, from the seventh to the tenth century, the Rule of St Benedict became the chief and fundamental law of monasticism in the West. Even so, when a few years ago the millenary of the reform of Gérard de Brogne was celebrated, people wondered whether the Rule of St Benedict was really the one the saint had adopted.

If there was no one single movement of reform, there were regional movements of reformation, in the wide sense of the expression. There were centers which served as nuclei for the spread of reformed monasticism. These centers of reform most often consisted of new or renewed monasteries, not those which were ancient and powerful but grown old, too much involved in the network of feudal, political, economic, or at all events temporal, institutions. It is nearly always young monasteries, like Cluny, Mont Saint-Michel, and Saint-Pierre de Pérouse, or rejuvenated ones, like Gorze, which reform monasticism, and some will reform ancient monasteries. Reform is, so to speak, contagious, and contacts are made between different monasteries wishing to take advantage of it. This kind of mutual attraction between reformed or reforming houses is seen in many regions. Mont Saint-Michel is a typical case. As in certain other places, reform consisted in importing monks where canons, possibly irregular, were living. It gained by contributions from Saint Wandrille, Brogne and Ghent. It had connections with monasticism in Brittany and England, with Cluny and Dijon, and through Dijon it got men, texts and ideas from Fruttaria in the subalpine region and from Ravenna.

Thus networks of communication were created, vast, but limited. They were not universal and they were neither organized nor institutional. They were made through personal relationships and sustained by the communion of the whole of new or renewed monasticism in the same ideal of reform. of reform.

Finally, if there were centers of reform like this, despite the lack of organization, certain of which spread their influence far, very far, afield, it was because a direct means of influence, human relationships, contact between man and man, existed. If ideas travelled, it was because monks travelled. Saint Romuald was a great traveller who went from one monastery to another, rousing fervor everywhere, and criticized for his instability. The abbots of Cluny also travelled a lot: Saint Odilo went to Italy five times, without any official mission, without power, but not without authority. He had his own personal authority, the prestige of his security and of the ideal life he represented. Jean of Fécamp went from Ravenna to Normandy. These saints and these abbots sacrified personal stability for the benefit of monastic stability.

In the century which runs from 950 to 1050, they took part in an intense fermentation of the reforming ideal, and it is this that gives profound unity to the whole reformation, despite the absence of organization among the different reforms. This fermentation could only be the effect of the monastic spirit, that is, the spirit of the monks, and so, ultimately, of the Holy Spirit in them. To reform monasticism and anything else, more important than organization, centralization and institutions, is fervor.

BOOKS AND READING IN MEDIEVAL CLOISTERS*

MEDIEVAL MEN liked to compare the abbey library with an arsenal, without which the monks could not carry out their combat for God, and a proverb declared:

> A cloister without a book-cupboard
> is like a camp without ammunition.[1]

Nearer to our time, Cardinal Schuster was in the habit of saying that monastic decadence sets in when the library is no longer frequented. The library, in all ages, has answered a double need of the religious life: there must be books, and they must be used. Let us then recall in turn the place which they occupied in the organization of claustral life, then the benefits which were expected and received from their reading.

The Books

To possess them was in no way a luxury. On the contrary, it was a prime necessity requiring effort and expense. Their production, maintenance and preservation raised problems of conventual life, economics, financial administration and, finally, architecture.

In order to make books, a dauntless spirit and the necessary resources were needed first. Copying was a work which many liked but all found costly. One may believe the case of the

283

monk of Lorsch to be exceptional: he put his name at the end of the work he had just transcribed as though to express his gratification at having finished, but did not add—as one of his brethren hastened to do—that they had had to chain him to his desk to help him overcome the temptation to give the whole thing up.[2] In addition to the continuous effort of concentration and fatigue of the eyes and fingers, there was the tension of the whole body. The position of the scribe was uncomfortable. Seated on a stool in front of a desk that was sometimes unsteady and to which were attached the full ink-horns, quills and scrapers, he had constantly to be preventing one or other of these instruments or receptacles or himself from toppling over.[3] A line drawing in the middle of a page at the end of a twelfth century copy of St Augustine shows us a copyist, Hildebert, in this position, one quill behind his ear and another in his right hand, holding in his left a pumice-stone to remove the rough patches on the parchment or to correct the mistakes in transcription. Near him sits his assistant, his *amanuensis,* preparing a sheet of parchment for him. And at his feet there is a low table—*mensa Hildeberti,* reads the caption—on which a mouse is prowling round a quarter of cheese and a piece of bread. The page spread on the desk announces the feelings of Hildebert, immobilized by his work and helpless to prevent his dinner from going down another throat than his own and his collaborator's: "Wretched mouse! How many times have you moved me to anger! May God destroy you!"[4]

The patience demanded by the labor of copying was perhaps more the virtue of nuns than of monks. From the time of St Jerome and Eusebius of Caesarea, there are known

2. This fact and others have been recorded by D. J. Dubois, "Les bibliothèques monastiques", in *Feuille des oblats de l'Abbaye Sainte-Marie de Paris,* n. 21 (January 1955) pp. 14-15.

3. See A. Dain, *Les manuscrits* (Paris, 1949) pp. 21-27.

4. "Pessime mus, saepius me provocas ad iram. Ut Deus te perdat! " This page of the MS A XXI-1 of the Library of the Chapter of Saint-Guy in Prague is reproduced in the catalogue of the exhibition *L'art ancien en Tchéco-Slovaquie* (Paris: Musée des Arts décoratifs, 1957) pl. 8.

examples of this feminine accomplishment.[5] In the eighth century, it was to Edburge and Saint Lioba that St Boniface sent his "book orders".[6] In the tenth century at the abbey of Saint-Gall, the recluse Wibonada, anxious over the approach of the Hungarian invasion, made this recommendation: "Save your books first of all, then the sacred vessels and the monastery's goods".[7] In the twelfth century, the nun Diemud of Wessobrun "copied in a magnificent hand about fifty manuscripts".[8] Many other cases could be quoted. Did nuns write more legibly than monks even then? One monk in the twelfth century sent a work of his to the nuns of Nieder-münster "to be transcribed legibly" (*ut legibiliter scriba-tur*").[9] They were not content to copy; they also composed, particularly poems, as the Carmels have long continued to do.

The making of a manuscript required considerable organiza-tion. It presupposed in the first place a sufficient supply from flocks and herds to furnish the skins necessary for the pre-paration of parchment and the leather required for the binding. In the ninth century, the wife of Geoffrey Martel, Count of Anjou, wishing to have at her disposal a collection of sermons, gave to the monastery where they were to be copied two hundred sheep and, in addition, several bushels of wheat. For the skin of the sheep was still only the raw material: the skins still had to be worked on in a workshop, then entrusted to the team of the *scriptorium*, that is, the writing room. If monks need to possess forests in which they had the rights over the game, particularly quadrupeds such as roebucks, stags and wild boar, it was not so that they could go hunting—which was forbidden clerks by canon law. If nuns were glad to accept game as rent, it was because they too had to think about their bindings. Geoffrey of Anjou, founding in 1047 the abbey of Sainte Marie of Saintes, set

---

5. See P. Schmitz, *Histoire de l'ordre de S. Benoît*, VII, *Les Moniales* (Maredsous, 1956) pp. 259-260.

6. Schmitz, p. 261.

7. Ibid., p. 263.

8. Ibid., pp. 264-265.

9. Ibid.

aside for this purpose the tithe of stags and doe caught on the isle of Oléron.[10]

The production of books demanded equally a certain division of labor. From this trade, from the thirteenth century, a term was borrowed which was destined to become frequent: piece, translating *pecia*, which probably comes from *pecus,* that is sheep, as in [French] "pécore", "pecque", etc. In the language of the tanners and parchment makers, the word designated a piece of parchment prepared so that it could be written on. This *folio* was folded across the middle, which made four double pages in 4° format, then it was folded again to make eight 8° pages, or a *quaternio*, a section. Each of these sections or pieces was given out to a different copyist. The sections were hired out by the parchment makers—whose name [parcheminiers] is still attached to a street in Paris in the school section—and each scribe copied a section, then came to get another. Finally they were joined together, with a fair chance of being put in the wrong order, which creates the problems facing editors of these texts today. From this university technique arose various expressions whose origin we have forgotten but which canon Destrez, that great specialist in the *pecia,* loved to recall: "to be all to pieces", to do "piece work", "to take to pieces" the model being shared between several copyists, after which each one *"emportait sa pièce"* [took his cut]. When the parchment maker who hired them out asked too much money, they said he was *"près de ses pièces"* [tight-fisted], and the student, in order to get things straight, had to *"accomoder de toutes pièces"* [give him a good dressing down].

The books were not museum pieces: they were used. So they had to be taken care of while they were in use and then their upkeep had to be seen to. When they got old, like people and institutions, they had to be looked after and rejuvenated. Sometimes they are found designated as very old: *veterrimos, vetustissimos.*[11] Pope Alexander III, confirming a gift to the Abbey of Corbie, specified as its purpose

10. J. Dubois, "Les bibliothèques", p. 9.

11. E. Lesne, *Histoire de la proprieté ecclésiastique en France,* IV: *Les livres, "Scriptoria" et bibliothèques* (Lille, 1938) p. 793.

"the repair and restoration of the books in your library, the which hath grown too old, and the making of new volumes".[12] Of course, when books accumulate, they become at times "embarrassing friends". But it is never right that they should smell of dust, or that, when they have grown old, they should be left buried in what have been called "necropolises of books". They must be kept healthy and in good condition and, to that end, taken care of, not harmed, out of respect for their content and because of the trouble taken over them. One copyist summed up in two lines the whole attitude we should have towards them:

> *Dulcis amice, gravem scribendi attende laborem*
> *Tolle, aperi, recita, ne laedas, claude, repone.*[13]

[Sweet friend, consider the hard work of writing 'this book'. Pick it up, open it, read it, do not damage it, close it, return it.]

Because books were expensive, they represented a capital investment. "That precious treasure that we love more than gold,"[14] as they affirmed. They were the real "riches of the cloister" (*divitiae claustrales*)[15] and the beauty of their content was greater than that of their cover (*splendidiore tamen intus honore micat*).[16] They read them and had them read aloud. Some monks always had a book on them: pocket editions are no modern invention. We read in the Life of Wedric, Cistercian prior of Aulne at the end of the twelfth century, *Vix sinus illius umquam fuit sine libello.* And the biographer added these two lines:

---

12. "Ad reparationem et emendationem librorum bibliothecae vestrae, quae nimis senuerat, et ad constitutionem novorum librorum", quoted by Lesne, *Histoire de la propriété* p. 792, n. 5. The care devoted to the binding and upkeep of books attracted the attention of visitors during the regular visit to Cistercian monasteries as may be seen by the *carta visitationis* that I have published under the title "Le formulaire de Pontigny" in *Miscellanea Populetana* (Poblet, 1966), no. XVIII: *De religatione librorum*, p. 247.

13. Quoted by Lesne, p. 794, n. 1.

14. Lesne, p. 24. n. 7: "Istum thesaurum quem diligimus super aurum."

15. Ibid.

16. Ibid., p. 25. n. 1.

> Often at his neck he carried a scrip
> bulging with books and covered by his ample cowl.[17]

This recalls the old monk who never moved without taking with him one or more satchels full of books. And when he was asked how he knew so much, he replied that it was by osmosis.

Books circulated in different ways, by means of loans, barters, exchanges, buying and selling, not to mention theft. Each one was worth a high price, calculated according to the time and the place in sous, deniers, talents or marks. They could be used to pay, at least in part, the keep of a child sent to a monastery. In one case of this kind, the father donated a piece of land and the mother gave a work of St Ambrose.[18] From the ninth century there existed book markets where they could be bought, or got rid of, whatever the means by which they had been acquired. Book theft, too, was already well organized. As in our day, men knew how to cross a frontier in order to get rid of a book in a foreign country if they did not want the owner to track it down. In the ninth century, a manuscript stolen from the abbey of St Hubert was sold at Toul for this reason (*quasi in extera provincia securius ibi celandum*).[19] Elsewhere, two old sections of a book found in a pilgrim's bag were bought back at a high price by Odo of Glanfeuil.[20] In the course of their invasions and their raids, the Norsemen were not so barbarous as not to know the value of books. They knew how to turn what they had taken the trouble to carry off into money, and sometimes the owner was able to buy back his possession from the middleman who had acquired it in good faith. A copy of the commentary of Chalcidius on the *Timaeus* of Plato was bought in this way from a pirate in the ninth century.[21] It

---

17. "Saepius et collo sacellum ferre solebat / Codicibus tumidum, quae lata cuculla tegebat," ed. in *Catalogus Codicum hagiographicorum Bibliothecae Regiae Bruxellensis,* I (Brussels, 1886) p. 448.

18. Lesne, *Histoire de la propriété,* p. 482.

19. Ibid., p. 481. n. 6.

20. Ibid.

sometimes happened that guests at monasteries put books in their luggage, and it could hardly have been by inadvertence. Such are the risks of charity. We even know that at Saint Denis in the ninth century a thief pretended to pray so he could get near the object of his theft, which had been put down not far from him (*fur specie orantis depositum rapuit*).[22] An inscription even tells us of such and such a work carried off by a thief from Fulda: *iste et iste sublata sunt a Fuldensi latrone.*[23] Fulda was a monastery. So the man who took them might have been a monk! One can understand the anathemas and imprecations still legible on so many manuscripts, or the inscription placed at the entrace to the Popes' library which began with these words,

> *Si quis sumpserit, rapserit, clepserit . . .*

> [If anyone has taken, plundered, or pilfered . . .]

Other works were lost in the course of removal from place to place. And so loans, which were frequent, were made under the guarantee of an oath or deposit, as a pledge of other books or a sum of money.[24]

How then was the preservation of books undertaken at the time? It presupposed a place and an responsible official. The first went through an evolution which took it from the library-treasury to the library-study.[25] At first, of course, the books were placed in one or several cupboards whose Latin name—*armarium, armaria*—determined the title of the keeper of the store of books, *armarius*. Each cupboard contained shelves called *gradus*. The main—sometimes the only—cupboard was often placed in the cloister near the entrance to the church, especially in Cistercian monasteries. In some Premonstratensian abbeys there were several in the sacristy,

24. See Lesne, p. 479. Letters making claims over books that had been lent and returned in a damaged condition are noted by S. J. Heathcote, "The letter collections attributed to Master Trasmundus," in *Analecta Cisterciensa,* 21 (1965) p. 217, n. 169; and 223, n. 186.

25. See T. Gerits, "A propos de l'organisation des bibliothèques médiévales dans l'ordre de Prémontré en Angleterre et en Allemagne," in *Analecta Praemonstratensia,* 37 (1931) pp. 75-84 with bibliography.

the refectory, the infirmary or the cloister. In some places they were given a special place, preferably on an upper storey of the building to preserve their contents from damp and theft. But most often the manuscripts were kept at the heart of the monastery, near the church or the sacristy, that is, in places where the monks worshipped or prepared for worship, as if to make the books share a kind of sacredness. Or again the place was inside or in the area of the Lady Chapel, which was often the infirmary chapel. More than once the *armarium* was put under the patronage of the Blessed Virgin. It has been said that this kind of library was of the "Romanesque" type; it answered the needs of a period when people had relatively few books. Of course, a cupboard with several shelves might have ten or more, which could represent about a hundred volumes. At least the value of these manuscripts meant that they were preserved with the same care as the things used for worship or other treasures, and sometimes with them. This lasted for a shorter or longer time according to the region, over a period which coincides roughly with the use of parchment. Then in the "Gothic" age, as the use of paper spread and books multiplied, there appeared the library in which volumes were no longer merely kept but where they could be written and above all used. This room was no longer generally near the church or sacristy, and in moving away from the place of worship, it lost its sacred character. Its construction was dominated by practical considerations, in particular the need for light and space. There had to be windows in sufficient number, at such a distance from one another that it was possible to read comfortably anywhere. Desks were installed enabling the copyists to do their work and readers to spread out the books; up to the time of the Renaissance—as may still be seen by the library of Lorenzo de Medici in Florence—the books were kept on these desks, called *plutei*. Where strangers had access to them, the books were chained.

Whoever was in charge of the books—the *armarius,* also called the *custos,* especially in the latter periods of the Middle Ages—had to ensure the increase and renewal of the stock. For this purpose, from the twelfth century, he sometimes drew a fixed revenue.[26] He held simultaneously the two posts which in the libraries of today are held by the assistant called the "librarian"—he is the *custos*—and the head of the department who is the "curator". At all events, he was the servant of the readers. He was not merely set to safeguard a treasure; he had to put it at the "disposal" of the brethren, on pain of a fault, at Prémontré. His task was a fine but delicate one: he obeyed *ad iussum abbatis*. Using his intelligence, he tried to adapt himself to the capacity of each one (*pro capacitate singulorum*). He had to be careful to give everyone the spiritual nourishment they needed, and then to change their book as soon as they had finished it (*distribuere, et cuique suum, quando perlegerit, mutare*).[27] A work of devotion and, all in all, of charity.

Reading

Such were the educational means that the life of the cloister offered religious: a store of books that was itself spiritual and an organized service. How did the users benefit by it? That cannot be answered briefly without making generalizations. So it is better to go back to one or two works which deal with particular cases. But first, a precise example—although perhaps idealized or simplified by hagiography—will give a picture of the conditions and demands of the religious education of an adult. The author of the Life of John of Gorze in the tenth century related that he, already a priest, made the acquaintance of two pious women of Metz, Fredeburg and Geisa. Among other penitential practices, one of them wore a hair shirt. Hearing this, John was seized with a "trembling" which brought about his conversion. Now if, at least in that community, the most austere were the most learned, these nuns were well educated. Jean set out at once to study with them, first of all the whole of the Bible, then

26. See Lesne, p. 792.
27. Texts in Gerits, p. 76.

the Liturgy—readings from the Mass, sacramental rites, computation, canon and civil law, homilies, commentaries on the epistles and gospels, lives of saints, and so to plainchant which even at that time seems to have offered singular difficulties. Although he was no longer a child, John was not ashamed to take a great deal of trouble in this field. Nothing could discourage him. They smiled at him, but he persevered and was victorious. His biographer concluded: "Such were the very full leisure hours which he shared with those handmaids of God".[28]

This extreme case can summarize the part played by books in the spiritual development of the majority of monks. A proportion of them, perhaps a high one, never learned to write. They did not fail to admit it, even to have it announced, when documents and contracts which they witnessed were signed for them.[29] But all were supposed to have—and many had in fact—the zeal for reading, the *studium legendi,* which, from the origins of monasticism in the West, was part of the contemplative's program. How, in this regard, did the libraries contribute towards maintaining in the cloisters a certain level of spiritual life? By providing for the mind something of a nature calculated to instruct, cultivate and expand it. The Bible and the commentaries which the Fathers had made on it nourished their faith. Prayer was fed by the varied texts of a private or liturgica character which consisted of phrases, sometimes with comments, of adoration, thanksgiving, humble confession or supplication. Fervor was stimulated by the examples presented in the *Lives of the Saints.* These legends, inspired by Holy Scripture, constituted a sort of exegesis of holiness, an interpretation of the mys-

28. MGH SS IV, p. 432: "Stadium itaque lectionis divinae cum eisdem ancillis Dei summa vi statim arripuit, et primum sacrae bibliothecae historiam Veteris ac Novi Testamenti percurrens ex integro. Cantibus ecclesiasticis sub idem temporis insudare nec erubuit nec desperavit.,. . . et licet nonnulli ut alienori aetate deludi tacite riderent ingenium, pertinacia boni desiderii, quamvis duro eluctato labor, prorsus evicit. Haec ei inerim sanctorum negotiorum ocia cum praedictis ancillis Dei fuere."
29. See A. Wenderhost, "Monachus scribere nesciens", in *Mitteilungen des Instituts für österreichische Geschichtsforschung,* 17 (1963), pp. 67-75.

tery and history of the Church through the resounding successes of those great models of Christian and monastic life, as they imagined them. The concern for interior and then institutional reform was made actual by the patristic tradition.[30] The whole realm of literature, the humanities and sciences, sacred and secular, "adorned the mind", raised it up, gave a sense of disinterested leisure, of the gratuitous.[31] The works of the Greek Fathers, read in translation, brought contact with the thought of the East.[32] The element of adventure found in the accounts of journeys in hagiography, the element of humor in the pictures which decorate so many manuscripts, the element of beauty which is added to truth and illustrates it in so many illuminations—an art in which the nuns excelled—all this "overflow" of joy was a relaxation and a comfort.[33]

Books were not only instruments of intellectual formation and reservoirs of ideas and information. They were food for something which is worth more than learning: spiritual education. They sharpened the mind and opened it to the action of grace. They were a meeting point between the effort of man and the gift of God. The place for reading was regularly blessed, and the Lord was asked that what was read might be "grasped" by an interior sense, and then transformed into action.[34] The giving out of books at the beginning of Lent was a sacred rite,[35] because reading them had a higher aim

---

30. See *Temoins de la spiritualité occidentale,* pp. 155-174.

31. See *L'amour des lettres et le desir de Dieu.,* 2nd ed. (Paris, 1963) *passim.*

32. See *Temoins de la spiritualité occidentale,* pp. 74 & 91, and above, p. 211.

33. See *Temoins,* pp. 264-287; "Un Missel de Montiéramey" in *Scriptorium,* 13 (1959), pp. 247-249 *et pl.*

34. PL 121, 851: "Ut quicquid hic divinarum scripturarum ab eis lectum fuerit, sensu capiant, opere compleant." May I quote once again the prayer for the "blessing of a new book", which is in MS Subiaco 275 (CCLXX), fol. 64: "Benedictio libri novi. Omnipotens sempiterne Deus, quaesumus ut virtus Spiritus Sancti descendat super hunc librum, qui eum mundando per invocationem tui nominis purificet et sensum ei mentis nostre aperiat. Dextera tua sancta illum benedicat atque sanctificet et omnium legentium corda illuminet et verum intellectum tribuat, sed et illuminata tua precepta conservare et implere secundum tuam voluntatem bonis operibus implendo concedat."

35. PL 66, 733: Ulrich, *Consuetudines Cluniacensus,* III, 52, PL 149, 697.

than the acquisition of learning or the simple development of the natural faculties. It was always a matter of going, by means of books, to Him who by a long symbolic tradition had been compared to a book, the book of life, the open book *par excellence,* dying with arms outstretched on the Cross, with pierced side, rising in glory and sending the Spirit, revealing the contents of all the Holy Books: Jesus Christ, God and Man.[36]

36. To the texts that I have quoted under the title "Aspects spirituels de la symbolique du livre au XIIe siècle", in *L'homme devant Dieu. Mélanges offertes au P. Henri de Lubac* (Paris, 1964) II, pp. 63-72, may be added the fragment that I have edited under the title "Pétulance et spiritualité dans le commentaire d'Hélinand sur le Cantique", in *Archives d'Histoire doctrinale et lettéraire du Moyen Age,* 31 (1964) [Paris, 1965] pp. 41-42.

ST IGNATIUS AT MONTSERRAT*

AT A TIME when the word ecumenism is often used, when people tend to emphasize what humanist and Christian groups have in common, Jesuits and monks have a right to remind themselves that they are united not only by the same ideal—a life consecrated to the service of God—but by memories of friendship. The new volume of the *History of the Company of Jesus* which Father Scaduto has just published tells how the contemplative orders immediately showed themselves well-disposed toward the new institute founded by St Ignatius, and how he and his successor, Father Lainez, liked to find prayerful respite in monasteries like Monte Cassino or Camaldoli, or to send religious there.[1] Fr Hugo Rahner years ago showed the "monastic" tendencies of St Ignatius.[2] Elsewhere he has pointed out that among the important sources of the *Exercises*, the Rules of St Basil and St Benedict, and the Conferences of Cassian must be included.[3] And recently a document has been discovered which will make it possible to confirm and clarify these views. It is still unpublished, but I owe my knowledge of its existence to the kindness of Fr Scaduto. The document in question con-

* Published in *Christus*, 50 (1966) pp. 161-173.

1. M. Scudato, *Storia della Compagnia di Gesu* 2, 1 (Rome: Civiltà Cattolica, 1964) pp. 533-537.

2. H. Rahner, "Die ignatianische Mystik der Weltfreudigkeit," in *Zeitschrift für Aszese und Mystik*, 12 (1937) pp. 124-125, where the word "mönchisch" is used.

3. H. Rahner, *Servir Dieu dans l'Eglise. Ignace de Loyola et la genèse des Exercices* (Paris: Editions de l'Epi, 1959) pp. 79-93.

sists of notes taken for St Ignatius by Father Polanco, his secretary, at the time the saint was preparing to write the *Constitutions*. Extracts from ancient Rules manifestly have a place in it, but so too have more recent constitutions.[4] In short, although it would be wrong to yield to a facile and artificial parallelism, mutual influences can be detected. They diminish neither the originality of each institute nor the personal genius of the founders; they simply prove that there is in the Church a common fund, as it were, of spiritual traditions, upon which each draws in his own way.

This material does not have purely a literary character. Over and above the texts, it includes experiments; and it is to one of these that I should like to draw attention. This is attested to by a little known but very suggestive document which it will be enough to introduce, then translate and comment upon briefly. It will show us St Ignatius at the beginning of a spiritual destiny which was to be unique—his own—living through spiritual states which other saints before him had experienced, although in different circumstances. Of these traditional preparations, some are ancient, others contemporary with him. The slow maturation of his work has its full meaning only if his spiritual itinerary is placed in the context of the vast and profound movement of reform which was working through devout Catholic circles at the end of the fifteenth century and in the course of the sixteenth. Men were witnessing at the time a renewal of all forms of religious life, those which entailed the common life and those which were characterized by the search for solitude.[5]

Even the title which was given at a very early date to St Ignatius' autobiography—The Tale of the Pilgrim—is signi-

4. The text has been discovered by Father Leturia. Father Scudato has been good enough to tell me, and to give me permission to make public, the fact that it is to be published; the same scholar undertook to read the MS of this present article, which owes him a number of useful suggestions. I wish to thank him here. I have likewise been helped in the translation and commentary of the text to be printed here by M. Maurice Jacques, assistant in the parish of Saint-Louis of Strasbourg, to whom I also express my gratitude.

5. On this point, I have quoted texts and examples in *Temoins de la spiritualité occidentale*, pp. 341-360.

ficant. When Iñigo left Loyola, he became a "pilgrim" because he had the intention (at least, he was to say later in
interpreting his past) of going to Jerusalem. But he also became a *peregrinus,* to use a word which in the ascetic tradition designated the voluntary exile who went away to a
foreign country.[6] In telling Father Polanco of the conversion
of St Ignatius, Father Lainez made no mention of Jerusalem.
On the other hand, he used exactly the vocabulary of voluntary exile and the Biblical themes which had always been
used in speaking of it: the departure of Abraham and the
evangelical renunciation.

> He decided to go away from his country and his house
> under the pretext of going to the court of the Duke of
> Najera. [cf. Genesis 12,1: 'Leave your own country, your
> kinsmen and your Father's house'] In order to renounce
> utterly his country, his parents and his friends [we are
> reminded of the call to renunciation in St. Matthew 19:29],
> and his own body ['the monk may no longer even dispose
> of his own body', says the Rule of St Benedict, Ch.58] he
> enters upon the life of penance."[7]

It is not only this way of feigning ("simulating", Polanco
would say) a visit to Najera (it was really a flight: think of
the "flight of Abraham" of which Philo, and afterwards
Christian writers spoke)[8] which was precedent in the
examples of Saints. Those "fugitives" for God had left their
home, sometimes their monastery, in order to lead, far from
home, far from all the facilities to which they were accustomed, an existence entirely devoted to more intense prayer and
more austere mortification.[9] The phrase "to enter upon the
life of penitence", applies exactly to all those exiles for

6. On this point, I have collected information in *Aux sources de la spiritualité
occidentale* (Paris, 1964) pp. 40-44.
7. Letter of the 16th June 1547, published *Scripta de S. Ignatio,* I (Madrid,
1904) pp. 101-103, and in *Fontes narrativi de S. Ignatio,* I (Rome, 1963) p. 74 ff.
8. See *Aux sources de la spiritualité occidentale,* pp. 37-40.
9. Ibid., p. 49.

Christ. *Peregrinari pro Christo* meant to become a voluntary penitent.[10]

And so after leaving Guipuzcoa for Catalonia, Iñigo conformed in everything to his program of prayer and mortification in solitude. On the way, he "bartered his clothes for those of a poor man",[11] as Lainez said. He put on a "sack, that is a tunic of skin",[12] the garment of penitents and of the first monks, which people liked to compare with the garb of St John the Baptist and the Prophets.[13] He lived on bread and water.[14] When he arrived at the monastery of Montserrat, he performed the vigil of arms before the altar of Our Lady, and the next day he opened his conscience to the pilgrims' confessor, Dom Juan Chanon, and gave his mule and his armor to the Abbey. Several people speak at this time of his "mendicity", his "severe austerities", his "continuous vocal prayers",[15] of the time spent "in a hermitage"[16] where he led "the contemplative life",[17] of his "retreat", that is, his anchoretic existence in penitence before going to Manrese.[18] All these indications are still of a very general character. But there is a more precise document: the testimony of Fr Araoz, who had known the saint well. Here is a translation of it which attempts to preserve in the text the disjointed conversational character of its style:

10. Ibid., p. 50-90. At the top of the first of his letters that we have, St Ignatius calls himself "El pobre peregrino", *Epistolae et Instructiones S. Ignatii,* I (Madrid, 1903) p. 73.

11. Letter of Lainez to Polanco, quoted above, p. 311, n. 7.

12. Deposition of Perpinyà at the process of canonization, *Scripta* 1, p. 388.

13. I have collected texts in *La vie parfaite* (Paris-Turnhout: Brepols, 1948) pp. 76-79.

14. Letter of Lainez, quoted above, ch. 7, n. 2.

15. Palanco, in *Fontes narrativi,* I (Rome, 1963), *Polanci complementum,* p. 507.

16. Charles Tapia, quoted by A.-M. Albareda, *Sant Ignasi a Montserrat* (Montserrat, 1935) p. 80, n.b.

17. Gonzales de Illescas, quoted ibid., p. 82 n.b.

18. Nicolas Blandini, quoted in *Sant Ignasi a Montserrat,* p. 82, n.b. "Secessit enim in Sylvam Montiserrato proximam . . . ibique paenitentiam egit, dein Manresam . . . concessit". On *secedere, secessus,* I have quoted texts in *Chances de la spiritualité occidentale* (Paris, 1966) pp. 329-337, and in *Etudes sur le vocabulaire monastique du Moyen Age.* Studia Anselmiana, 48 (1961) see index, p. 164.

1. Among the many things which Fr Aroaz thought should be put in the book of the life of the blessed Father Ignatius, the Father Minister of the house at Madrid, and some others, tell us the following. Shortly after Father Ignatius arrived at Montserrat, he asked to stay at some hermitage while he was there. As he was so young, I believe, the monks of that holy house did not want to accept him. So it was that Father Ignatius went off to find on the mountainside a cave in which to live in seclusion, with the intention of going down to the monastery sometimes to make his confession and communion. Finding a hollow under a rock, he settled down and stayed there for a while. As he intended, he went regularly from time to time to the monastery for confession and communion. He would ask for alms at the gatehouse of the monastery like the other poor, then go back to his cave with the small piece of bread given him. He lived on that, together with roots and herbs.

2. After some time, the Brother who gave out the alms noticed our Father. He looked at him very carefully and saw that he behaved with great humility. I think too that he taught much good to the poor, so that they spoke very well of him. So this monk went off to tell the abbot that the pilgrim who had given them his clothes and the mule with which had come to the house, had been coming from time to time to ask for alms for a long time. He had to be taking refuge in some part of the mountain, and the monk was afraid the wild beasts might eat him. He suspected that he might have gone mad, although he seemed to be a man of noble birth and good circumstances. That was why he wanted to send a boy after him to find out where he was hiding. The Abbot gave the brother this permission, and he sent the boy. Walking behind him, [the boy] saw that he went in under a rock. Full of admiration, he came back to the monastery and told the brother who had sent him where he was hiding.

3. The monk went again to the abbot and, in front of a doctor who cared for the sick in the house, told him what the boy had said. This doctor was from Barcelona. The abbot told the monk that the next day he could go with the boy and ask the pilgrim who he was and rebuke him for being there. The doctor I mentioned told the abbot that he too wanted to go with the monk. Later on he knew Father

Araoz at Barcelona very well, was very familiar with him, and, as an eyewitness, told him what happened then.

4. So the monk and the doctor went off with the boy to look for our Father. At a great distance from the monastery they saw him under a rock. They called and our Father came out, I think Father Araoz said "on all fours", with a grave and humble expression. The monk was well prepared and he began to admonish him and to tell him that to live and dwell in that place was a piece of great temerity, for he was exposed to the great danger of being eaten by the wild beasts; that this seemed to be a desperate case, for it was tempting God to preserve him miraculously in this way, and so his eternal salvation would be in great danger if he died there; and since he seemed to be a man of good circumstances, he should come with them and take up another way of life, and other things which I don't remember. Our Father listened with great humility without speaking and, when the monk had finished his discourse, Father Ignatius began to reply point by point to what he had said with great prudence and wisdom. He said so many and such things that the monk and the doctor were filled with admiration. Without making any other reply except to bid him remain with God, they went back to the monastery. And Father Ignatius went back into his cave.

5. When they arrived at the monastery, they told the abbot what had happened and that the stranger had become a fool for Jesus Christ. All marvelled at what he had said to them. Thanks to this reputation and to this opinion of our Father which they had been told of, the monks intended to give him presents and to honor him when he came. Our Father came at the usual time and, at the monastery, people who had previously taken no notice of him began to show him great courtesy and honor. When the Saint saw that, he went back to the mountains whence he had come.

6. Father Araoz used to say that on that mountain something important happened to our Father which is not in the book of his life either. On this mountain there was a cross, and our Father was in the habit of going to the place where it was and praying the seven canonical hours at the proper time. After he had continued in this holy exercise for some days, for a long period there appeared to him in the air,

above the cross, bands of serpents and scorpions and other horrible visions. Our Father persisted in his holy exercise and so conquered the evil spirit.[19]

And so, there was Ignatius in solitude. There had been hermits around Montserrat for centuries, looked after by the monastery, and the cave—*cueva,* say the Castilian texts, the Latin ones *specus*—where the Saint is supposed to have lived is still pointed out. The very nature of the place and its designations conform to the eremitical tradition. To quote only one example, there is venerated to our day at Subiaco the *sacro speco* where Saint Benedict spent three years in solitude before becoming the father of a monastery. Everything recorded in paragraph one conforms to the type of the solitary life of all times: poverty, austerity, the practice of prayer and the sacraments. The Fathers of the desert, at the beginning of monasticism, went to the eucharistic synaxis. The testimony of Father Araoz has been given somewhat divergent interpretations by historians. It will suffice here to retain what is essential and common to all. In the life of Saint Ignatius, there was a period of solitary life, the length of which has not been established with certainty.

What emerges from paragraph two is not merely the poverty of the saint—on which however there is a fresh emphasis—but the fact that in his solitude he began to shed spiritual influence. He spoke of God to the other poor. He was not able to live in such a fervor of charity without wanting to share, to communicate, his love. This again occurred in the lives of many holy hermits. Saint Benedict at Subiaco did good to the shepherds on the mountain from the time they discovered his presence.[20] Let us pick up the allusion to "wild beasts". They inhabit the desert: Our Lord had met them during his fast in the desert, on the mountain of temptation. "And he was among the wild beasts".[21] They

---

19. The text has been published in *Scripta* 1, pp. 731-738, then with notes and bibliography, in *Font. narr.* 3, pp. 198-208.
20. Saint Gregory the Great, *Dialogues* 2, ch. 1.
21. Mk 1, 12-13.

are mentioned in the lives of many holy hermits. When the shepherds saw Saint Benedict for the first time, "clothed in skins in the midst of the undergrowth, they took him for some wild beast".[22] Finally, let us note a first allusion to the possible madness of Saint Ignatius. In passing, the solicitude of the monks for this poor man, their concern for his physical and mental health, and their anxiety to prevent his life being in peril is admirable.

In the next part of the text (paragraph three), the abbot's envoy questions the saint about his identity, because he had remained incognito, except to Dom Chanon, who had kept his secret. This desire to pass unnoticed, anonymous, as inconspicuous as possible—especially if one was of noble birth— also belongs to the spiritual tradition of the *peregrini*, the voluntary exiles, who left the country where they were known in order to be forgotten.[23]

In the fourth paragraph, let us single out Ignatius' devotion to silence and humility. He listened "without speaking" to the reasonable speech which the monk had prepared with such care, then, filled with the "wisdom" of the spiritual man, he replied and convinced his questioner. The two enquirers could only exhort him, in the admirable expression they invented at the time, to "remain with God". How can one fail to be reminded at this point of the other phrase used by St Gregory to describe what St Benedict was doing in his cave after the monks had tried to make him live with them at Vicovaro: *habitavit secum*. In the context which gives it its meaning: "He returned to his beloved solitude, and there, under the eyes of the heavenly Observer, he lived with himself.[24] So Ignatius returned to his cave, no doubt "on all fours" as he had come out.

His visitors knew now that he was not mad, just as the shepherds of Subiaco had discovered that St Benedict, in

---

22. *Dialogues* 2, ch.1.
23. See *Aux sources de la spiritualité occidentale*, pp. 50-51.
24. *Dialogues* 2, ch. 3. On the idea of being present to God that this phrase suggests in St Gregory and traditionally, there is an excellent study by J. Winandy, "Habitavit secum," in *Collectanea OCR*, 25 (1963) pp. 343-354.

spite of his hairy appearance, was a man of God. "Many of them passed from the instincts of a beast to the grace of devotion", added St Gregory.[25] To be exact, the envoys of the Abbot of Montserrat understood the folly with which St Ignatius was possessed (Paragraph five). He belonged to that long line of "fools for Christ" to whom St Paul had given their title to nobility,[26] and of whom examples would be known in every century, not only up to St Benedict Labre, but to our own time.[27] This theme of "folly for Jesus Christ" was to occupy a place in the Tale of the Pilgrim and in the other writings of St Ignatius. Between Ferrara and Genoa, when Ignatius was captured by Spanish soldiers, their captain took him for a madman. This happened after he had had "led forth, as it were, the representation of Christ" at the time of his Passion.[28] Rule XI of the *Summary of Constitutions* would require that a man accept "being treated as insane", without, of course, having given grounds for it. And in the *Exercises,* in the third degree of humility we read: "I prefer to be regarded as a fool and a madman for the sake of Christ, who was taken for such first".[29] One could quote, among other things, the definition given by a seventeenth century Jesuit—"The Company of Jesus is the company of fools and of those who make profession of folly" and the verse of Father Surin, which begins with these lines:

> "All I wish now is to imitate the folly
> Of Jesus, who on the Cross one day . . ."[30]

25. *Dialogues* 2, ch. I.

26. "We are fools for Christ's sake", 1 Cor. 4, 10.

27. Texts have been collected by D. Mollat and A. Derville, "Folie de la Croix", in *Dictionnaire de spiritualité* 5 (Paris, 1966) col. 635-650, and by T. Spidlik and F. Vandenbroucke, art, "Fous pour le Christ", ibid., pp. 752-770.

28. *Le Récit du pèlerin,* n. 52-53, trans. A. Thirty, DDB (Bruges: Desclée de Brouwer, 1956) pp. 92-93.

29. *Scripta* 2, pp. 262-272. These texts are quoted in *Dictionnaire de Spiritualité* 5, col. 768-769. In an inquiry held at Montserrat at the time of the process of the canonization of St Ignatius, it was said that when the latter, already well on in years, was attending classes at the Gymnasium (we would say the Grammar School) at Barcelona, the schoolboys used to make fun of him and insult him; all of which he bore with patience, even asking their help. The text seems to say: "ipse omnia patienter ferebat et cum magna humilitate et charitate ab eis petebat et [probably for ut] lectiones ei repeteret [probably for repeterent]", ed. C. de Dalmases, in *Analecta sacra Tarraconensia,* 15 (1942) p. 144.

30. *Cantiques spirituels* (Bordeaux, 1660) p. 26.

Finally, the last paragraph (six) gives us the key to several tempter. There had been a serpent in the first Paradise, Jesus come into his cave to do, if not to participate in the mystery of the death and resurrection of Christ? He went to pray by the cross, the symbol of mortification and of victory. He had the vision of those wild beasts which are the symbol of the tempter. There had been a serpent in the first Paradise, Jesus had been "with the wild beasts" on the mountain of temptation where he had triumphed over the devil; the scorpion mentioned in the liturgy of Lenten Psalm 91 is trodden under foot. Reminiscences of the same theme.[31] Saint Anthony in his temptations had had "horrible visions" of the same kind and Saint Benedict in his cave, before becoming a spiritual father, had had to overcome a temptation whose onset was accompanied by the flight around him of a "little black bird".[32] Like all the great hermits, Saint Ignatius was subjected to violent temptation and he overcame.

Thus the testimony of Father Araoz is full of the sap of tradition. Its value is in literary allusions which are not, with him, reminiscences of hagiographic themes but memories which came from the source itself, the saint. And he indicated the religious and theological significance of these facts: Ignatius, like Christ, trod the path of temptation and the cross in order to attain renewal, regeneration in the mystery of the Resurrection, and to receive the spirit of the glorified Lord.

With regard to his stay at Montserrat, problems of chronology could arise. Let us leave to the specialists in Ignatian history the task of placing these events in relation to the other data which preceded and followed them.[33] Let us simply ask ourselves in conclusion whether the document analyzed here in any way throws light on the spirituality of the saint.

31. See D. Dufrasne, "Le thème biblique. Satan," in *Assemblées du Seigneur. Troisième dimanche de Carême* (Bruges, 1964) pp. 39-50; and J.-C. Guy, "Le combat contre le démon dans le monachisme ancien", ibid., pp. 61-71.

32. St Gregory, *Dialogues* 2, ch. 2.

33. See P. de Leturia, *Estudios Ignacianos,* 1 (Rome, 1957) pp. 157-165.

If spirituality is essentially apostolic, it does not exclude solitude. We know how often, in the annotations and additions to the *Exercises,* Ignatius stressed the importance of the retreatant's detaching himself as fully as possible from his ordinary occupations in order to find himself alone with God. Thus transformed, he will return to his environment to keep and communicate his fervor there. The life of Ignatius, likewise, saw an alternation between times of solitude and service to men, up to the great vision of *la Storta* which, at the moment when he was about to enter Rome to settle, was a direct call to the apostolic life. Up till then, there had been periods of eremitical life, in particular that period to which Father Araoz bore witness. Did they leave any traces in his life and above all in his spirituality?

The *Exercises* rest entirely upon the absolute aloneness of the retreatant. From the outset he is warned that the fruit of his spiritual effort will depend upon the generosity with which he separates himself from the environment and the occupations familiar to him. He can only emerge transformed. During the whole duration of the *Exercises,* this condition of solitude and isolation must be carefully safeguarded. It is even suggested at times that the retreatant plunge himself into darkness, withdraw into the most utter silence, in order to dispose himself to listen to the word of the Lord.

Anything to do with the formation and spiritual life of the sons of Ignatius must rest entirely upon this experience of solitude and silence which occurs twice in the course of formation, at the beginning and at the end, and is renewed every year in the course of a week's retreat in solitude.

This solitude is always accompanied by penance. But in this field, St Ignatius had freed himself to a large extent from his first experiments. The great penances which he permitted Favre and Francis Xavier to perform in the course of the great Exercises are exceptions. In his instructions St Ignatius recommended physical penance and fasting, but practised with moderation. We know how much he was opposed to Francis Borgia, whose penances always seemed to him excessive. In the *Constitutions* and in the famous letter on obedience, he placed physical mortification after the holocaust of self-will in obedience. He did not regularly impose bodily penances.

Solitude and moderate physical mortification therefore form a part of Ignatian spirituality but they do not take first place. As in the previous monastic tradition, they are a means to an end. In the life and teaching of St Ignatius, these practices are means of liberation from self. They should help in seeking and finding the divine will, which consists in service finding expression in apostolic mission. Ignatius did not neglect the absolute search for God but for him the man who has found God, who has learned to talk to him "as a friend talks to his friend", should go and speak about it to men and teach them what he has learned. This is by no means as foreign to the monastic tradition as one might think, particularly in its eremitical form. Many contemplatives have experienced the need, felt the call and received the grace to pass on what they have received. The hermit does not make his solitude and his asceticism ends in themselves, any more than he sees in the world an image of damnation. But he uses solitude and asceticism with an end in view which the spirit of the world would not allow him to attain directly. It is the same ideal that the apostle pursues under different forms: seeking, finding and following perfectly the will of God, to bring about the salvation of his soul. The difference lies in the means employed. The hermit keeps to solitude and asceticism, like Jesus of Nazareth. He knows that the Lord went farther than Nazareth. After the poor, hidden and humiliated life, the Lord entered on paths which led to public life in the boroughs and villages inhabited by men who were sinners and whom he had come to save. It was by those paths that he came to the Passion, to Calvary and the Resurrection. The hermit will pass through the same stages, but without leaving the solitude and humiliation of Nazareth, in an interior martyrdom maintained by asceticism. When the hermit deprives himself of sleep to devote himself to vigils, he certainly does not do it out of contempt for weak nature, knowing well enough that it needs rest to renew itself. He knows himself to be a watchman waiting through the sufferings due to sin for the resurrection. At the end of his career the hermit will see himself surrounded with disciples. The experience of God will make him a spiritual father. At that moment he joins the apostle.

The apostle has embarked earlier on the career of spiritual action. His martyrdom is to live constantly with a world that is indifferent, even hostile, to the ideal which he sets before it. But if he has the audacity to confront the powers of sin, not in the solitude of single combat but in the human mass quivering with life, he has it after carrying off a profound victory over himself.

Thus there are two very different forms of life based on solitude and asceticism. Both lead alike to the singular love of God and man. The hermit takes one, the Jesuit takes another.

AFRICAN MONASTICISM TODAY*

HAVING IN THE COURSE of the last three years visited twenty-three Benedictine and Cistercian monasteries, and some Carmels and convents of Poor Clares, in thirteen African countries and in Madagascar, I have been asked to draw my conclusions from the experience.

A difficult, or rather a delicate task, because my sojourn in each of these houses was brief and permitted only a fleeting acquaintance with the peculiar situation of each. Everywhere, however, I have witnessed such confidence—for which I remain profoundly grateful—that I have been able to estimate the efforts achieved and the results obtained, and to glimpse in addition the problems posed and the difficulties still to be surmounted. The cases are extremely varied: Madagascar and Africa are two worlds between which there are nevertheless links, if only in the economic and political fields—which means that I landed on Red Island with a whole convoy of presidents and prime ministers arriving for a meeting of the O.C.A.M. [Organisation Commune Africaine et Malagache]. In addition, in every continent and even in every country, the conditions for setting up monasteries vary according to the level of economic, political, social, religious and cultural

* Opening address at the second congress of superiors of African monasteries held at Rome in September 1966; published in *Rythmes du monde*, 40 (1966) pp. 165-176; in *Parole et mission*, 10 (1967) pp. 480-499;s in Italian in *Vita monastica*, 21 (1967) pp. 38-47, 97-106.

development—and the difference between one country or group of countries and another is sometimes very great. Finally, each monastery results not from a theory but from contingent circumstances, and it would be premature to lay down laws for the future on the basis of an inquiry into these data. But at least we have the right to ask ourselves whether, in this apparently disparate unity, we can discern common problems and common elements for their solution. We may suppose so *a priori* for, in spite of diversity, a real unity may be seen in the deep concepts, the religious values, the basic traditions, the behavior patterns which are very important, for example, in the education of children, and even in the details of human conduct. These similarities we perceive in so many parts of the immense African continent, between African and the Malagasy world, and which we know exist between them and the Asiatic countries or even the areas of pre-Columbian civilization in Latin America, lead us to believe that, on many points, the ideas and practices of the West, which we are inclined to think universal, constitute no more than an exception in the world as a whole.

Given the complexity of the problem, our answer cannot consist in finding the happy medium between necessarily diverse solutions. But at least we can try to get a view of the whole, and so round out the information which each can acquire about the place with which he is linked. Without generalizing from any particular case, we must try to place them all in as objective a synthesis as possible. We can here only make suggestions and give impressions, none of which pretend to be authoritative and all of which must inevitably be somewhat general. They need to be illustrated with individual testimony, examples, accounts of vocation or foundations, which discretion would not always allow us to quote even if we had the necessary time and space. The future historian of these young African and Malagasy monasteries will have a glorious time studying their beginnings.

Even now we have every right to yield to enthusiasm. We know that this was Cassian's reaction when he visited the first monasteries in Africa. The renewal is no less fine than the beginnings. What infinite admiration these foundations, these adventures of the Church, deserve! How difficult it is to speak of them, bearing in mind all the factors operative in each place! At least believe—for I say it in all sincerity—that I have marvelled at all of them.

Existing to Endure

The first proposition to be accepted is this very general fact: African and Malagasy monasticism exists. It must not be spoken of in the future tense, as though it were expected in time to come. It belongs to the Church's present.

1. First and foremost, there are African and Malagasy monks and nuns.

2. In addition, the Africanization and Madagascanization of monasticism have begun and in some places are complete.

a. On the one hand, indeed, the existence of African and Malagasy monks and nuns constitutes what may be called monastic successes: genuine vocations seeking God in separation from the world and the recollection this solitude encourages; life in fraternal charity; the activity of prayer and, sometimes, advanced states of prayer; finally a spiritual influence exercised by the communities and, to a greater or lesser degree according to circumstances and vocations, by a few monks and nuns. To have enabled the appearance of such blessings, the flowering of such gifts, to have formed such Christians (if only few in number) would in itself be a real enrichment for the Church and would achieve the very goal of monasticism. And the fact that there are adult vocations, not resulting from any propaganda, is enough to give confidence for the future. The Holy Spirit who raises them up is present in this monastic event.

b. On the other hand, monastic institutions and ways of thought arising from a tradition previously formed in the West have already been influenced, modified and, one may say, improved, enriched and made more flexible by African or Malagasy ideas and customs.

Because vocations are the work of the Spirit who blows

where he wills and is free with his gifts, we have to wait for them on him, sometimes a long time. In order to prepare for them, it is necessary to have begun to exist. To bemoan, for example, having come twenty years too soon would be to misunderstand one of the laws of action: the more time a necessary thing requires, the more important its undertaking without delay.

On the whole, it may be observed that the monastic life begins more easily among women than among men, perhaps because, made for the home, they more readily hear the call to seek God in the life of prayer in community. This should not surprise us. Christian literature knew of consecrated virgins before there were monks. The Spirit does not only work at the level of theologians; girls from the bush have already given evidence that they are able to practise a high degree of theological prayer.

The vocations of nuns, moreover, like those of monks, vary considerably from one region to another for many reasons. But we must be beware of making comparisons between monasteries which already have them, or which have a great many, and those which are still awaiting them, or have only a few: To speak of the "success" of the first and of the "failure" of the second would show that we were judging by quantity, according to statistics, and not by the monastic authenticity of persons and institutions. The patience of God should be a lesson and a source of encouragement to all. A monastery which has not yet acquired any indigenous recruits has not lost its *raison d'etre*. It, like the others, will acquire them in God's good time if it remains faithful to the role of monasticism as defined by Vatican II in prescribing its establishment in young Churches.

Finally, in the realm of institutions, the "particular statutes" of the monastery of Hanga, in Tanzania, which have been added as an appendix to the constitutions of the Benedictine congregation of Sainte Odile, and which were approved by the Congregation of Religious on 18 June 1963, have already introduced into the legislation of the Church "a Benedictine monastic way of life adapted to the conditions of Africa".

Africanization and Madagascanization

It is natural that one of the first problems we are led to consider in a life in which prayer occupies a primary place should be its Africanization and Madagascanization. The problem is a delicate one. In considering it, we must avoid any over-simplification. In finding a solution, we must avoid any excess. But although we must beware of being hasty, we have no right to evade the question. The factors are complex and it would be as foolish to reject the whole of Western contribution as it would be to show too little confidence in traditional culture. We need to discern several things here. First of all, we may distinguish what may be called levels of reality. "Everything that is Western is far from being anti-African or anti-Malagasy. There is in the West an element which is *common* because it is universally human. There is an element which may be adopted by any African or Asian or Malagasy without his having in the least to renounce his national heritage. Finally, there is an element that is *marked with the stamp of the West,* with the turn of mind, the more marked tendency peculiar to human beings from that part of the world which we call the West. It is at the level of this third point that the originality peculiar to every people, to every continent, is to be found."[1] It is at this level that the Africanization and Madagascanization of forms of expression in prayer must be brought about—at the cost of a certain "dewesternization", so to speak.

But in point of fact different levels of development must also be distinguished. They vary from one country to another, and in the same country, at times from one region to another. We may also say that, generally speaking, a certain degree of westernization is an accomplished fact. To a certain extent this has been beneficial, and it is irreversible. A number of Christians—clerical, lay and religious—have been educated in the West or by Westerners, and have more or less

---

1. R. Ralibera, SJ, "Théologien-pretre africain et développement de la culture negro-africaine," in *Presence africaine, IIe congrès des écrivains et artistes noirs, 1959,* vol. II, p. 164, no 27-28.

lost contact with and confidence in traditional values. These values have not however disappeared; they remain latent in some, very lively in many, while still others are rediscovering them by degree. At the moment, the situation is confused. It is important to have confidence in the Holy Spirit, to take into account the situations created by history, and to respect men as they are.

The solution can only come from the indigenous peoples themselves, and certain indications may already be seen. Thus the *Festival de la négritude* held in Dakar in 1966 aroused interest, as did the announcement of its repetition bienally, a project towards which the Holy See has shown itself favorable. Competent Africans and Malagasy are already at work in episcopal conferences and liturgical commissions. The monks will have a similar work to do in areas which concern them. The attitude of Westerners among them should be marked by confidence towards what is African or Malagasy, if only to make up for what may have been negative in the conduct of some of their Western predecessors, and to help their black brothers to emerge from the inferiority complex which they still have and which some admit openly. I have heard it said more than once that "Christianity is the religion of the Whites". Shall we see a Christian *"négritude"*? Our duty is, at the least, to want it and to make it wanted. Better for the indigenous peoples to have to moderate our desire for africanisation than to reproach us for holding them back.

Even now, observations made in monasteries—to speak only of them—make it possible to foresee that development will lie in two fields, (1) liturgical rites properly speaking—and on this point, monks and nuns will have to take into account the decisions of national and diocesan commissions on liturgy, and (2) gestures, attitudes and expressions corresponding to aspects of monastic demeanor—position during prayer, marks and titles of respect, way of entertaining guests. Where traditional, natural and meaningful modes of behavior survive it would be out of place to impose others which, even in the West, only date from a bygone—often recent—age and now have little meaning. It is even more inappropriate to import ideas, spiritual concepts or practices of asceticism or piety too strongly marked by one period or one region (whether it be seventeenth century France or central European Baroque) while giving the impression that they are universally accepted in Europe and necessary. The Africans are sometimes astonished when they discover that something they believed to be "European" and on that account good comes only from one country, or even from one province.

Problems of the Spiritual Life.

Vatican II declared that those who establish the religious life in the young Churches should "assimilate to Christianity the ascetic and contemplative traditions whose origins were placed by God in the ancient culture, sometimes before the preaching of the Gospel" (*Ad gentes* n.18). It prescribed that contemplatives should "lead their lives in a way suited to the religious traditions of each people" (*ibid.,* n.40). What problems does this requirement raise for monasticism in Africa and Madagascar?

The first thing to be noted is that vocations are no different than they were from the first. Today as in the days of St Anthony, Christians hear as a call addressed to them this saying of the Lord: "If you wish to go the whole way, go, sell your possessions, and give to the poor . . . and come, follow me." They know that they are drawn to a life of prayer, solitude, silence and humble work in a community. You even meet here and there an aspirant to the eremitical life with guarantees that inspire confidence. The primacy of the gratuitous, of adoration, is sometimes felt with great purity by souls which are not attracted by any system or by rapid methods. In comparison with existing forms of religious life which do so much good everywhere, they understand quite easily that to become a monk means to commit oneself to the quest for union with God, and the prayer of supplication will be its consequence, or rather, its fruit. An often acute sense of justice—which can inspire vengeance! —likewise favors an understanding of reparation, penitence and the solidarity of all men in sin and in redemption.

The training given should take account of these "probes", as people say today, and of many others. In this way the intercession they ask of their ancestors helps towards understanding the veneration of saints. The prayer for peace—that peace which is part of the greeting given daily in many regions—soon becomes spontaneous. The repetition of melodies and phrases of which they never tire encourages a contemplative way of talking to God. The practice of mutual aid, the habit of common labor in the rice fields and other plantations, prepares for family life in the convent. Moreover their taste for the concrete, but human, in its humble and everyday form is another value which can be a grace.

Vocation gains by being explained not in abstract terms such as the search for an Absolute, but as a call to enter into that community of life which is the mystery of the Three Persons. If the wealth of symbolical expression, as it appears in the proverbs of a region, is respected and used, it is possible to find means of making many realities of a spiritual nature understood. In Madagascar, for example, rice growing can be the symbol of interior activity: water and rice, which are inseparable, signify Christian solidarity. Oxen on the one hand and, on the other, those white birds whose movement is imitated in folk dances, suggest faithfulness. The whole profane world is spontaneously associated with the religious. They must not be separated, but made to give each other meaning. The liturgy should be eloquent. There is nothing to be gained by suppressing gestures or devotions and substituting for them forms of prayer in which image and representation have not an adequate role.

Whatever may be the transpositions that patristic and biblical symbolism may or may not have to undergo in the technical civilization of the West, and in spite of the difference that exists in certain groups of images (those that come, for example, from the flora and fauna) in the biblical world and the African and Malagasy world, many minds find themselves in tune with the style in which the Holy Scriptures and the works of the Fathers, both ancient and medieval, are written, and with the way of thinking in which they originate. They like the similes, the leisurely development and the delight in parallelism. They find that the Bible refines the spirits that live on it, and are capable of reflecting on it, of digging deep into the text and, in the best sense of the word, studying it. God worked on those souls, he prepared them, and monastic vocations existed. The catachesis had not satisfied all spiritual needs; it had put their hearts in expectation of a deepening that was being brought about by contact with Holy Scripture. This presupposes more sense of God and more understanding than learning. Learning is completed and assimilated in the course of the training, during which there is often occasion to admire the progress of Grace.

Saint John is widely appreciated. In one community every new commentary on that Gospel, as soon as it arrives, is immediately asked for by a good number of young nuns. And indeed the author surely gives an important place to the idea of "life" which is so important in the Bantu concept of the stream of life and the Malagasy of sharing life in brotherhood-friendship? Whether they work in the fields or travel for long hours in the bush taxis, Madagascans love singing Christian folksongs, *Zafindraony*, which are poetic paraphrases of Biblical sayings. As done in our liturgical responsories, they unite verses from different part of Scripture, and from this association springs new light. We have reason to think that there are great resources there for future Malagasy liturgy. Divorced from the controversies he creates among orientalists, Evagrius is in some places a living reality, as moreover are the books of Fr Hausherr. *The Lives of the Fathers* are full of details which are perfectly familiar to those who have lived in the bush. Dorotheus of Gaza describes several situations well-known to many. The tales of the *Exordium Magnum* of Cîteaux have the same quality and meet the same response. As for St Bernard, it is enough to quote this delightful reflection: "He speaks as we do in Rwanda: he takes his time". Finally, one cannot help noticing in more than one place the influence exercised by the writings of St Theresa of the Infant Jesus, no doubt on account of her message of simplicity.

Community is conceived spontaneously as a family in which blossoms the innate sense of brotherhood, of respect for the elders, of the meeting—Madagascan *palabre* or *fivoriana*—where everyone has the right and sometimes the duty to speak. The difference between the races can give rise to rivalry and jealousy; but also, consequently, to the exercise of forgiveness. Many of those who had to suffer in their own person or in their families from tribal wars appreciate the peace and understanding which they enjoy now. And to some the union of the races in one country seems like an ideal of solidarity, which gains all its meaning from the charity in the Church. Duties of hospitality are taken very seriously in a place where every house is an inn, where they have been used to seeing relations, friends, and passing strangers appear at any hour of the day—as St Benedict says—and especially in the evening. To demand notice, especially in a place where the telephone and mail service are inadequate, would likely shock people greatly. But the poor themselves know how to give and they would be offended if you refused a gesture of that kind. Men who have highly developed, sometimes leisurely, forms of politeness are taken aback by what we call frankness but what seems to them brusqueness.

There is a special problem which can arise here. The African or Malagasy has a profound need for a family community. So it seems that he must, right from his postulancy, be integrated into the community. On the other hand, in a group of whites he is easily intimidated. Moreover, the way in which certain Westerners understand the observance is so rigid that there is no transition upon entry into this life. We may ask whether it would not be desirable to have a separate novitiate, where life would be simpler and the real character of each person would better be revealed. There could be a progressive apprenticeship in the office—part-time attendance at first—in the work and in reading. This solution should not be thrust aside entirely nor should it be regarded as authoritative. The whole community trains newcomers and this demands a great deal from it. The important thing is that the one or two monks responsible for training the younger ones should always be with them, sharing their work and their whole life.

The question raised by the practice of silence cannot be evaded. It is with good reason considered by some contrary to nature in a place where words and gestures are the necessary expression of the heart's movement, where moods need symbols, and where the spoken word not only is the sign of life but has a sacred character. The gift of the heart is seen in little presents which people give one another, even among the poor, and in Madagascar, if they give as a present only half a basket of rice, this is because the heart is taken to fill up the other half. "In our innumerable proverbs", said a monk of that country, "we have none like your 'speech is silver but silence is golden' ". Many Africans and Malagasy shrink from opening their hearts in a *tête-à-tête*. They do it more easily in a group, even if it takes time, and then there must not be too many whites in the company, and the whites must let them have their say. These conversations are necessary for the Africans or Malagasy and the Westerners to learn to understand one another. Both sides should ask themselves how their brethren are reacting to their ideas, and what on both sides they should keep in their customs or what modify. It is important to thrash out problems in council where everyone is present. The decision taken by the head of the monastery, whose authority must not be questioned, will be seen then as the responsibility of all.

Poverty is a formidable problem everywhere. In an underdeveloped country, an austere standard of living can seem affluent, especially if because of the enclosure there is little contact with the people of the neighborhood. Wealth, even relative, far from being understood will be exaggerated. In theory two solutions are possible: either admit to being rich but make others benefit effectually from this boon; or else, in more complete isolation from populace, practise poverty in a way that will be more readily perceptible. In point of fact, a situation of wealth is likely to cause scandal even if it does not yet scandalize because of the backwardness of the mass of people and because the charity dispensed retards its development. In practice, many foundations are conditioned by their past, even recent, and any solution must take account of the facts. In the future, there will be reason to pay heed to developmental conditions in each region before establishing a house there, and to try to do so in such a way that the "collective witness" to poverty recommended by Vatican II (*Perfectae Caritatis* No.13) weighs with some, even if it is not possible for everyone to grasp it. Of course, to the example of poverty should be added that of productive work to serve as a model and educate those who see it. But if the distance between the development of a monastic economic enterprise and the capacity for training the men of a region is too vast, they will not understand the lesson. So one bishop recommends, rather than a "model farm" which demands great resources to begin with, and whose material and methods might be too discouraging, a "pilot-field" which would serve as an example at a level accessible to all. For all or almost all can come to love work if they can be brought to understand its nobility. The future will perhaps see, around a centre that has developed, "cells" occupied by fraternities whose economic situation would be close to the standard of living and productivity of the average population. At all events, the place where the mother and daughter houses were placed would have to be carefully chosen. And in places where it can already be foreseen that African monks will take over, setting up enterprises, economic or other, which would be too heavy a burden and for which they do not, like us, feel the need, should be avoided. From now on we should be careful not to let them dissipate their energies in multiple activities or in diverse and numerous forms of work. Nor is it right to impose upon them a rhythm of production which can never be theirs, even when they have learnt from us methods which they appreciate but will apply according to the temperament given them by the Creator.

This leads to a last consideration, that of time, whose value is relative to different representatives of the same human race. The Africans and Malagasy who enter our monasteries are on the whole sensitive to rhythms of nature which are not the same as on our continents. They come from circles which have a sense of the transitory, for example with regard to habitation. They have a great capacity for suffering and for patience. Their reactions are not always immediate: they wait and they look before saying things that have matured in their minds and make good sense. All these temperaments have their advantages, as do those which are made differently. And so all men should understand and respect one another, and the quick should acquire enough virtue to be slow with the slow.

Thus we have no right to destroy the gifts of nature and temperament, or cultural and religious traditions, when they have survived and can be beneficial. They do exist, profoundly and we can say luckily, even beneath the veneer of western influence. It is our duty to help them to become Christian values.

Observances and Institutions

In this field, we find ourselves faced with two tendencies which seem contradictory but which are complementary and can lead us to return to tradition. On the one hand, a need is felt for putting spiritual attitudes into concrete form in observances of prayer or penitence—fasting for example, in this there is nothing that is not healthy and an opportune reminder for us. Indeed, by dint of spiritualizing observances—which sometimes boils down to intellectualizing them under the pretext of interiorizing them—we are in danger of having nothing left of them. On the other hand, Africans realise the necessity for a real flexibility in the institutions that prescribe observances, and this too is excellent. It is a question of personalizing them, rather than materializing them by making them the subject of obligations imposed, as it were, from the outside, minutely fixing the details without leaving room for any discretion or initiative.

We must help our African and Malagasy brethren to recover that part of spiritual liberty that monasticism has partially lost in recent times under the influence of a highly developed juridicism. Timetables can become less rigid, less precise, less heavy. We must avoid lending truth in the monasteries to the proverb that "the whites are born with a bracelet on their arms", meaning a wrist-watch. Do not let us allow constitutions to enter into too many minutiae and lay down serious sanctions for infractions that appear minor, for example concerning silence. Rather than forbidding speech under pain of punishment, let them set forward positively the value of recollection and *taciturnitas*. Similarly, simply because exclusion from refectory (that is, from the common table) still has its full force in a society where family life is intense, it would be well to impose it only for serious lapses.

What our African and Malagasy brethren need in order to open out is first and foremost a broad and solid structure, an environment that will be familial, huge, hierarchic and organized, like theirs. Clearly divisions into different classes of monks would be a bad thing. From this point of view the community structure established by St Benedict in social and cultural conditions very similar to those of many regions of Africa today retains all its value, and there is something to be gained by returning to it, by-passing institutions like lay brothers and sisters, which the late Middle Ages introduced into the West. This consideration dictated for example the Statutes of Hanga, in which the number of priests present is conceded to be of less importance than the number of solemnly professed, provided that the sacerdotal ministry is safeguarded. What is needed next is the continuity and security given by a tradition. Unless it is strictly necessary, let us avoid bringing up again either convictions or the authority of those exercising it, in particular the head of the monastery, who should be the superior living on the spot. It is for us to enter into the problems of our brethren, not to burden them with ours. Sometimes Westerners make a kind of game, almost a sport, of universal criticism which is hardly intended to have any consequences but which can cause damage where the game is taken more seriously. Similarly, certain intricate theological problems, already so difficult for the specialists who formulate them in Europe and America, should not be tackled without preparation by those who speak and those who listen. Taking into account unforeseen matters of health and other circumstances, everything is to be gained by maintaining as far as possible the continuity of superiors and members of the communities. Instability in the exercise of authority brings nothing but disadvantages. You have to be able to have confidence in a man and give him his chance. The head of the monastery and his council should have real responsibility, and frequent appeal to remote jurisdiction including habitual interference, should be ruled out.

More and more, hope is increasing for a measure of union between monasteries, a sort of organization for which the institutional formula is yet to be found, but which would insure cohesion and mutual aid. Some think that African and Malagasy monasticism could be conceived not as a family of the Western type, independent and limited, but like a huge clan of which each member has a fellowship with every other and is bound to bring him help. In this, they are thinking of a fellowship in the style of the Bantu *Jamâa* or the Malagasy *Fihavanana.*

Finally, it would be sad if, in meetings where African or Malagasy monks were discussed, they were either not represented or barely represented, whatever the legal status that these witnesses and delegates enjoy or do not enjoy. Whether they are "simple" or "conventual" priors or neither is of little moment, provided they can listen to us and let us hear their voices.

In short, the situation demands flexibility and humility of us. Let us learn how to avoid imposing our authority and importing without adaptation our ways of thinking, of acting, of being Christians. Jesus Christ was not a Westerner. On what authority should we tie down his message to the psychology and the culture of a limited part of the world, even if it happens to be our own? By means of the mutual understanding already evident, institutions and observances, together with the concepts and practices of the spiritual life, are little by little finding the form that charity demands. Then the clothing imported from the West can be modified, the habit perhaps replaced by the *lambana* or some other local garment. The scapular can disappear, as it already is, if what is essential remains. Similarly, the diet can be adapted to local food, provided it is carefully considered, balanced and sufficiently varied. Certain western forms of abstinence should be sacrificed; the spirit of sacrifice will remain and even be deepened.

The Art of Waiting.

At the close of this paper which has drawn attention to more problems than solutions, two facts must be recalled which dominate the whole discussion. First, the slow pace of history and second, respect for what is. We must set out from what is in order to bring about what will be, at the pace of eternal God and in spite of human dullness.

To begin with, it is natural that African and Malagasy monasticism should raise problems. We are dealing with a new enterprise, almost a new creation, which does not yet have the advantage of enough past for us to be able to deduce any laws from it. Moreover, it is comforting to see the heads of institutions which have already stood the test of time likewise asking themselves questions. Are methods of spreading the Gospel and setting up schools which proved their worth a hundred or even fifty years ago still valid? There are missionaries who are asking themselves this and they do not disguise the difficulties of their task nor the real or apparent failure of their work. And so monks should not be afraid either to discuss their problems publicly or to ask Christians outside their institution what they think. They can always decide later which of these observations and suggestions can be retained.

One of the major difficulties in African and Malagasy monasticism arises from the fact that, generally speaking, it has been launched during the last fifteen years, which means at the height of a world crisis, at a time of decolonization, at a period when Africa has passed from an old historical state to a new one. The ground is shifting. Monasticism needs a certain stability.

Amongst the forms of courage such a time requires must be counted those which include trying, taking risks, even failing, really or apparently, wholly or partially, and starting again, in the same place or elsewhere. Every failure which teaches a lesson is a success. But on the other hand we must remember this saying of St Francis de Sales: "God sometimes wants us in a craft he did not put us in." Even if there have been mistakes at the beginning, we must be able to accept a situation which already exists, and begin by adapting ourselves to it in order to make it progress as soon as possible as much as possible. So we appreciate increasingly the importance of preparing the ground. Before making a foundation we must patiently and on the spot collect information about all the conditions affecting settlement and expansion. Even after this there will be some surprises but at least we have a duty to eliminate the major unknowns.

The best condition of success, insofar as the word has meaning in a Christian system, is undoubtedly modesty. I have had cause to be humiliated in a refectory full of African monks, where they were reading a *History of the Church* written by an English Catholic prelate. The topic was the Renaissance, during which the See of Rome was the subject of rivalry between a number of Roman families, and I was reminded that these tribal struggles had lasted the whole of the Christian Middle Ages, causing numerous schisms which at the time troubled the whole Church as well as the Papacy. An African monk converted from paganism remembered having seen during his studies in Europe, in a Christian family, a sorceress going through all sorts of grimaces and incantatory rites around a sick woman. No doubt such cases are rarer now in one continent than another, but they were very frequent indeed in ours for centuries. And God was patient. Let us be likewise.

Let us avoid accusing of infantilism (because they are

primitive) things that are profound but upset our intellectual pretensions. Wésterners have, through contact with Africans and Malagasy, simplified their life already, eliminated unnecessary requirements and rediscovered what is essential and sufficient. Many of them recognize that they have learned something from their brothers. The Africanization of Europeans has begun. That alone would not be an inconsiderable result. Rather than sending Africans to train in Europe, something from this perspective might be gained by sending Europeans to Africa, for example a religious being prepared to be Novice Master. We have something to learn from one another in developing a more universal and hence richer monastic spirituality and culture. And in this work of exchange, contemporary African and Malagasy monasticism is itself a source to the extent that it is a beginning—African monasticism, as in the fourth century begins in the twentieth. History has not yet dulled it. But African monasticism can benefit by the contribution of the western tradition if those who transmit it can keep it authentic, purify it if necessary to make it a means of fresh progress for all.

I conclude with two Bantu proverbs to remind us of two special needs of the youth of African and Malagasy monasticism. The first is fidelity to a vocation in which you cannot give light unless you are on fire. "He who has no fire can give none to his neighbour". But this ardor goes hand in hand with patience, and the second saying teaches us a lesson in confidence: "What you will eat tomorrow, God spends the night finding for you." Finally, let us not forget this Irish dictum, which might be African or Malagasy, and which is so encouraging: "When God created time, he created plenty of it".

THE ROLE OF MONASTIC SPIRITUALITY

CRITICALLY DISCUSSED*

T O TREAT OF THE ROLE OF MONASTIC spirituality from a critical point of view does not merely
imply bringing out its content, but likewise marking its
influence. It does not mean solely acknowledging both its
content and influence, but appraising them. Monasticism has
more than once in the past been a subject of discussion.
Today, however, the question takes on a new significance:
monasticism is discussed outside and inside the Catholic
Church, even by monks, and rightly so. We have here an
aspect of the activity and a manifestation of the vitality of
the Church in our time which seeks—*ecclesia quaerens*—better
to grasp the meaning and to justify the values it has received
from tradition, so as beter to transmit them, and ever more
faithfully to respond to their demands.

Some general notion of monasticism must be the point of
departure in such an inquiry. Monasticism must therefore be
considered in all its breadth. To restrict it to ancient or
recent forms of the Benedictine institution would be unduly
to limit its scope. The Trappists, the Carthusians, the Camaldolese, the Hieronymites, the Poor Clares, the Dominican
nuns, and others offer many manifestations of the "monastic
phenomenon". They represent sometimes extreme forms of
that phenomenon, but forms which, by the very fact of being
extreme, are clear and significant. The fact of monasticism
must likewise be considered in all its traditional depth by

* Published in *La vie spirituelle*, 114(1966)623-644; in Spanish in *Cuadernos
monasticos*, 2 (1966); in English in *Worship*, 39 (1965) 583-596.

bringing to light all the elements common to it in its successive periods from its origin in the fourth century to our time. The studies that have been made in our generation by excellent theologians and historians of monasticism will greatly facilitate the present study.

Finally, beyond all those varied historical manifestations the essential element of monastic life must be discerned. We will find it expressed in the well balanced and impartial considerations of an Italian Benedictine:

> If we consider past tradition, there is no doubt that Benedictine monasticism belongs to the *contemplative* type of religious life even if, as history shows, it has never excluded a certain amount of varied activity. But in our time activism threatens to upset everything and to do away precisely with that contemplative character which seems essential to monasticism in every age. In some instances, we may wonder if the monastery and the monk still preserve the essential of a life which in itself is, at least in a certain measure, a contemplative life, and which, at all events, must favor the contemplative life. Who can deny that, precisely in our world of today, monasticism is called upon to incarnate values that are above all contemplative, and to bear witness to their importance and their preeminence? "[1]

Let us now try to make this rather general notion definite and to view it in the light of history, or better, tradition. It will then be possible to form a worthy judgment and to indicate the role which monasticism can play in the contemporary Church. Let us consider its chief elements and show what were and what are their advantages but also their dangers, nay even their ill-effects.

Essential Elements of Monasticism

If we wish to consider these elements as a whole before giving attention to each one in particular, we can say that monasticism has simply given an institutional form to

---

1. F. Visentin, in C. Vagaggini, *La preghiera* (Rome, 1964) pp. 946 f.

practices and aspirations inherent in every life in Christ. In addition to the laws the Church imposed on all, the monks made obligatory for themselves those institutions they had created within the Church. In so far and in so far only did they go beyond Christians in general. They pledged themselves to practise the Christian life according to those particular norms which they had freely established or chosen under the inspiration of the Holy Spirit and under the control and with the approval of Church authorities. There was no question of an ideal different from that of all Christians, nor of a Christian life more perfect than that of the generality of Christians, but of a complex of means designed to favor the quest for perfection imposed on all Christians, and to make clear and concrete certain demands of that imitation of Christ which the Gospel proposed to all men, and which, from their origin, monks have always made their essential aim.[2]

What were the principal means they chose? In the first place, the fundamental Christian attitude which consists in not being *of this world* made them leave the world. They no longer wished to be *with the world.* Spiritual death to the world of sin, detachment from this passing world, became for them separation from the world. They went into the desert, into solitude. This flight from the world, this search for solitude, gave rise to the terms "monks, monasteries, cloisters," used to designate their persons and their homes. The ascetics who did not leave the world, even if they practised celibacy, voluntary poverty, and a life of prayer, were not regarded as monks.[3] Dom Guéranger's concept remains true: "Separation from the world in itself makes the monk."[4] The life of a monk is a life of solitude. Whether he is alone as in

2. Texts are cited by U. Ranke-Heinemann, *Das frühe Mönchtum, Seine Motive nach den Selbstzeugnissen* (Essen, 1964) pp. 83-100 ("Das Motiv der Nachfolge").

3. Cf. J. M. Leroux, "Monachisme et communauté Chrétienne d'après S. Jean Chrysostome," in *Théologie de la vie monastique* (Paris, 1961) p. 149.

4. An unpublished conference given at Solesmes, which has been quoted several times.

the case of the hermit, or whether he lives in community, he has set himself apart from ordinary and even Christian society.

When he leaves the world, it is in order to be with God. He goes into solitude to "seek God," according to a biblical principle unceasingly repeated in monastic tradition. Seeking God and his kingdom manifests itself an effort toward keeping "the remembrance of God." These expressions, drawn from scripture, and the reality they inspired were illustrated through a vocabulary that had lost the philosophical meaning it had had when the language of ancient Greece spoke of "contemplation" and "contemplative life." This new element explains the predominant part which was always given to prayer in monasticism. The life of monks is a life of prayer and in this sense it is a contemplative life.[5] Theirs is a prayer of adoration and praise, but also a prayer of intercession and supplication for all those whom God loves and wishes to save. This sense of universal solidarity appears in maxims such as those of Evagrius: "Happy is the monk who regards as his own the salvation and progress of all men,"[6] and, "The monk is one who, although separated from all, is united to his fellowmen."[7] A third essential element of monasticism consists in an intense awareness of the need of "conversion," *metanoia*, inherent to every life in Christ. It was usually expressed in self-accusation inspiring a constantly renewed effort with a view to mortifying "sinful flesh," and not only avoiding sin, but repressing inclination to sin. This accounts for the importance given confession and penance. The life of a monk is a life of penance. The monk is a voluntary penitent and, on this point also, he is responsible for others. We need only cite a dictum of Saint Jerome which became classical

5. The demonstration has been made for the Rule of Saint Benedict by A. de Vogüé, "La Règle de S. Benoît et la vie contemplative," in *Collectanea Cisterciensia* 37 (1965) pp. 89-107, and, for the remaining part of the Middle Ages, in the pages I have written on the same problem under the title: "La vie monastique est-elle une vie contemplative? ", *Collectanea*, pp. 108-120.

6. *De oratione*, 122; P.G., 79, 1193.

7. *Ibid.*, 124; 1193.

and entered the manual of medieval canon law generally called the *Decretum Gratiani*: "The role of the monk is not to teach, but to weep over his sins and those of others."[8]

Detachment from the goods of this world became for monks a renunciation of all property, voluntary poverty. The life of a monk is a life of poverty; the monk is a "poor man of Christ."

Submission to the will of God in imitation of Christ who always did the will of his Father became obedience to a superior who represented God. That obedience tended to be total, absolute, but was always free and voluntary. It was practised at first toward a "spiritual father" and later in cenobitic life toward the father of the community, whose authority was well defined and limited by a rule. Obedience was regarded as necessarily bound up with renunciation, for it seemed at least as important and difficult to renounce one's own will as to renounce one's own goods. It seemed likewise required by charity. Monks voluntarily submitted to one another, those among them who exercised authority themselves submitted entirely to the law of God in order to discern and carry out together God's design on each and every one of them. Monastic life is a life of obedience; the monk is an obedient man.

Until now no mention has been made of celibacy since originally celibacy was not strictly a monastic concept. It had existed before monasticism was established: consecrated virginity is attested in the epistles of Saint Paul and throughout the first three centuries of Christianity. However, as soon as monks adopted the various essential elements of monasticism that have been pointed out, they likewise adopted that form of complete and definitive chastity which is voluntary and perpetual celibacy. Chastity could be practised in other states of life, as, for instance, in marriage; it could take on other forms. The monks adopted a specific form. To be alone in the way they understood it, to be a "monk" (to be single),

8. Jerome, *Contra Vigilantium*, 15; P.L. 23, 351.

necessarily meant to practice continency in celibacy. Monks
were often referred to as "continent" men.

Notwithstanding variations in modes of application, such
were from the very beginning and throughout history the
chief characteristics of monastic life. Having stated them, we
can now attempt to pass critical judgment on them.

Advantages and Dangers of Monasticism

Let us try to ascertain the advantages of monasticism, the
better to estimate afterward the consequences they entailed.

We may say that the principal advantages were the following:

Monasticism helped the Church discover or perceive more
clearly certain demands of the spiritual program proposed by
the Church.

It showed monastic life as an example, one of the possible
realizations of life in Christ, illustrating certain aspects of the
evangelical message.

It offered thereby a possibility, a help, to generous Christians who wished to adopt the same practices.

It set up examples of sanctity. Apart from the martyrs,
most saints venerated in the ancient and medieval Church
were monks.

It brought forth a spiritual literature that transmitted and
elaborated the experiences and the teachings of monks.
Ascetic literature of all times, but especially of the Middle
Ages, strongly bore the influence of great monastic authors
such as Saint Jerome, Saint Basil, Cassian, Julian Pomerius,
the compilers of the Merovingian age (e.g., Defensor of
Ligugé), the writers of the Carolingian epoch (e.g., Smaragdus
of Saint-Mihiel), and later those of the twelfth century,
particularly Saint Bernard.

But it is fitting to lay stress on two chief services monasticism rendered the Church. In the first place, it introduced
into the life of many Christians, both clerics and lay persons,
spiritual practices that had been proper to the Christian life
at the beginning. Retreat (meaning is, as the term itself in-

dicates, a certain anchoretism for a period of intense solitude and recollection), spiritual direction, manifestation of conscience to a spiritual father, meditation, spiritual reading, had of monastic origin.

Self-accusation in particular contributed greatly to revivifying penance. From the very first monastic generations, as the most ancient of the *Apophthegmata* of the Fathers bear witness, a deepening of the Christian conscience had been observed among them. Little by little, everyone acquired a more and more intimate and intense conviction of his sinful condition and experienced the need to acknowledge it and to mortify himself in order to do penance.

It was in the same period—late fourth and early fifth century—that a new concept and practice of penance began to prevail. Public penance was not given up officially; but because of the length and severity of the penitential practices imposed and above all because of the non-repeatable character of the sacrament and its humiliating aspect and disabling consequences, there was a strong tendency to postpone it until proximity of death seemed to urge it and at the same time to preclude occasions for further sin. These considerations were similar to those which often caused the delay of baptism. It is not necessary to enter into the controversial question as to how early so-called private penance was introduced into the Church. It is probable at any rate that St Basil, St Augustine, and other Fathers of that time had the inadequacies of public penance in mind, when they insisted so strongly on the biblical and earlier ascetic conception that a true spirit of penance should extend far beyond gross sin to everything which is not pleasing to God. And this was one of the great functions of monasticism: to demonstrate in practice that spiritual perfection and complete detachment from sin are ultimately one and the same thing, that the safest way and perhaps the only way to cease being a sinner is to become a saint. It is in the ascetic-monastic milieu, therefore, that the beginnings of what today is called private penance, and even repeatable confession and absolution, are to be found.[9]

9. Gerhart B. Ladner, *The Idea of Reform* (Cambridge, Mass., 1959) pp. 309f.

Another important role of monasticism, was reaction against the spiritual emptiness engendered gradually in some milieux with the development of institutions and even with the appearance of a certain "legalism," as well as with the material growth of the Church. Monks exercised a sort of "prophetic" protest against every form of mediocrity.[10] It has been remarked with regard to Cassian that in some of its representatives monasticism was not unlike Protestantism.[11] There have been striking voices, like those of St Jerome, St Peter Damian, St Bernard, Blessed Paul Giustiniani and, today, Thomas Merton. But there was also—and there is still—the silent protest of many unknown monks and nuns proclaiming in their own way, by their life, the message to which writers give expression. By the very fact that they exist and are known to exist, such contemplatives set all Christians on their guard against the temptations of an easy or superficial activism. That prophetic function is a form of witness on the part of monks to the eschatological character of the Church. More consciously than others, they already live for the other world, and they remind everyone that beyond this world there is another; that beyond the present, there is the kingdom to come. They remind Christians not to be satisfied with this world, although they may desire to make it better. They remind them that human progress and "development" under all its forms and in all domains remain ordained and subordinated to a personal encounter with God in Christ.

Finally, one of the secondary roles of monasticism was to put at the Church's disposal a generous personnel, ready to be employed in the difficult works of evangelization or reform of morals at times and in countries in which others were not assuming those functions. So it happened—less than is said at times, but in a way that cannot be passed over in silence—that bishops or popes in particular circumstances asked monks to enter the clergy or to become members of

---

10. Cf. J. Fontaine, art. *France,* in *Dictionnaire de spiritualité,* col. 792.

11. A. de Vogüé, "Monachisme et Eglise dans la pensée de Cassien," in *Théologie de la vie monastique,* pp. 220 and 223.

the hierarchy of the Church, or again to devote themselves to agricultural, cultural, pastoral, or missionary activity.

Now, what were the dangers to which monasticism was exposed and to which it yielded?

The first was to go too far in the realization of a legitimate ideal, and in the first place to exaggerate the practice of asceticism. Hence the excesses, the abuses and extravagances of certain forms of mortification in ancient monasticism or at the time of St Peter Damian, de Rancé, or Dom de Lestrange. On the whole, these excesses were not so serious as a free literature likes sometimes to assert today. Those who read the sources and know how much to attribute to their literary genre and to their humor admire the moderation and the good sense with which the *Apophthegmata* of the Fathers of the desert or the writings of subsequent great authors are filled. But the danger of exaggeration was real and was not always avoided.

In the realm of ideas, there was the temptation to give too much value to human effort, at the expense of the efficacy of grace. Pelagius was a monk, and Pelagianism is a typically monastic error.

Another danger was to regard as an absolute, as an end, what was only a means, and consequently to present monastic life as the model for all Christian life, and as a point of reference against which Christian life should be judged. That accounts for a certain fashion, nay, a certain snobbishness in the fourth and fifth centuries, for example, for what has been called the "Egyptian way of life."[12] It is clear that this engendered pride and vain self-complacency in many a monk.

History also witnessed instances in which monks tended to separate themselves from the greater church, either by having no hierarchy, by opposing authority of a charismatic nature to that of ecclesiastic institution, or again by rejecting the doctrine of the Church on certain points, or by living without the sacraments, even strangely enough the Eucharist. Others gave in to an individualism or, what is worse, an egoism

12. J. Fontaine, *Dict. de Spiritualité*, col. 792.

which impelled them not to care for their neighbor and his salvation, nor for the good to be done the neighbor here and not. The prophetic protest at times resembled an Adventism or a Millenarianism ignorant of the concerns of the Church. At times, monasticism gave the impression of being related to the Church, as sects are to Churches.

Moreover, when spiritual fervor disappeared or diminished among certain monks, there was a tendency to think that the institutions which that interior fervor had produced were sufficient in themselves, without the continuance of the enthusiasm which had brought them into existence. This could lead to community life without charity, to a life of celibacy without chastity, to poverty without privation or detachment.

Consequences of the Benefits and Disadvantages

Having observed the advantages and dangers monasticism presents, we can note a few of the facts that can be explained by them.

The advantages enable us to understand why the authority of the Church has always encouraged the monastic institution as a whole, insured its protection, and undertaken its defence when necessary. It was a bishop, St Athanasius, who wrote the *Life* of St Anthony, the father of all monks; a pope, St Gregory the Great, did the same for "the patriarch of western monks," St Benedict. Both wished to illustrate and comment that way of life. We might cite many instances in which leaders of the Church, from St Augustine to Paul VI, affirmed the legitimacy and the high value of monasticism.

The benefits of monasticism explain also why Christians have always discerned its significance and have seen in it an example of Christian generosity and an incitement to fervor. This accounts for the vast diffusion of monastic literature, to mention only one of the signs of the importance attributed to monasticism. Lives of monks and texts written for or by monks have nearly always enjoyed a certain prestige and have exercised an influence on spiritual writings up to our own day.

On the other hand, the drawbacks and the dangers of monasticism account for the criticisms directed against it. We have seen that one of its functions was to criticize, in the measure in which it protested; but it also needed to be criticized, and indeed it was by monks themselves as well as by other Christians. At all times there have been churchmen who reproved certain monks for the abuses, the excesses, and the deviations that have already been pointed out. To cite a few examples taken from different periods will make the point.

In antiquity, in the fourth and fifth centuries, a reaction of sorts against monks can be observed, a certain mistrust on the part of Christians, both lay and cleric, living in the world and satisfied with the established Church. They opposed the diffusion of the ideal of continence, which threatened to permeate even the lives of married people. Who would give the Church new sons? They worried about the ideal of voluntary poverty. Who would come to the aid of the needy? Who would administer the properties of the clergy? They feared that the ideal of separation from the world would deprive it of men experienced in the work to be done. Who would preach and convert the world?

We notice some opposition to St Martin from bishops and members of the clergy of Gaul, and an opposition to both St Martin and St Jerome from members of the Roman clergy. [13] We also see monks finding fault with other monks: St Jerome found St Martin and his disciples too moderate. [14] St Basil criticized Eustathius of Sebaste and his groups of ascetics. [15] St John Chrysostom rebuked certain monks for their melancholy, for the relaxation of discipline, and for their tendency to believe their observances were infallible means of sanctification; [16] he reproved them for their indifference to

13. Cf. A. de Vogüé, "La Règle de S. Benoit," p. 231.

14. Cf. J. Fontaine, *Dict. de Spiritualité,* col. 795, and "Vérité et fiction dans la chronologie de la Vita Martini" in *S. Martin et son temps.* Studia Anselmiana, 46 (Rome, 1961) p. 232.

15. J. Gibromont, "S. Basile," in *Théologie de la vie monastique,* p. 113.

16. J. M. Leroux, "Monachisme et communauté chrétienne," pp. 167f.

the salvation of their neighbor,[17] and for their want of charity.[18] St Augustine upbraided slothful monks who did not want to work and for them he wrote his treatise *De opere monachorum.* The praises Cassian reserved for the Egyptian monks were nothing else than indirect criticisms addressed to the monks of Gaul. He put the Gallic monks on their guard against gyrovagues, sarabaites, and false hermits.[19] Rules were written to preserve monks from the exaggerations and deviations to which they were exposed. Thus the Rule of St Benedict begins with a censure of bad monks. The function which doctrinal definitions filled in the domain of faith, the exclusion of errors, was performed by monastic legislation in what concerned discipline, the condemnation and elimination of abuses. So a continuous criticism of monasticism was carried out in antiquity both by monks and by churchmen.

In the Middle Ages criticism of monasticism was at the bottom of all those efforts at renewal that we call reform, whether the initiative was taken by a prince, as in the case of the Carolingian reform, or by bishops or councils, by monks like St Odo and the abbots of Cluny, St Peter Damian, the Cistercians and St Bernard, or again by popes like Gregory VII in the eleventh century, Alexander III in the twelfth, and Benedict XII in the fourteenth. Monasticism was in a state of continual reform, which supposes a constant self-criticism. One of the roles of monasticism in the Middle Ages was to keep alive in the Church the idea and ideal of reform.[20] A historical phenomenon such as the Gregorian reform in the eleventh century was not accomplished only by new legislation; it was helped by a renewal and a deepening of the religious mentality contributed in large part by monasteries.[21] Again in the thirteenth century, we see monasticism

---

17. *Ibid.,* p. 169.
18. *Ibid.,* p. 171.
19. A. de Vogüé, "La Règle de S. Benoit," p. 221.
20. G. Ladner, *The Idea of Reform,* pp. 319-426 ("Monasticism as a vehicle of a Christian idea of reform in the age of the Fathers").
21. I gave some indications on this point in *Témoins de la vie spirituelle en Occident,* (Paris, 1965).

criticized and called back to the demands of its vocation by Odon de Cheriton[22] and by the theologians of the mendicant orders.[23]

The epoch of the Reformation was one of those times when monasticism was subjected to virulent criticism. In the life of Luther himself we observe an evolution on this point. At first he tended to reinforce laws, to re-establish observances in the Augustinian Order to which he belonged; later he made a complete break with vows and observances, and elaborated a theology to justify such a rupture. This radical criticism has been maintained in Protestantism and reinforced in our times by new arguments borrowed from history. An attempt was made to explain the appearance of monasticism through religious or philosophical foreign to Christianity, or by economic circumstances or an opposition to the hierarchical Church.[24] But the problem has just recently been taken up again on its true ground, theology.[25]

In our time, monastic life is the object of critism, some of which comes from historians, philosophers, and theologians who attribute to certain traditional attitudes of monasticism —such as separation from the world, "contempt of the world," contemplative life—a Platonic, pessimistic, dualistic, "anti-incarnational" origin or savor. Others react against a monasticism too well established, too inconspicuous as to solitude, austerity, poverty, and simplicity of life. A book like Louis Bouyer's *The Meaning of Monastic Life* represented a protest of this kind. Recently, the *American Benedictine Review* has published articles questioning concepts and practices of monasticism as a whole[26] and that of the

---

22. I have furnished evidence under the titles "Pétulance et spiritualité dans le commentaire sur le Cantique," in *Archives d'histoire doctrinale et littéraire du moyen âge,* 39 [1964] (Paris, 1965) pp. 43-47, and "Hélinand de Froidmont ou Odon de Cheriton? ", ibid. 32 [1965] (Paris, 1966) pp. 61-69.

23. Let us think for example of the sermons of Humbert de Romans, OP.

24. An "aperçu" of these various attempts is given by U. Ranke—Heinemann, *Das Frühe Mönchtum,* pp. 9-12.

25. R. H. Esnault, *Luther et le monachisme aujourd'hui* (Geneva, 1964).

26. "Problems Facing Monachism Today," in *American Benedictine Review,* 16:I (1965) pp. 47-56 (German translation in *Geist und Leben,* 1965).

United States in particular.[27] Thomas Merton did not hesitate
to bring up problems which the Cistercians of the Strict Observance have to face.[28] In a letter he affirmed, "I have con-
sistently held that a monk can speak from the Desert, since
there is no other place from which he has a better claim to be
heard." And one of his latest essays ended with the following
sentence which vibrates with the tone of the great prophetic
and protesting voices: "But one thing is certain, if the contemplative, the monk, the priest, the poet merely forsake
their vestiges of wisdom and join in the triumphant empty-
handed crowing of advertising men and engineers of opinion,
then there is nothing left in store for us but total madness."[29]

·Regarding the *nabis,* those prophets who were at times
"charismatic leaders" of the people of Israel, a comparison
has been made between "the efficaciousness of their protest
against an excessive attachment to terrestrial goods and that
which monasticism and other ascetic movements of the same
kind exercised in the Middle Ages." The historian who made
the comparison also offered the following observation, which
we ought to be able to apply to monasticism of any period:

> By walking out of the circle in which they had hitherto
> lived, by making palpable both in their dress and in living a
> secluded life in special colonies their opposition to any
> kind of comfortable worldliness or cultivated self-interest
> so that they might dedicate themselves utterly to the reli-
> gious idea, they brought home once more with unmis-
> takable severity to a nation that had become too flabby
> and soft, that 'life is not the highest good,' and that there is
> something greater than earthly progress and the enjoyment
> and multiplication of worldly goods.[30]

27. A. Thaick, "The Twentienth Century Monk," *ibid.,* 16:2, pp. 242-246.
28. "The Monk in the Diaspora," in *Commonweal* (1964) pp. 741-745, and in
Blackfriars (1964) pp. 290-302. H. Urs von Balthasar and others have remarked
that in our last generations, some of the Christian voices that were most listened
to were monastic voices, such as those of St Theresa of the Child Jesus, Sister
Elizabeth of the Trinity, Charles de Foucauld, Dom Marmion, and Thomas
Merton.
29. *Symbolism,* published in the Indies in 1965, p. 29.
30. Walther Eichrodt, *Theology of the Old Testament* (Philadelphia, 1961) pp.
326ff.

Actuality of Monastic Spirituality

If we wish to form a comprehensive judgment on the role and the value of monastic spirituality, we must distinguish which practices, observances, and modes of existence are proper to the life of monks, and which are ancient, traditional, sound and applicable to everyone. The latter come from Christian sources common to all members of the Church, from scriptures, the liturgy, and patristic literature. The way in which monasticism has utilized and lived by these has remained simple, a stranger to the methods, techniques, and at times the complications which more recent "schools" have introduced to answer altered needs. The monastic way of serving God and praying to him lies at equal distance from the individualism that appeared in the writings of many spiritual authors from the end of the Middle Ages to the nineteenth and even the twentieth century, and on the other hand from the tendency to collectivism, signs of which are discernible today.

But the monastic life has its limitations. If sometimes in the past it has been presented as *the* model of Christian life, that was a deviation or an abuse of terms which might well be explained in part by circumstances. We see better today that it is only *a* model, one of the possible realizations of life in Christ, one of the means of carrying out and illustrating some of its demands. The movement of ideas provoked by the Council will contribute to this equitable re-evaluation, this re-equilibration, if we may so speak. Monasticism is not made to answer all the needs of the Church. In itself it is neither oriented toward the priesthood nor turned toward evangelization or any other ministry. Many of its authentic representatives, beginning with cloistered contemplatives, are strangers to clerical life and to any exercise of direct apostolate. *Non omnia possumus omnes*: we cannot all do everything.

What is essential and in this sense specific to monasticism is the primary place it gives to prayer under both its forms: private and communal. In the nineteenth century, the second was sometimes regarded as a sort of monkish, and especially Benedictine specialty, by the fact that the celebration of the liturgy was seldom performed by any others. The role which Dom Guéranger and others in Europe played in the liturgical renewal from the middle of the nineteenth century to the middle of the twentieth, and which the Benedictines continue to play in the United States in our times, should not make us forget that traditionally the divine office is only one of the forms of prayer for monks, one of the observances by which they seek union with God. Today, in proportion as the liturgy is again becoming pastoral, the leadership of the liturgical movement is gradually passing into the hands of those charged with pastoral work, and these are not monks. At the same time monasticism is laying more and more emphasis on the *lectio divina,* and many incline to think that an institution of religious life which grants less time to reading than to the office cannot claim to be Benedictine, since it does not conform with one of the fundamental prescriptions of the Rule of St Benedict. Moreover, that element of solemnity which developed in the Benedictine liturgy at the time of the baroque and in the nineteenth century tends everywhere to be reduced. This evolution cannot but bring monasticism back to its true function in the Church.

Its role is to permit certain forms of piety, what we might call "pietist movements," to be realized within the Church itself. In them, the monks sustain their fervor. They are in the Church without entirely breaking away from the world. They detach themselves from the world but their culture has always exercised an influence on the world.

Their role is to affirm at the same time and in their own way the lordship of Christ over everything that exists, the primacy of eschatological anticipation, docility to the charisms of the Spirit, and obedience to the Church and its institutions. When one of these elements tend to weaken, monasticism loses some of its vigor. It runs the risk of becoming a well established institution, but one devoid of fervor, or of being a group of fervent persons whose enthusiasm is uncontrolled and lacks continuity. If the values of monasticism are no longer or not sufficiently found in some institutions which ought to preserve them, they appear in new foundations and institutions. The whole history of monasticism, and certain of its manifestations of vitality in the Church today, illustrate this fact. But it would be as fallacious to wish to depend on a purely spiritual tradition without any connection with history as it would be illusory to think that fidelity to the past suffices to justify an institution.

Finally, the principal role of monasticism is to remind everyone that the first condition to be fulfilled in transforming society is the transformation of ourselves by leading the life in Christ as fully as possible, and to do this for the glory of God. This is particularly true during a period marked at the same time by a return to sources and by the emergence of new forms of Christian fervor and action, more and more "secular" in appearance in that they are practised in the world. If monasticism remains different, it does not for that reason judge others. It admires them, learns some lessons from them, and helps them as much as possible. Nevertheless, monks and nuns know that for them the best way of preaching the law of the Lord is to reform themselves with total generosity.

Translated by Sister Marianne Pomerleau OSB
Convent of St Benedict
St Joseph, Minnesota